Shakespeare's *face*

Shakespeare's *face*

Stephanie Nolen

WITH JONATHAN BATE, TARNYA COOPER, MARJORIE GARBER, ANDREW GURR, ALEXANDER LEGGATT, ROBERT TITTLER AND STANLEY WELLS

PIATKUS

Published by arrangement with Alfred A. Knopf Canada, Toronto, Canada

First published in the USA in 2002 by Alfred A. Knopf Canada,
a division of Random House of Canada Ltd

First published in the UK in 2003 by
Judy Piatkus (Publishers) Limited
5 Windmill Street
London W1T 2JA
e-mail: info@piatkus.co.uk

A catalogue record for this book is available from the British Library

ISBN 0 7499 2391 1

This book has been printed on paper manufactured with respect for the environment using wood from managed sustainable resources

Printed and bound in Great Britain by
Mackays of Chatham Ltd, Chatham, Kent

Contents

A Note to the Reader

Lloyd Sullivan, whose mother was Kathleen Hales-Sanders, represents the family members who own the Sanders portrait. They believe it to have been painted by their ancestor John Sanders (it is possible that John's brother Thomas, or another family member, was the actual painter, if not the original owner). Lloyd Sullivan has worked tirelessly to authenticate the portrait, and his exhaustive research, provided to the author, has been invaluable.

What I claim here is the right of every Shakespeare-lover who has ever lived to paint his own portrait of the man.

— ANTHONY BURGESS, *Shakespeare*

Foreword

Like the painting that inspired it, this book can be read in different ways. One way is as a work of investigative journalism in which Stephanie Nolen goes behind the story she broke in May 2001 about a then-unknown portrait possibly of William Shakespeare. Her six chapters, which form the spine of the book, take us along on her voyage of discovery. As she notes, she is neither a Shakespeare scholar nor a trained art historian, but rather a curious layperson who attempts to unravel the mystery of the painting and to seek answers to the many questions it poses. From time to time, she calls on an expert to assist her in solving a particular puzzle or in separating fact from fiction.

Read another way, *Shakespeare's Face* is a fascinating work of literary and art historical scholarship in which a distinguished group of experts from Canada, Great Britain and the United States bring all their wit and learning to bear on a very old picture. They look at the Sanders portrait as an artifact, as a work of art, as a cultural icon and as a fascinating window into Shakespeare's world. I've met only two of these scholars in person, but I like to imagine them gathered around the painting as I saw it when it went on display at the Art Gallery of Ontario, in Toronto, in the summer of 2001.

The portrait sits on a pedestal in the middle of a small gallery. The scholars form a circle around this enigmatic object—are some of them trying to catch its eye?—each one with a different point of vantage. At first the room is quiet, as each of them looks for the clues that mean the most to her or him. One scholar moves up to look at the painting face to face. Another inspects the back of the panel under a magnifying glass. Still another seems to be as interested in his *Collected Works of Shakespeare* as in the picture. Finally one of them offers an opinion. Another chimes in. And soon the room is filled with animated discourse. (Involved in this conversation and yet separate from it is Stephanie Nolen, who is writing furiously in her notebook and missing not one crucial detail.) The conversation they might have had if they had met around the portrait is the one they now hold in the pages of this book.

But perhaps the most satisfying way of reading *Shakespeare's Face* is as a historical detective story in which some of the evidence is four hundred years old, some is still warm and some may still turn up. In this version of the book the skills of all its writers—ten scholars and one journalist—are needed: investigative reporting; art historical analysis; paleography; literary deduction; genealogy; cultural anthropology; scientific analysis; painstaking archival research, to name a few. All their skills combine in an attempt to answer the question that all of us must ask of the slightly naughty-looking fellow in the Sanders portrait: Are you Shakespeare, or aren't you? Is yours the face of genius?

If your experience of reading *Shakespeare's Face* is anything like mine has been as its editor, charged with bringing all these pieces together into what I hope makes for a coherent whole, then as you turn these pages, and move from one point of view to another, you will change your opinion time and again on its central question. In the process you will learn a great deal about a great many things, ranging from the forensic analysis of old works of art to the hidden messages in obscure Elizabethan poems. But most of all you will gain a new and more intimate sense of William Shakespeare.

However you read this book, you will always come back to Shakespeare and the extraordinary staying power of his genius. He is omnipresent in our world even if he comes from a place and time quite alien to our own. He is where we least expect him, including, some would argue, in a painted face on an old and somewhat battered oak panel that has gone unnoticed for most of its life since perhaps a fledgling player in Shakespeare's company applied the paint, layer on layer on layer, until it formed a face—a face of which one thing can be said for sure: it looked upon the same England that Shakespeare saw four centuries ago.

Rick Archbold
Toronto, Spring 2002

A Note on the Writers

Jonathan Bate ("Scenes from the Birth of a Myth and the Death of a Dramatist") is King Alfred Professor of English Literature and Leverhulme Research Professor at the University of Liverpool. Among his books on Shakespeare are *The Genius of Shakespeare* (1997) and *The Oxford Illustrated History of Shakespeare on Stage* (2001). He is currently writing the volume on the Elizabethan period for the new Oxford history of English literature, of which he is also general editor. He is a regular reviewer for *The Sunday Telegraph* and *The Times Literary Supplement*. His reviews have also appeared in *The New York Times* and *The Wall Street Journal*.

Tarnya Cooper ("A Painting with a Past") studied at the Courtauld Institute of Art and the University of Sussex, where she specialized in non-courtly English portraiture of the sixteenth and early seventeenth centuries. She earned her D.Phil. in the History of Art for her dissertation, "*Memento Mori* Portraiture: Painting, Protestant Culture and Patronage by Middle Elites in England and Wales 1544-1630." She works as Assistant Curator of Art at University College, London, and is the art historical adviser to the exhibition on the world of Queen Elizabeth I at the National Maritime Museum, London, which will open in the spring of 2003. She is the author of a number of articles on Elizabethan portraiture.

Marjorie Garber ("Looking the Part") is William R. Kenan Jr. Professor of English and Director of the Humanities Center, as well as the Chair of the Department of Visual and Environmental Studies and Director of the Carpenter Center for the Visual Arts at Harvard University. She also chairs an international organization, the Consortium of Humanities Centers and Institutes. The author of three books on Shakespeare, *Dream in Shakespeare* (1974), *Coming of Age in Shakespeare* (1981) and *Shakespeare's Ghost Writers* (1987), she has also published critical articles and books of cultural analysis, criticism and theory. Among her latest is *Sex and Real Estate: Why We Love Houses* (2000), a cultural analysis of the way desire for material things functions in our relation to homes. Her latest book is *Academic Instincts* (2001), a discussion of key issues in the humanities, including the relationship between "amateurs" and "professionals," the relationship between one academic discipline and another, and the relationship between "jargon" and "plain language." Forthcoming is a new book called *Quotation Marks*.

Andrew Gurr ("Picturing Shakespeare in 1603") is a Professor of English at the University of Reading and, until recently, Director of Globe Research at the Shakespeare Globe Centre, London, England. He was educated in New Zealand at the

University of Auckland and in the U.K. at Cambridge. His teaching has taken him to England (the Universities of Leeds and Reading), Kenya (the University of Nairobi), New Zealand (the Victoria University of Wellington and the University of Auckland) and the U.S. (UCLA and the University of Connecticut). He has also held research fellowships at the University of Nairobi, the Folger Shakespeare Library, the University of Canterbury and Cambridge University. He has been a director of the Globe project in London since 1983. His many publications include *The Shakespearean Stage 1574-1642* (1970, 1992), *Playgoing in Shakespeare's London* (1987), with John Orrell *Rebuilding Shakespeare's Globe* (1989), *Shakespeare's Globe Rebuilt* (1995), *The Shakespearian Playing Companies* (1996), and with Mariko Ichikawa *Staging in Shakespeare's Theatres* (2001). He has edited several Renaissance plays, including *Richard II* and *Henry V* for the *New Cambridge Shakespeare*, and the Quarto *Henry V* for the *Cambridge Quarto* series. He has written extensively about the design, the archaeology and the sociology of the London theatres of Shakespeare's time.

Alexandra F. Johnston, Arleane Ralph and Abigail Anne Young ("The Conundrum of the Label") bring their combined expertise as paleographers to bear on all manner of Elizabethan handwriting in their work for the Records of Early English Drama project (REED), based at the University of Toronto. REED is an international research project that is revolutionizing scholarly understanding of Shakespeare's dramatic context. Its aims are to locate, edit and publish systematically all evidence for drama, music and ceremony in Great Britain from the earliest surviving record in any location up to 1642, when the Puritans closed professional theatres. So far, nineteen volumes have been published in what has been called "one of the few remaining miracles of humanistic scholarship." Alexandra F. Johnston, who has published widely in the field of early theatre, is Professor of English at the University of Toronto and Director of REED. Arleane Ralph is a Research Associate at REED and a specialist in the English hands of the sixteenth and seventeenth centuries. Abigail Anne Young is a Research Associate at REED and a specialist in both Latin and English hands from the twelfth to the seventeenth centuries.

Alexander Leggatt ("The Man Who Will Not Meet Your Eyes") is Professor of English at University College, University of Toronto. He has published extensively on English drama, mostly on the work of Shakespeare and his contemporaries. His examination of the literature of the English theatre includes *Shakespeare's Comedy of Love* (1974), *Shakespeare's Political Drama* (1988), *Jacobean Public Theatre* (1992), *English Stage Comedy 1490-1990* (1998) and *Introduction to English Renaissance Comedy* (1999). He is editor of *The Cambridge Companion to Shakespearean Comedy* (2002). He has held the Guggenheim and Killam Fellowships. In 1995 he won an Outstanding Teaching Award from the Faculty of Arts and Science, University of Toronto, and in 1998 the Faculty Award in the University of Toronto Alumni Awards of Excellence.

Robert Tittler ("An Actor's Face?") has taught British and European History at Loyola College in Montreal and its successor Concordia University since 1969, taking time out to serve as a Visiting Professor of History at Yale University in 1998. His training and early research interests lay in the political and narrative approach to Tudor and Early Stuart English History, interests that have broadened since the late 1970s to include research in Early Modern English Urban History, culminating in the publication of his sixth book, *The Reformation and the Towns in England* (1998) and of *Townspeople and Nation, English Urban Experiences, 1540-1640* (2001). His involvement since the mid-1980s with the role of visual and material forms in the context of Early Modern England led to his monograph, *Architecture and Power, the Town Hall and the English Urban Community, 1500-1640* (1991). Since 1995 he has researched and taught the subject of portraiture in the Early Modern Period of English History. He is currently engaged in a project to investigate the role of non-courtly English portraiture, c. 1550-1640, as a form of social and political discourse.

Stanley Wells ("'The God of Our Idolatry'") is Emeritus Professor and an Honorary Fellow of University College London, where he took his first degree in 1951, Emeritus Professor of the University of Birmingham and an Honorary Fellow of the Shakespeare Institute, where he served from 1988 to 1997 as Professor of Shakespeare Studies. Since 1995 he has held the honorary position of Chairman of the Shakespeare Birthplace Trust in Stratford-upon-Avon. He is Vice-Chairman of the Royal Shakespeare Company and was Chairman of the International

Shakespeare Association from 1996 to 2001. He is a Trustee of both the Rose and the Globe Theatres. In 1995 he was awarded the Walcott Award of the Library Association for services to bibliography. He served as General Editor of the Oxford edition of *Shakespeare's Complete Works* (1986), and as General Editor of the multi-volume *Oxford Shakespeare.* His publications include *Royal Shakespeare* (1977, 1978), *Shakespeare: The Writer and His Work* (1978), *Shakespeare: An Illustrated Dictionary* (1978, 1985), *Re-editing Shakespeare for the Modern Reader* (1984), *Shakespeare: A Dramatic Life* (1994). He is Associate Editor of the New Penguin edition of Shakespeare and edited the annual Shakespeare Survey for Cambridge University Press from 1980 to 1999. He is also an Associate Editor of the forthcoming *New Dictionary of National Biography* and co-editor of the *Oxford Companion to Shakespeare* (2001). Forthcoming is *For All Time: Shakespeare and His Legacy.*

Stephanie Nolen is a foreign affairs reporter for *The Globe and Mail,* Canada's national newspaper. Born in Montreal, and raised there and in Ottawa, she studied journalism at the University of King's College in Halifax and subsequently earned a master's degree in economic development from the London School of Economics. From there, she moved to the West Bank, where she learned Arabic and spent four years covering the Middle East for publications including *Newsweek, The Globe and Mail* and *The Independent* of London. She has recently reported from the war in Afghanistan, the new *intifada* in the Middle East and the AIDS pandemic in sub-Saharan Africa. She is the author of *Promised the Moon: the Untold Story of the First Women in the Space Race* (Penguin Books, 2002).

The Mystery Uncovered

SHAKESPEARE KNEW US. His characters, with their foibles and their failings (and their ribald inside jokes) are people we recognize as soon as they walk onto a stage. It is not simply that Shakespeare's plays are the most performed of any playwright's—rather, it is that Hamlet and Juliet and Othello are people just like us. We do not poison, behead or banish with quite the same frequency as did Shakespeare's medieval Italians and Danes or his early English Kings. But we plot, we pine and we fall disastrously in love with quite the wrong person every bit as often as do his creations. We are as darkly ambitious as Lady Macbeth, as jubilantly lusty as Bottom, as embittered as Iago. Shakespeare's first audiences loved his plays as much as we do today because they too saw themselves beneath the cloaks and helmets of his actors.

He knew us, but what do we know of William Shakespeare? Before I encountered the painting at the heart of this book, my knowledge of the playwright was sketchy, like most people's, and it came from predictable sources. I had an enthusiastic high school English teacher (who tried to get her surly teenage charges to speak in iambic pentameter in the lunch line), and I clutched a dog-eared copy of *The Winter's Tale* in earnest coffee-fuelled debates as an undergraduate. I knew that in recent years the union of Shakespeare studies and pop culture had produced not just state-of-the-art movies but also glossy magazine articles on some of the long-running debates (Shakespeare as misogynist or closet revolutionary).

Like most young North Americans with a reasonably good education, I knew Shakespeare came from Stratford-upon-Avon. I could name his wife, Anne Hathaway, and seemed to remember something about, shall we say, a hastily arranged marriage. I knew that many of the phrases he first penned had taken permanent root in English—"love is blind," for example, "it was Greek to me," "neither here nor there" and "to catch a cold." And as Hollywood directors competed to film his plays, it was obvious Shakespeare's influence on culture continued to extend well beyond the realm of literature.

I didn't know the man. I didn't know I wanted to.

Then I met the man in the Sanders portrait and fast found myself in the thick of a detective story, one that drew its clues from genealogy, art history, forensics, great literature and old family tales.

The story of the portrait begins more than four hundred years ago—but I made my entry from stage left only recently. It started with a phone call from my mother. We were having one of our regular chats, me in my kitchen in Toronto, she in hers in Ottawa, on a spring evening in 2001.

"Here's a funny thing," she said. "Dad was talking to Lloyd Sullivan"—a neighbour who lives up the street, in a suburban house much like her own. "Well, he's got this picture—he inherited it from his mother, I think. It's a portrait of William Shakespeare—or maybe it's *by* William Shakespeare. Anyway, it's the only one of its kind. It might even be worth a million dollars. I thought it might make a good story."

My mother knows a good story when she hears one. She has been sending them my way since I was fifteen, when she helped me get my first job at a newspaper. But this one sounded like a bit much: a million-dollar picture of—or by, or something—Shakespeare, in a sleepy suburb of Ottawa? Not likely. My mother didn't know much more than these vague details. She had heard about the painting from my father, who had heard the story from the neighbour. My father was coming home from a jog one evening, saw Lloyd Sullivan fixing his brakes and stopped for a chat. They were discussing the stock market, when Lloyd quipped that *his* retirement plan was an oil painting—and he told my father about an old picture he had. It seemed like a rather fantastic tale, and my dad didn't take it too seriously. But a few days later he mentioned it to my mother, and she passed the story along to me.

I put down the telephone, both amused and intrigued. It is an axiom of the news business that the best-sounding leads are invariably apocryphal. And this one seemed *really* far-fetched. I was working on other stories, solid stories with real deadlines. I stored this one away.

And William Shakespeare did not cross my mind again for a week or two—until one morning a few hours before a weekly story meeting at *The Globe and Mail*, the newspaper where I report on international affairs. This was at the height of a ferocious newspaper war that then gripped Toronto, and I knew I had to come up with something: a new idea, a recycled idea, a lead I was still "nailing down." But all I could think of was that conversation with my mother. In the morning I tried several times to get hold of the man who owned the portrait, but in his retirement he occasionally drove a school bus and was hard to reach.

That afternoon, when I faced the lineup of hungry editors, I knew better than to make too much of this bizarre little tale. For if it turned out to be a fraud—and that seemed almost certain—I would be left making hollow excuses to the same testy bunch. Quickly I summarized what I knew: that my parents had this neighbour, that the neighbour had this picture and that the picture might possibly be of Shakespeare. Or by him.

The Globe's editor-in-chief, Richard Addis, a recently transplanted Englishman, was delighted with the notion of an undiscovered Shakespeare portrait. My reporter colleagues met it with skepticism: Shakespeare didn't paint. If he did paint, what were the odds that a retired engineer in Ottawa owned his lone masterpiece? Whoever the guy was, he had obviously seen one too many episodes of *The Antiques Roadshow*.

But Richard Addis was intrigued. I left that meeting with strict orders from the boss to find out more and report back. The next evening I finally caught up by telephone with Lloyd Sullivan, the representative acting on behalf of the family members who own the portrait. I started with neighbourly chitchat—"Don't know if you remember me, Barb and Jim Nolen's daughter"—and then got around to the painting my father had told my mother about. His story spilled out: there was indeed a picture. Not by Shakespeare, but of him. The only one painted from life. Handed down through

Lloyd's family for four hundred years. He had put the past ten years of his life and most of his savings into establishing its authenticity. And he had proved it: he was absolutely convinced that he owned the only genuine picture of the world's greatest writer.

Finally I asked the crucial question: would he let me come and see the painting? Could I write about it in *The Globe and Mail*? Lloyd agreed cautiously, on the condition that I not identify him in the newspaper. He was worried about security, since a painting he believed could be extremely valuable was stashed in his dining room. It seemed a little odd that he had not put the portrait in a bank vault, but then, from what I remembered, he was a regular-folks kind of guy. Maybe he didn't trust banks.

I was starting to get that prickle on the back of my neck that a good story always brings. But I was puzzled by Lloyd's assertion that his was the "only" picture of William Shakespeare. I knew what Shakespeare looked like: bald guy in a ruff; bit of a sourpuss, actually—not the type you imagined writing *Romeo and Juliet*. And if I knew that face of Shakespeare, there must be at least one portrait.

That night I holed up in *The Globe*'s cramped but rich library and started thumbing through the reference books. It took me only a few minutes to learn an astounding thing: we don't know what Shakespeare looked like. Not really. The only two reasonably reliable images we have—one of them the ubiquitous grump in the doublet—were created after his death. No portrait exists that was painted while Shakespeare was alive—at least none on which most scholars agree.

This was the knowledge I carried with me on the morning of May 9, 2001, when I knocked on the Sullivans' front door. Lloyd and his wife, Mary, live in an unpretentious four-bedroom house in an Ottawa suburb built around a crossroads: school, church, grocery store, hockey rink. Lloyd answered my knock and greeted me warmly. He was older than I remembered from our last encounter about ten years before—snowy haired now, but still jovial. He introduced Raymond du Plessis, an old friend who had been helping with "The Project."

Mary brought tea, and the four of us sat down in the living room for a chat. The room was a rather unlikely setting for a story about a Renaissance painting, for its walls were adorned with religious icons and, hung above the sofa, just one painting: a standard-issue-Canadiana oil of a snow-topped red barn at sunset. Lloyd and Mary asked after my brother and sister, and I inquired about their two daughters, with whom I had played hide-and-seek as a child. The Sullivans wanted to know all about my job with *The Globe*, and we talked about the places I had travelled and the stories I had covered, while my mind raced forward to the questions I wanted to ask.

Finally I cracked a fresh notebook and tried to start at the beginning. Where did Lloyd get the portrait? And who painted it? And what made him think it was Shakespeare, of all people? He began to tell his story, speaking with a mixture of gravity and enthusiasm that soon made it clear this painting was a consuming passion for him. The tale he told was a long and complicated one that jumped back and forth over four centuries and two continents. Raymond, a thin, serious, retired constitutional lawyer, interrupted periodically to correct Lloyd on dates and times and proper names. Ray's analytical mind clearly relished the puzzle of it all. And a few times Mary joined the conversation too, usually to correct some detail of the family history. She had the many branches of a sprawling Catholic clan clear in her mind.

We talked well into the night, and by the time I headed home, I had the skeleton of a fascinating story. But I had seen no sign of the painting, and somehow, I didn't like to bring it up: I needed to earn more of Lloyd's confidence before I asked to meet the man the family called "Willy Shake."

Very early the next morning, I made a series of rather ludicrous phone calls. Richard Addis had instructed me to seek comments on the painting from Shakespeare scholars and art experts. But I was not to reveal the specific portrait behind my questions or any details about its circumstances for fear that someone would scoop *The Globe*.

My first call was to Jacob Simon, chief curator of the National Portrait Gallery in London. The Gallery is one of Britain's premier art institutions, and I reckoned that if anyone would be knowledgeable about pictures of England's great writer, it would be their curators. Although I did not know it at the time, the Gallery has a Shakespeare of its own, called the Chandos portrait, a leading contender for the life-picture title. To my surprise, Simon actually picked up the phone. I introduced myself and launched into a brief, mortifying conversation.

I asked the British curator to assess the significance of a new, authentic life portrait of Shakespeare. He replied rather frostily that people are forever thinking they have found a Shakespeare, and they never have. "You're calling from where?" he asked at one point, his tone conveying that he considered it most unlikely that a plausible picture of Shakespeare would turn up in Canada, of all places. He was unimpressed. Three minutes into our conversation, Simon hung up on me. I could picture him shaking his head, wondering why the switchboard always put the nutcases through to him.

Mentally readjusting my reporter's armour, I turned to the Shakespeare scholars on my list. First I dialled the office of Stanley Wells, a professor of English literature who chairs the Shakespeare Birthplace Trust in Stratford-upon-Avon. The Trust is Shakespeare mecca: it maintains the poet's various homes and fosters much of the best Shakespeare scholarship today, keeping a precious archive of historical records for the town of Stratford. Over the telephone, Wells sounded just as one imagines a retired professor in a small English town ought to sound: wise, a bit posh, terribly polite. He was more kind than the curator had been and told me that a new portrait would of course be exciting, but like Simon, he warned that "new" portraits turn up frequently. Reasonably enough, he asked for details about this latest picture. Sworn to secrecy by the newspaper, I could give him only the most general information, quickly undermining the last of my credibility.

After my conversations with Jacob Simon and Stanley Wells, I called several more academics, a handful of art historians and a few auction houses to try to get a sense of the potential value of the picture. Talking to the art experts, I cagily posed such questions as, "If somebody had a picture of—oh, say, Jesus—and it had been scientifically authenticated and had a solid provenance, what would that be worth?" Jesus was the only remotely comparable figure I could come up with; someone revered all over the world but of whom we had no verified image. After a few hours of this, I had collected a couple of useable comments and had left a trail of experts in a variety of fields across Canada, the United States and Britain convinced that I was a complete lunatic.

By mid-morning I was back in the Sullivans' living room, barraging Lloyd and Ray with more questions. We spent hours going through the mountain of documents they had amassed and consulting genealogical charts spread across the dining room table. I sat on the thick beige carpet with files stacked around me and ticked through my list of queries, gradually filling a fat notebook.

By late afternoon, I had pieced together the following story. In 1972, Lloyd's mother, Kathleen, had died in Montreal at the age of sixty-nine. She left everything she owned to her husband, who outlived her by seven years—everything except her painting of William Shakespeare, a family heirloom that had come to her from an older brother, and then passed into the custody of Lloyd, her only child. He was then a practising engineer, a busy father, a man active in his church, a pitcher for the local softball team. For a while he hung the painting on his dining room wall. When he entertained colleagues at home, they would invariably ask about it. Who's the fellow with the twinkling eyes? That's William Shakespeare, Lloyd would tell them. "And they'd say, 'Have another drink,'" he recalls with a chuckle. Then one day a couple of friends suggested the portrait might be valuable; Lloyd thought it over and concluded the picture might best be put away for safekeeping. So Willy Shake went into the cupboard in the upstairs hall.

But Lloyd did not forget about the painting. Shortly before his mother died, she had advised him to give the portrait some attention—there was more to it than just a story. A retirement project, she suggested. And he thought, Damn it, when I retire and I've got nothing to do, I'm gonna research this. I'm not going to sit in a rocking chair and read newspapers. And, I mean, nobody in the family moved the yardsticks on this in the whole four hundred years.

This much Lloyd believed he knew from family tradition: the portrait was painted by his ancestor a dozen generations back, one John Sanders, born in 1576, the eldest son of a family in Worcester, England. Young John left home to make his fortune in London. There he became an actor, or at least a bit player, in Shakespeare's company—the Lord Chamberlain's Men, which was formed in 1594, when Shakespeare was thirty. John Sanders also dabbled in oils and did odd bits of painting around the theatre. He liked to try his hand at portraiture. And sometime in 1603, he prepared a sturdy oak panel and some bright oil paint and recorded the face of his colleague, William Shakespeare—then a writer of limited but burgeoning renown. Sanders or one of his children labelled the picture "Shakspere" (in a spelling the poet himself used) and included the playwright's birth and death dates, noting that this was his likeness at the age of thirty-nine. The portrait was handed down, passing from the first John Sanders to his son, and so on through the family.

At the beginning of the twentieth century, when the Sanders family left England for Canada, the portrait followed them. It passed from a school principal to his children and eventually to the gentle youngest sister—Lloyd's mother—and then to Lloyd. Since he had removed the painting from the wall where it had originally hung, Lloyd had kept it in that upstairs hall cupboard. For years, he had been researching the origin, provenance, history and authenticity of the portrait on behalf of the family. This work was still in progress and was expected to be concluded sometime within the next few years.

As I neared the end of that second long day at the Sullivans', my head ached with complicated details and a surfeit of unanswered questions. How did he know it wasn't a very good fake? If John Sanders painted well enough to record Shakespeare, why was none of his other work known? Why had the picture never become public before? Why hadn't some enterprising Sanders in the past four hundred years sold it for the fortune it was likely worth?

But Lloyd showed me wills and letters and a list of the rolls of actors from the Lord Chamberlain's and the King's Men from Shakespeare's time, a list that included a "J. Sanders." He gave me a thick sheaf of results from painstaking forensic analysis of the painting, which certainly looked persuasive. He appeared to have done a thorough job. I could not report the existence of a definite portrait of Shakespeare, but I could certainly report on a picture with an extraordinary claim. There was just one crucial thing I needed.

"Is he here?" I asked, suddenly a little nervous.

Lloyd got up from the dining room table, took a few steps to a nearby cabinet, reached down beside it and pulled out a brown parcel about four inches thick and a little bigger than an old-fashioned vinyl LP. He laid the package on the cluttered table, then casually pulled back the kraft paper wrapping and a layer of bubble wrap to reveal his treasure.

It was a rogue's face, a charmer's face that looked back at me with a tolerant, mischievous, slightly world-weary air. There was nothing austere or haughty about him, nothing of the great man being painted for posterity. The portrait was small, much smaller than I had imagined, but it was extraordinarily vivid. The colours in the paint seemed much too rich to be four centuries old.

Lloyd flipped the painting over and pointed to a three-inch-square patch near the top of the unpainted wood. This was what remained of the label that once identified the subject as "Shakspere"— but by now much of it had flaked away, and none of the writing was legible. The only identifying mark on the painting itself was a date, "AN° 1603," which appeared in small red letters in the top-right-hand corner. The right edge of the board seemed to have been damaged, and a faint line visible just inside the perimeter of the painting suggested that it had once been framed. There were three gouges across the top—I would learn later that someone sometime in the past had crudely attempted to attach the picture to a frame with nails.

I stood and gazed into those beguiling eyes, stifling an instinctive urge to pick up the portrait and hold it in my hands. And as my professional skepticism crumpled for a moment, I found myself wanting desperately to believe that this was indeed Shakespeare's face.

"He's . . . lovely," I said.

"Isn't he?" Lloyd agreed, with a paternal sort of smile. "Much better-looking than the others. You should see the Chandos portrait! It makes Shakespeare look . . . Italian! The guy in that picture is wearing an earring!" Shaking his head at the very idea, Lloyd bundled his Shakespeare back into the bubble wrap and tucked it in beside the cabinet.

I made my farewells and emerged into the late afternoon sun, feeling slightly stunned. It was hard to get that face out of my head. The evidence appeared solid, yet it didn't seem possible that a real picture of Shakespeare was here in the innocuous neighbourhood where I grew up.

Just as I arrived at my parents' house, a taxi pulled up bearing *The Globe* photographer Patti Gower, who had flown to Ottawa to take a picture of the picture. But when I called Lloyd to tell him I was bringing the photographer over, he told me he preferred that Patti not know who he was or where he lived. So I trundled back to his house, took charge of his precious heirloom and started home. I was hardly down his driveway when a light spring shower began to fall. I broke into a run and sprinted down the block, terrified the painting would get wet and be damaged. With the portrait safely within my parents' walls, Patti took over, promptly converting the living room into her photo studio.

While she worked, I called Richard Addis in his office in Toronto. Feeling a certain unreality even as I said the words, I told him that as far as I could ascertain from the little information I had, the picture had a possible claim to authenticity. I would need, of course, to call Lloyd's sources myself, and I would need to verify many of the details with Shakespeare scholars and experts on art. But I felt we could confidently report the discovery of a possible life portrait of William Shakespeare. Addis was ecstatic: "Marvellous!" he said. "Tell us everything!"

Then I started making calls: to the Canadian Conservation Institute, which had done the forensic tests, to the Folger Shakespeare Library in Washington, D.C., to professors in Liverpool and California, checking as much of Lloyd's tale as I could. And while Patti shot the picture from every angle, I paced, trying to calculate the likelihood of the house getting hit by lightning. An hour later, with enormous relief, I carried the Sanders portrait back to the Sullivans.

It was now the afternoon of May 10, 2001. Barely two weeks had elapsed from the time my mother first told me about the painting that had something to do with William Shakespeare. For the better part of forty-eight hours, I had been immersed in one of the strangest and potentially the most wonderful stories I had ever covered. I now had a day and a half to produce a news story for the paper.

At four o'clock, I sat down at my parents' dining room table and stared at my laptop screen, acutely conscious of the gaping holes in my knowledge of both Shakespeare and art history. But the life of a newspaper reporter is a repeated exercise in quickly learning enough to write authoritatively about something you previously knew nothing about. I had brought a towering pile of photocopied references with me from Toronto, and they were festooned with Post-it notes from a crash course self-administered late into the previous night. I began to write.

At five o'clock, Richard Addis called. *The Globe*'s editor-in-chief had decided the paper could not risk waiting another day, and he wanted the story for *tomorrow's* paper—which meant I had to file it at six o'clock. I had one more hour to tell the story of the painting that just might show us Shakespeare's face.

"The God of Our Idolatry"

Stanley Wells

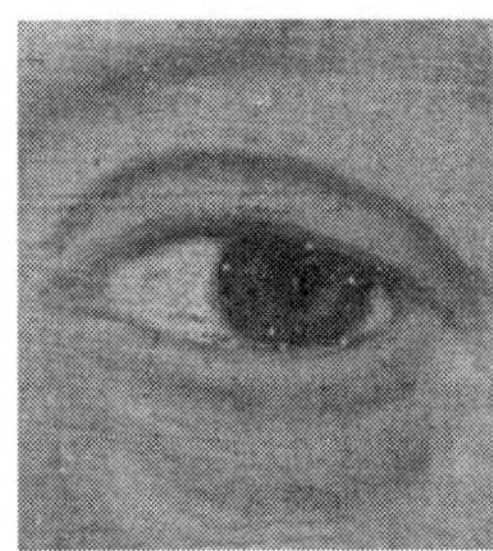

WHAT IS THERE about William Shakespeare that causes any news about him to be treated as a matter of global interest? Why should the recent reappearance of a portrait purporting to be of Shakespeare, and to have been painted while he was alive, have made headlines and nightly newscasts around the world?

In part Shakespeare's fame is a self-generating process, stemming from the acceptance of the view that he stands above all other writers, even all other creative artists, that he is on a par with pop stars, Hollywood celebrities, Olympic athletes and world leaders as a fit subject for media attention. But this does not explain the fact that he has come to attain the status of a universal cultural icon. The cards might well seem to have been stacked against the idea that an English poetic dramatist of the sixteenth century should occupy this position. His plays are written in a language that grows increasingly archaic, that even native speakers of English find hard to understand and that indeed may well have seemed difficult to some of those who first heard it.

His writings are rooted in earlier literature, especially the ancient classics and the Bible; it's a paradox that during the past hundred or so years Shakespeare's plays have largely superseded the classics as the basis for a literary education, and that during this period too the study of the Bible has declined, even though familiarity with the classics and the Bible might seem to be an essential foundation for the understanding of Shakespeare. What's more, his plays were written for theatres we know only too little of, and they employ dramatic and theatrical conventions very different from those of our own day. If in spite of these apparent disqualifications Shakespeare has become as famous as Elton John, Tom Cruise or Bill Clinton, it must have something to do with qualities in his work that transcend temporal and geographical—and therefore linguistic—boundaries.

We have no evidence that he ever travelled outside his own country. But, as he says in his Sonnet 27, he made many journeys within his head:

> Weary with toil I haste me to my bed,
> The dear repose for limbs with travel tired;
> But then begins a journey in my head
> To work my mind when body's work's expired.

Shakespeare's plays are the result of journeys of exploration within his head, voyaging in time as well as in space. He is conspicuously unconcerned, at least on the surface of his work, with present time and contemporary society. Only one of his plays, *The Merry Wives of Windsor*, and the framing scenes of another, *The Taming of the Shrew*, come at all close to portraying life in his own time, and even in them it is romanticized. Otherwise, all his plays except, unavoidably, the English histories, are set overseas, and none of them in the period during which he was writing.

Conspicuously too, Shakespeare depended largely for his narrative material on stories that had already proved their worth in mirroring and exploring situations common to large proportions of the world's population. He is a more literary dramatist than is often supposed. The legend perpetuated in the film *Shakespeare in Love*, that he invented the plots of his plays in between energetic bouts of lovemaking in the rafters of the Rose Theatre, was a charming embellishment. George Bernard Shaw, in one of his not infrequent moments of exasperation with Shakespeare, referred to his "gift of telling a story (provided someone else told it to him first)." There is more than a little truth in this. Shakespeare was not above all an inventor of plots. Many of the stories he drew on were the stuff of myth and folk legend. Even in so relatively slight a play as *The Comedy of Errors*, he complicates a mechanical, classical farce of mistaken identity with the romance story of the old father, Egeon, searching for and eventually finding his twin sons, so that the multiple reunions and reconciliations of the final scene touch deep chords in the audience's imagination. A simple story of mistaken identity becomes an exploration of the human need for a sense of personal identity and of the frightening, potentially tragic consequences of a withdrawal of this sense. Farce becomes, however lightly, serious drama: it is not far-fetched to compare Egeon's dismay at finding himself apparently rejected by the son he loves with King Lear's "Who is it that can tell me who I am?" when his daughters seem no longer to know him. One of Shakespeare's favourite books, which he drew on time and again, was the Roman poet Ovid's collection of myths, the *Metamorphoses*, and some of his own plays have acquired the status of myths.

To show that Shakespeare's plays are closely related to the work of other cultures does not in itself explain why these works, rather than other versions of the same myths and legends, should have become globally influential. There must be something about his handling of myths, legends and folk tales that has established them not only as classic embodiments of their narratives but also as works that can cut across national boundaries in the way that French and German classics, such as plays by Racine and Goethe, largely do not. (By contrast, Ibsen and Chekhov have travelled widely.) Shakespeare's broader appeal is due partly, I think, to the richness and density of his work, the way that it ignores traditional generic boundaries so that a single play can be understood on many levels at once—indeed, we might even suggest each play contains within it an almost infinite number of other plays that can be mined from it.

His tragedies work both outwardly and inwardly, offering profound psychological studies of individual persons while at the same time relating these to no less profound examinations of issues of government and statecraft—examinations that would be less astute than they are were they not projected in terms of the personalities of those involved in them. As a result, they offer multiple choices to their interpreters, so that productions of *Macbeth* and of *Hamlet* may stress the personal and the political in varying proportions; in these times, at least in Britain, directors tend to lay their emphases on the inner states of mind of the chief characters, but at other times, and in other places, the political dimension has been stressed. Similarly, directors vary in the degree to which they emphasize serious elements in the comedies. At the end of *Measure for Measure,* the chaste heroine, Isabella, in some productions accepts the Duke's proposal of marriage, in others ignores it and in others wordlessly rejects it.

Important too is Shakespeare's genius for plotting his narratives in ways that can work in their own right, so that, for instance, it is possible to enjoy *Macbeth* as a murder mystery or *Hamlet* as a ghost story without being conscious of the psychological and political depths that Shakespeare plumbed in his particular dramatizations of these stories. The plays can, as it were, be stripped down to their basic narrative structures yet still have meaning, as we can see in the enduring and international success of Charles and Mary Lamb's *Tales from Shakespeare* and similar prose retellings; or of the series of animated tales created for television and much used on video in schools, in which the texts are so drastically reduced that they last no more than thirty minutes each; or even in silent films and balletic versions such as Prokofiev's *Romeo and Juliet* and Robert Helpmann's *Hamlet,* which dispense with words altogether.

A too often repeated cliché about Shakespeare says that his greatness lies "all in the poetry," and it is true that some of his verbal effects, such as those relying on rhythm, rhyme and wordplay, may be variously untranslatable into other languages. But this is not to say that in the hands of skilful translators, such effects may not be replaceable by a poetry which, inspired by the original and attempting to recreate its linguistic theatricality, is nevertheless native to the language into which the translation is being made. Translation need not be mere banal paraphrase. Listeners and readers who rely on a modern translation, into any language, of

Shakespeare's text have the advantage over those who read or hear the original in that the translation will attempt to render intelligible the difficulties that those of us who have to hear or read it in English are obliged to put up with. It is even possible to argue that translation can improve on Shakespeare; in any case, it does Shakespeare a disservice to suggest that there is no more to his language than a meaningless shimmer of word music.

A. L. Rowse's half-hearted attempts to modernize aspects of the play's language are mercifully forgotten, but the modern version that Peter Brook imaginatively commissioned from Ted Hughes for his film of *King Lear* would surely be worth reading—and fascinating to see on stage or screen. Brook did not use it, and it seems to have disappeared. English-speaking readers may feel that they cannot judge the success of translations into wholly foreign languages, but the following Scots version, published in 1992, of the opening lines of Macbeth's "Is this a dagger" soliloquy will indicate something of the poetic power that translation can achieve:

What's this I see afore my een—a bityach [dagger]
Heftit [pointed] towart my haund? Come, let me cleik [clutch] ye—
I grip ye no, but ey can see ye yet!
Ar ye, weird vision, oniething at may
As weill be ticht as seen? Or ar ye but
A bityach o the mind, a fenyit [feigned] craitur
Ingenrit [engendered] o the heat-afflickit harns [mind]?

Cultural translation is perhaps even more difficult than linguistic, and may be impossible for some plays into some cultures. Since the eighteenth century, a few of Shakespeare's plays have entered the dramatic and literary mainstream of Russia and other Eastern European countries, but they have made slower headway in Africa, in Muslim countries and, until recently, in the Far East. We should not claim that every play that Shakespeare wrote is so deeply rooted in basic human reality that it is infinitely susceptible to cultural transference. Even nearby France has been slow to embrace Shakespeare; not until late in the twentieth century was *Henry V*, with its satirical portrayal of the French army, performed in France in French translation. And if we were being scrupulously fair, we should have to admit that some areas of the globe—such as parts of Southern America—still tend to find Shakespeare resistible, and that even in countries—including England—where he is appreciated in the language of his own time, it is by only a minority of the population. Yet in a sense the plays have constantly shown themselves amenable to cultural translation every time they have been performed, even in English, since Shakespeare's time, and it may be felt that geographical difference poses no greater obstacles to translation into foreign cultures than the passage of time to their performance in England—that, in other words, audiences in modern Beijing or Tbilisi are no less remote in their cultural expectations from those of Shakespeare's time than are the Londoners who watch *King Lear* or *Macbeth* in the reconstructed Globe Theatre today.

A thorough attempt to explain why Shakespeare is more international in his appeal than other authors would require an exhaustive comparative exercise that is beyond my capacities, but I am sure that part of the explanation lies in the fact that he was so committed to writing for the theatre, and that this caused him to write with a constant awareness that he was engaged in a profoundly collaborative exercise. He knew that he depended for success on the efforts of his co-workers, especially his actors, and he wrote for them in a way that permits them to make a creative contribution to the finished product. There is, as it were, an unwritten dimension to his plays, an openness to reinterpretation, which helps to explain the endless fascination they have exercised on audiences and performers alike. The actor playing Hamlet may emphasize the lyrical or the harsher aspects of the role, may choose to suggest that the character grows in maturity during the course of the action or that he is ultimately defeated by the burden he bears. Shylock may be presented as a figure of satire or may take on tragic dimensions. Othello may be a noble Moor or a self-deluded murderer. Shakespeare knew that the texts he wrote would take on a life of their own as soon as they were put into rehearsal, and as scholars have become increasingly ready to acknowledge in recent years, he himself allowed them to be reshaped during the rehearsal process. This helps to explain why his plays are endlessly self-renewing, why they can go on reshaping themselves on the world's stages.

I have stressed the mythic and legendary nature of Shakespeare's narratives, the richness and density of his work, the self-sufficiency of his dramatic structures, his plays' susceptibility to cultural translation and his theatrical openness. It is needless to say that he portrays situations that affect all of us, both personally and politically, that he creates—or gives his actors the stimulus to represent—characters in whom we can believe, that he deals with fundamental human concerns—love and marriage, birth and death, relationships between individuals and between levels of society, the need for good government on a personal and a national level. Many other dramatists do these things too, but Shakespeare is concerned not only with human beings in society but also with our place in the universe. He is in the most important sense of the word a *religious* dramatist—not a proponent of any particular religion but a writer who is aware, and makes his spectators aware, of the mystery of things, of humankind's need to seek, however unavailingly, for an understanding of how we came to be on earth and how we should conduct ourselves now we are here. That is why he often deals with the explicitly supernatural—in *Hamlet*, or *Macbeth, A Midsummer Night's Dream* or *The Tempest*—and why even plays that are not directly concerned with otherworldly matters may nevertheless invoke a sense of a world elsewhere, as, for example, Antipholus of Syracuse fears that "[t]here's none but witches do inhabit here" (*The Comedy of Errors*, 3.2.162), or, in *Twelfth Night*, Viola, reunited with her brother, can say, "If spirits can assume both form and suit / You come to fright us" (5.1.232–3). And this is why, too, *King Lear*, with its constant battering at the gates of the unknown, its examination of what differentiates human beings from the beasts, has come to be regarded as Shakespeare's greatest play.

But having said this, we must say too that Shakespeare would not command his global audience were he not also, in the fullest sense of the word, the greatest of entertainers, capable of engaging the hearts and minds of those who watch his plays, of absorbing them into the worlds he gives the illusion of creating, of making people laugh even as they deeply feel, of transporting them from beginning to end of a story and leaving them with a sense of profound artistic satisfaction. The journeys that began in

Shakespeare's head have carried him and his works around "the great globe itself," and we are their inheritors.

No wonder, then, that the appearance of a "new" Shakespeare portrait should cause such a stir. And given the human need to gaze on relics of the holy and the great, the Sanders portrait joins a long and not always distinguished lineage of authentic and supposed relics of William Shakespeare.

Even intrinsically worthless objects may be treasured because of their associations with the mighty dead. Museums and birthplaces all over the world bear witness to the quasi-religious adoration that may be bestowed on great men's relics—the clothes they wore, locks of their hair, the pens they wrote with, the musical instruments they played, chairs they sat on, the cups they drank from. Books signed by the author, or even by a famous owner, are prized. For artists of the relatively recent past, such relics often abound: whole houses may be filled with possessions of Goethe or Dickens or Verdi. But the further we go back in time, the less likely it becomes that relics will survive, so those that do are correspondingly more highly valued.

The early-nineteenth-century painter Benjamin Robert Haydon became almost hysterical with excitement when he heard of the discovery of a ring that might have belonged to Shakespeare. In March 1818 he wrote to the poet John Keats, "I shall certainly go mad! In a field at Stratford upon Avon, in a field that belonged to Shakespeare; they have found a gold ring and seal, with the initial thus—W. S. and a true lover's knot between. If this is not Shakespeare who is it?—a true lover's knot.!! As sure as you breathe, & that he was the first of beings the Seal belonged to him—O Lord!" Whether the ring actually belonged to Shakespeare is not proven; it is now on exhibition in Stratford-upon-Avon at the Shakespeare Centre, headquarters of the Shakespeare Birthplace Trust, and cheap reproductions of it may be bought in the gift shop.

Though the instinct to venerate relics of great artists is especially associated with the Romantic period, for Shakespeare it can be traced back at least to the middle of the eighteenth century. In 1759 the Reverend Francis Gastrell, who had bought Shakespeare's house, New Place, in Stratford-upon-Avon, became exasperated by requests for cuttings from the mulberry tree that Shakespeare was supposed to have planted in its garden. As a result, he had the tree cut down and sold to a Birmingham dealer who manufactured and sold more souvenirs purporting to be made of its wood than could possibly have come from a single tree. In 1768 the town councillors successfully made approaches to the famous actor David Garrick in the hope that he would present them with a statue of Shakespeare to adorn the niche at the front of their new town hall, where it still stands. As reward, Garrick was made the first freeman of the borough (a freeman was a paid-up member of one of the city's guilds, a status that gave him certain rights of access); the scroll conferring the honour was enclosed "in a small neat chest constructed from a mulberry tree planted by Shakespeare himself." It is a beautiful example of the woodcarver's art, bearing a representation of Garrick as King Lear. The deification of Shakespeare was confirmed in the ode that Garrick wrote and performed for the 1769 Jubilee, in which the playwright is invoked in the words "'Tis he! 'tis He! / The god of our idolatry!"

Some faint evidence that portraits of Shakespeare may have existed in his lifetime is supplied in the second of the so-called

Parnassus plays of unknown authorship written around 1600 for performance by students of St. John's College, Cambridge. A ridiculous character named Gullio (the name means "a gull," or "a fool") hero-worships Shakespeare, boasting of how he woos his mistress with speeches larded with quotations from *Venus and Adonis* and *Romeo and Juliet*. His adoration reaches a climax as he exclaims, "O, sweet Master Shakespeare! I'll have his picture in my study at the court." This is Shakespeare as pin-up. Gullio's effusions are of course being mocked; even so, they indicate that by this point in his career Shakespeare had become a cult figure among certain sections of society. The author of the play is satirizing excessive adulation, but his mockery may be mixed with envy. How Gullio might have hoped to acquire Shakespeare's picture is not clear. A portrait of his fellow playwright Ben Jonson, later used as a frontispiece to two of his books, had been issued as an independent print sometime during the 1620s. Conceivably, paintings or engravings of Shakespeare, too, were on sale from London printmakers' or painters' shops, and possibly one of them formed the basis for the engraving by Martin Droeshout that graces the title page of the First Folio of 1623 (the first comprehensive edition of Shakespeare's plays). If so, none has survived.

The degree, if any, to which personal appearance may be an indicator of character clearly both fascinated and puzzled Shakespeare himself. "There's no art to find the mind's construction in the face," says King Duncan of the treacherous Thane of Cawdor (*Macbeth*, 1.4.11–12). In *Twelfth Night*, Viola speaks meditatively to the Sea Captain of the extent to which a man's appearance may reflect his personality (1.2.43–7):

There is a fair behaviour in thee, captain,
And though that nature with a beauteous wall
Doth oft close in pollution,
I will believe thou hast a mind that suits
With this thy fair and outward character.

The paradox that "Thersites' body is as good as Ajax' / When neither are alive" is profoundly explored in *Cymbeline* (4.2. 253–4). And most poignantly, personally and enigmatically, in Sonnet 94 Shakespeare writes,

They that have power to hurt and will do none,
That do not do the thing they most do show,
Who moving others are themselves as stone,
Unmovèd, cold, and to temptation slow—
They rightly do inherit nature's graces,
And husband nature's riches from expense;
They are the lords and masters of their faces,
Others but stewards of their excellence.

Was Shakespeare himself the lord and master of his face, giving away no hints of his feelings through his personal expression, like Claudius in *Hamlet*, or Angelo in *Measure for Measure*? Would we feel that we knew him any more deeply if we had a portrait of him comparable in excellence to, for example, the wonderfully dashing Lothian painting of the great poet John Donne, who died only fifteen years after Shakespeare, in 1631, which surely shows Donne exactly as we should like to imagine him? And as he would have liked to be imagined, too, because the frequently represented Donne had a genius for self-projection, nowhere more apparent than in his decision during his last days to have himself painted wearing his shroud in preparation for the erection of his funerary effigy in St. Paul's Cathedral.

Of the countless images that have laid claim to be of Shakespeare over the four centuries since his death, the vast majority seem to have been based on the two "portraits" generally accepted as authentic: the bust by Geraert Janssen that marks the place where Shakespeare is buried in Holy Trinity Church, Stratford-upon-Avon, and Martin Droeshout's engraving for the First Folio. Both are indifferent works of art, inferior to many of the imitations and fakes they have inspired. These range from fine paintings to the trivial souvenirs that can be seen in the gift shops of Stratford and of countless other places all over the world—the bottle stoppers, the tea cloths, the key rings and the erasers. A passion for objects of associative interest that have little if any value in themselves is of course easily mocked. Shakespeare himself makes Benedick in *Much Ado about Nothing* speak satirically of such instincts when he offers to scour the world for curiosities rather than converse with Beatrice: "Will your grace command me any service to the world's end? I will go on the slightest errand now to the Antipodes that you can devise to send me on. I will fetch you a tooth-picker now from the furthest inch of Asia, bring you the length of Prester John's foot, fetch you a hair off the Great Cham's beard, do you any embassage to the pigmies, rather than hold three words' conference with this harpy" (2. 2. 246–53). More seriously, in *Twelfth Night* Sebastian asks Antonio, "Shall we go see the relics"—that is, the religious relics—"of this town?," suggesting that they "satisfy [their] eyes / With the memorials and things of fame / That do renown this city" (3.3. 19–24). Shakespeare understood the tourist's desire for contact with the past.

Shakespeare and Donne are not the only writers of their time to be memorialized through portraiture; others besides Ben Jonson include George Chapman and John Fletcher (see "The Picture Gallery," page x). Some claims for visual authenticity are more secure than others. It is easy to feel that the portrait of a beautiful young man painted in 1585 and found among a heap of rubble in Corpus Christi College, Cambridge, in 1953 ought to represent Shakespeare's great and exact, though short-lived, contemporary Christopher Marlowe, but the identification has only circumstantial evidence to support it. Marlowe studied at Corpus Christi, and was twenty-one in 1585, but his humble origins make it unlikely that he should have had his portrait painted at this age. Desire may breed belief.

There is, however, no reason why Shakespeare should not have been painted during the year 1603. He was already well known to the literary and theatrical public and in aristocratic and court circles, his name is mentioned in numerous printed and manuscript writings, and he was known as the author of around twenty-five successful plays. His narrative poems, frequently reprinted, were highly fashionable, especially among young people; various complimentary references to his work had appeared in print; his name had started to appear on title pages five years previously, and John Manningham, a young law student, had recorded a racy anecdote about him in his journal: "Upon a time when [Richard] Burbage played Richard III there was a citizen grew so far in liking with him that before she went from the play she appointed him to come that night unto her by the name of

Richard the Third. Shakespeare, overhearing their conclusion, went before, was entertained, and at his game ere Burbage came. Then message being brought that Richard III was at the door, Shakespeare caused return to be made that William the Conqueror was before Richard III." In any case, and in spite of the doubts that have reasonably been cast on the portrait of Christopher Marlowe, it was not exceptional for persons of Shakespeare's social class to have their portraits painted (though understandably fewer of them have survived than of aristocrats). For example, the will of Shakespeare's colleague and friend John Heminges bequeathed to one of his sons-in-law, Capt. William Smith, "his wife's picture set up in a frame in my house" and to another, Thomas Sheppard, "his wife's picture which is also set up in a frame in my house."

The Sanders portrait that has inspired this book will, of course, be read in many different ways. Whether it really offers us a new direct line of communication with Shakespeare is probably something we shall never know. In that case, it will retain among portraits the status enjoyed in the dramatic canon by plays of uncertain authorship, such as *Edward III*—increasingly regarded as having been written at least in part by Shakespeare; *A Yorkshire Tragedy*—which has its supporters but is more generally attributed to Thomas Middleton; and *The London Prodigal*, for whose Shakespearean authorship there is little if any support. But even if the portrait's authenticity were to be disproved, the excitement that its discovery has provoked is itself a sociological phenomenon of considerable interest. If this had been a possible new portrait of, say, John Milton or John Dryden or Alexander Pope, it would have been of interest to scholars, might even have been reported in the more intellectually inclined newspapers, but would not have been a media event on anything like the scale of the supposed Shakespeare portrait.

As in so many other categories, when it comes to the quasi-religious veneration of writers and their relics, William Shakespeare stands alone. A true picture of his face would make the greatest relic of all.

Prime Suspects

A PRECIOUS RELIC: Lloyd Sullivan suspected as much when in 1991 he set out to prove that his picture really portrayed William Shakespeare. Not that he embarked on the project with any serious agenda; in the beginning, it was just a diversion. At fifty-eight, he had taken early retirement from Bell Canada, the large telecommunications firm where he had worked for thirty-five years. In his first few months of retirement, he spent a lot of time on the golf course and at gatherings of his charismatic Roman Catholic prayer group. But he was still a relatively young man and he had plenty of energy. One morning he got old Willy Shake out of the hall cupboard and remembered his mother's admonition to "do something" with the portrait. But what exactly? And where to start?

The obvious question was whether his portrait looked anything like the other pictures of Shakespeare. But it didn't take Lloyd long to make the same discovery that so astonished me a decade later: we really don't know Shakespeare's face.

We have thirty-eight of Shakespeare's plays (including possible collaborations); two poems and 154 of his sonnets; we have his will, his court testimony in a lawsuit and the records of his purchases of property and grain in Stratford. But we have no picture of his face when he was writing his great works. Not the face as it furrowed over half-filled pages; not the face that looked out at the audience as *Hamlet*'s Ghost; not the face that bowed before Queen Elizabeth I after the performance of *The Merry Wives of Windsor*, a play that, legend holds, the sovereign commanded him to write.

But the only two images of William Shakespeare that have near-unanimous scholarly approval were both created after his death. There are no contemporary descriptions of Shakespeare, either. The earliest written account of what Shakespeare looked like dates from about 1680, more than sixty years after his death in 1616. The account was written by the seventeenth-century antiquarian and essayist John Aubrey, who sought out people who knew or knew about the poet as research for his *Brief Lives*, which was posthumously published in 1813. The Stratford neighbours told Aubrey that Shakespeare "was a handsome, well-shap't man: very good company, and of a very readie and pleasant smooth witt."[1] Not what you might call an evocative description.

If readers or playgoers picture a face when they read or hear Shakespeare's words, it is nothing like the rakish countenance I gazed on that day in May in a suburban Ottawa dining room. The face you and I most likely think of when we picture Shakespeare is the engraving by Martin Droeshout printed on the title page of the First Folio of 1623. The Folio was the fruition of a long-planned memorial project undertaken by two of Shakespeare's friends and former business partners, John Heminges and Henry Condell. Their friendship went back at least as far as 1595, when the three appear together in the records of the Lord Chamberlain's Men, and the poet left money in his will to buy each of them, as well as the actor Richard Burbage, a commemorative gold ring.

For the First Folio, Condell and Heminges collected thirty-six plays by Shakespeare—half of them never before published—under the title *Mr. William Shakespeare's Comedies, Histories, and Tragedies*. Were it not for this book, which sold for about £1 a copy and whose first print run is unlikely to have been more than 750 copies, much of Shakespeare's work would almost certainly have been lost. The Folio went through four printings, the last in 1685, for a total of about three thousand copies. Every edition bore the same portrait engraving, though by the fourth and final edition it was so darkened and smudged as to give Shakespeare a suggestion of five-o'clock shadow.

In the Droeshout engraving, Shakespeare looks to be a man of firm middle age, with a bald pate and hair curling over his ears. He wears a handsomely embroidered doublet (a heavy Elizabethan jacket) with a stiff white collar that curves up to frame his face. He has a long nose, narrow lips, deep-set eyes and fine arched brows. It is the face of an observer, refined and intelligent—but with little life to it. Art historians concur that the First Folio portrait represents just about the least skilful example of the work of a not terribly talented artist. Droeshout's other known engravings, of assorted people of note, are more clear and vivid.

Many questions about this image intrigue scholars, but chief among them is this: why did Heminges and Condell, who by that time in their careers certainly could have paid the fees of a decent artist, choose a mediocre journeyman to immortalize their friend? Droeshout was a Protestant refugee born in Belgium in the 1560s. He moved to England with his Flemish family as a young man. Perhaps, as the Victorian critic J. Hain Friswell speculated, "the engraver was the artist readiest to hand"[2]—someone the actors already knew. Others have suggested that Droeshout had earlier created, possibly from life, the original sketch or painting on which the engraving was based and so was the natural person to do the engraving. Other scholars argue that Droeshout modelled his engraving on a sketch or painting by his Flemish colleague Marcus Gheeraerts. The records show the two worked together, and it was reported in the 1750s that Gheeraerts had painted a life portrait of Shakespeare in oil,[3]—so Droeshout may have had access through his colleague to an original from which to work.

The important question, though, is whether the engraving is an accurate portrait of the poet. The scholarly consensus? Not really. As many critics have pointed out, the picture has a host of flaws: one eye is lower and larger than the other, and the hair is not balanced. The body is too small for the head, and the arms are weirdly placed. The picture has a "childish clumsiness," is "inept and wit-less looking";[4] the vast expanse of forehead resembles "a horrible hydrocephalus development."[5] Some scholars have excused Droeshout's lack of skill on the grounds that he may have been working from a poor original drawing. In the 1800s, the leading theory was that he worked from "a mere daub by Burbage, done in the theatre."[6] (The actor Richard Burbage, one of Shakespeare's closest theatrical colleagues, also seems to have been an artist of middling ability.) Whether or not Droeshout worked from an original, he simply was not very good at what he did.

Nonetheless, the engraving has one simple but powerful argument in its favour: Shakespeare's friends accepted it. Heminges and Condell obviously gave it their approval, and the playwright Ben Jonson wrote this brief tribute, which appeared on the page facing Droeshout's portrait:

The Figure, that thou here seest put,
It was for gentle Shakespeare cut;
Wherein the Graver had a strife
With Nature, to out-do the life;
O, could he but have drawn his wit
As well in brass, as he hath hit
His face, the Print would then surpass
All, that was ever writ in brass.
But, Since he cannot, Reader, look
Not on his Picture, but his Book.

Given its approval by Shakespeare's contemporaries, the engraving presumably represents a passable likeness of the playwright in the later years of his life. For Ben Jonson, John Heminges and Henry Condell, this was a recognizable William Shakespeare.

The second of the two widely accepted images of the playwright is less well known but has a similarly strong claim. This is the memorial bust nestled in the north wall above Shakespeare's grave in the chancel of Holy Trinity Church in Stratford-upon-Avon. The bust was carved by Geraert Janssen (his name is often anglicized as Gerard or Garret Johnson), a stonemason whose Dutch carver father immigrated to London and set up shop not far from Shakespeare's Globe Theatre. Gerard was the youngest of the carving Janssens, and was, in the estimation of scholars, the least skilled of the clan. The bust was erected in 1620, four years after Shakespeare's death. It is made of soft bluish Cotswold limestone, carved then painted. It is life-size and shows a middle-aged man from the waist up. He is bald except for a tuft of curls over each ear but sports a pointed goatee and a thin, curling moustache. The face is fleshy and painted to a ruddy complexion. The hair is reddish brown, the eyes originally likely a dark hazel. The figure in the bust wears a burgundy doublet with a thin black gown atop it, a white collar and white cuffs—appropriate for a dignitary in a provincial town. The hands are fine and thin; one holds a quill pen, the other rests on a sheet of paper. Overall the bust bears a reasonable family resemblance to the Droeshout engraving—the faces are similar in shape, fleshy with a broad forehead and small mouth—so there has been speculation that the two artists worked from the same model.

This portrait in stone is a typical piece of funerary statuary—formal, expressionless, with vacant eyes—and has found little favour with Shakespeareans who have made the pilgrimage to Stratford to see it. One disappointed scholar sees a "self-satisfied pork-butcher," while another complains that the "dull eyes and fat jowls seem to offer no clue as to what might be within, whether soul or imagination, telling us only that this man was a worldly success."[7]

The bust was almost certainly commissioned and paid for by Shakespeare's family—by his widow, Anne Hathaway, or his daughters and son-in-law, who could certainly afford to uphold such social conventions as gravesite monuments—and to do so in some style. (The playwright left his wife and family a substantial estate, and his son-in-law, John Hall, was the town's respected physician.) And whether or not the sculptor himself knew Shakespeare, his workshop's proximity to the Globe Theatre and to Shakespeare's former theatrical colleagues gave him access to men who remembered him well. "Bad as it is, it is the most universally accredited and beloved likeness of the poet," the critic Friswell wrote in 1864. But as an image of genius, the bust is even less edifying than the Droeshout engraving—neither displays any of the wit that Ben Jonson so revered. No one who seeks clues to the man's greatness will find much satisfaction here.

This realization only strengthened Lloyd Sullivan's belief that the Sanders portrait could be immensely important. But how to prove that it was genuine, as (so his mother had told him) each generation of the Sanders family had believed back to the 1600s? He was going to have to venture into the unknown world of art scholarship.

If Lloyd did not know much about Shakespeare when he started his project, he knew even less about fine art and the rituals of its authentication. But that summer of 1991, at a family reunion, he happened to mention the unusual family heirloom to his cousin Allan Sullivan, a diplomat then serving as the Canadian Consul General in New York. Cousin Allan had inherited a number of paintings from his own father. He had taken them for appraisal to Christie's auction house, where he had met Lord Anthony Crichton-Stuart, the firm's specialist in Old Masters. Allan now offered to seek his advice. Accordingly, Lloyd gratefully turned over the file he had amassed so far—the letters and wills and a few photocopies from some art books at the local library.

Lloyd waited a year for a reply. In the meantime, he continued his reading, wading through biographies of Shakespeare and studies of Elizabethan theatre. Then one day in the spring of 1992, Cousin Allan called to say that Lord Crichton-Stuart was coming to Ottawa on business with the National Gallery, and he would be willing to grant Lloyd an audience, at which he would examine the Sanders portrait and return his supporting documents. "That was sort of a big deal," Lloyd says shyly. "I mean, this was the first big break."

On the appointed day, Lloyd removed the portrait from its cache in the cupboard, placed it in a tan vinyl suitcase and put the suitcase in the trunk of his white Chrysler sedan. On the way downtown he picked up his security force, two burly guys he knew from the local football team. He found his way to the underground parking lot beneath the swank Westin Hotel, then proceeded with his escorts to the hotel lobby, where he and the Christie's specialist had agreed to meet. He instructed his bodyguards to melt discreetly into the crowd, then strode forth to shake Crichton-Stuart's hand. The two men rode the elevator to the floor where the expert had taken a room. Lloyd unpacked Willy Shake and laid him on the bed.

Anthony Crichton-Stuart was a dashing, dark-haired aristocrat, everything Lloyd imagined an art expert from Christie's should be. He turned up the hotel-room lights and bent over the picture. Lloyd rocked on his heels and looked nervously out the window. The expert scrutinized the picture for several long minutes, then delivered his verdict. The picture was in very good condition—not the work of an Old Master, of course, but almost certainly from the seventeenth century, and not a bad piece, actually. He figured it would likely fetch about $100,000 at auction, regardless of its subject, but if it could be proved to be Shakespeare, it might be worth millions. Crichton-Stuart promised to send some information on how one might go about authenticating it. Lloyd thanked him profusely and packed his painting back in the suitcase. Down in the lobby, he gave the football players the nod and, quietly elated, bundled everyone into the car for the drive back home.

Lord Crichton-Stuart does not remember the occasion now. He declined to discuss it, in fact, sending word through an apologetic minion that each year he sees dozens of pictures that have unusual stories. And a genuine portrait from the reign of James I, while uncommon in Canada, is not, in his world, such a rarity. A picture of Shakespeare does not come along every day, the underling agreed, but Crichton-Stuart is a man who sees a lot of extraordinary art, and this was, after all, almost ten years ago.

The expert's encouraging assessment gave Lloyd new purpose. He was more determined than ever to prove that his portrait was genuine. What had started out as a hobby was gradually taking up more and more of his time: it seemed every book he read led him to five more, and none of them was easy going. But he had not read much before he realized that the Sanders portrait was in decidedly mixed company. There have been, over the years, stacks of portraits said to be William Shakespeare—some 450 all told. Many were deliberate fakes, but some have quite solid pedigrees. In other words, the Sanders portrait had serious competition. Even with the known fakes and the forgeries removed from the field, there were a handful of contenders with reasonable claims to have been painted when Shakespeare was alive.

Not that there was much of a market for portraits of the Swan of Avon during his lifetime or in the years immediately following his death—it took some time for his fame to grow. But the First Folio and its subsequent editions did much to increase Shakespeare's celebrity. By the 1660s, no more than fifty years after his death, the scant details of his poorly documented life began to be embellished into legend. Expanding ranks of admirers claimed all manner of connections: Shakespeare slept here, he drank here, he taught here, he befriended my father, he wooed my mother.

Alexander Leggatt, a Shakespeare scholar at the University of Toronto, would later explain to me how difficult it is to get a firm sense of the playwright's popularity in the seventeenth century. There was, it seems, a mix of tremendous admiration, as evinced by Ben Jonson, and a feeling that, as Leggatt summed it up, "The old guy was pretty good, but we've moved on." Shakespeare was compared with younger playwrights such as Francis Beaumont and John Fletcher (twenty and fifteen years his junior respectively) and deemed quaintly old-fashioned.

But by the middle of the eighteenth century, Shakespeare had moved from obscurity to reverence. He was acclaimed as England's national poet, and the cult of his personality—Bardolatory, as George Bernard Shaw later declared it—was entrenched. With the cult came the Shakespeare industry that Stanley Wells has described. Admirers wanted an image of their demigod. "A visible figure-head was necessary," writes the art historian David Piper. "The interest in Shakespeare's portraits, though waxing and waning, and shifting in nature, has always been there, and the demand has brought forth an ever-increasing flood of images."[8]

In about 1770, a wave of "original" pictures of Shakespeare began to appear, and dozens more followed over the next two centuries. These portraits were concocted by artists and dealers of limited scruples and consumed hungrily by a public content not to ask many questions. "It seems to be the rule with picture-dealers, that, should they meet with an English face, possessing brown hair, dark eyes, and an ample forehead, concomitants not at all unusual, to at once insist that a new portrait of our great national poet has been discovered," sighed J. Hain Friswell.[9] The new pictures often bore a resemblance to the Droeshout engraving or the bust, and this in turn was used to bolster their claim to authenticity.

In the nineteenth century, a number of rogues specialized in altering portraits of other people into likenesses of Shakespeare. The masters of this art, Edward Holder and F. W. Zincke, are thought to have created at least sixty Shakespeares between them in careers that spanned two decades. Holder, a sometime art dealer, is said to have altered a portrait by scraping off existing detail rather than by painting on top of it. Later, feeling either sadistic or repentant, he would sometimes reveal his methods to trusting buyers, but they in turn often outright ignored his confession, so determined were they to believe they had a genuine portrait. Zincke once confided to a dealer from whom he bought a large family portrait that he was going to cut it down and convert every last family member into the playwright Will. On another occasion, Holder claimed that he gave his buyers plenty of hints: "I have never been inclined to dupe the world as many in my situation in life have done. I have a wife and nine children to support; and had I the advantages which others have made by my works, I should not be the poor man I am now."[10] Holder and Zincke were quite proud of their skill in transmogrification, once demonstrating their method to Abraham Wivell, a student of Shakespearean iconography in the 1820s. Before Wivell's eyes, Holder neatly turned a portrait of a clergyman into a recognizable Oliver Cromwell. Zincke then took it to an art shop and sold it for £4.

Holder and Zincke were but the most prolific among a company of nineteenth-century forgers and fakers. Marion Henry Spielmann, the acknowledged expert on images of Shakespeare at the turn of the twentieth century, explained the situation thus: "Others were at work as well, for the market was too brisk in its demand, even if the trade was not exactly regular in its nature, for the commerce to be kept between the pair [Holder and Zincke]. Furthermore, it must be remembered that it did not always need a painter for the creation of Shakespeare portraits; all that was required was a man who could paint upon a background the name of the poet, or dates sufficient to establish a suggestion that the likeness might be his, to do the trick sufficiently well to satisfy the more credulous whose only desire it was to find some—indeed any—panel or canvas that might offer an opportunity for pandering to the weakness of unreasoning hero-worship."[11] In 1827 a Mr. Hilder is reported to have "furnished whole families of Shakespeares . . . happening to buy a capital portrait of an alderman and his wife, he cruelly separated the pair, and had the alderman turned into Cromwell and the wife into a most magnificent Shakespeare."[12] A public content with the collective fiction waited for Hilder's handiwork; the paintings, in the words of the art historian William Pressly, were "willed to be Will."[13]

The alderman's wife may not have made a terribly credible Shakespeare, but over the years there have been contenders that convinced even the experts of their time. A few, because of the strength or romanticism of their story, endured until the latter half of the twentieth century, when modern science or contemporary scholarship exposed them. These include pictures of unknown men who were declared to be Shakespeare; pictures of other people altered to look more like Shakespeare was supposed to; and outright forgeries.

They are worth a closer look, these most enduring of the contenders, for their claims to fame—and their debunking—charted the course that lay ahead for the Sanders portrait. Imagine these pictures hung on the wall of a long gallery, a dozen Shakespeares looking out from heavy frames. They are arranged in a row, starting with the "authentic" portraits now known to be fakes, through to, at the other end, the only two contenders—the Flower and the Chandos—apart from the Sanders, that have so far survived the inquiries of modern experts. The walk is an exercise in the Darwinian evolution of Shakespeare's faces, where only the strongest portraits survive. (See "The Picture Gallery" for these images.)

Pause first at a picture now known as the Zuccaro, because it was long said to be the work of the Italian artist Federigo Zuccaro, a painter who did considerable work in Florence and Rome. Zuccaro is also known to have travelled to England in the late 1500s, and he has been nominated as the creator of a number of Elizabethan portraits, including pictures of Queen Elizabeth herself; her favourite, Robert Dudley, the Earl of Leicester; and her cousin, Mary, Queen of Scots. The Zuccaro

Shakespeare shows a mysterious and romantic-looking man with the high, domed forehead and heavy eyelids of the Droeshout engraving, a suitably dashing image for nineteenth-century tastes. It surfaced in Bath in the early 1800s and was immediately proclaimed a long-lost portrait of the playwright from 1602. This picture enjoyed a long life as Shakespeare's face; it was acquired as an authentic life portrait by the Folger Shakespeare Library in 1926.

In style, this Shakespeare does resemble Zuccaro's English paintings, and the sitter wears an elaborate white ruff that mimics the courtly collars in this artist's pictures of the Queen and her courtiers. Most convincing of all, the picture is inscribed on the back "Guglielm Shakespeare." But a little art historical sleuthing in the twentieth century drastically undermined the portrait's claim. It turns out that Federigo Zuccaro spent only six months in England in 1575, the year William Shakespeare turned eleven. Zuccaro would have needed a clairvoyant's powers in addition to his skill with a paintbrush to sense the future greatness of a dusty schoolboy in a provincial town and to imagine how that boy would look as a man in his thirties. In 1988 a restoration of the Zuccaro portrait revealed an authentic Elizabethan portrait that was overpainted in the nineteenth century to look suitably Shakespearean. (The term Elizabethan applies to the period of Elizabeth I's reign, which ended with her death in 1603. Her nephew, James VI of Scotland, succeeded her as James I of England, ushering in the Jacobean era.)

A similar fate befell the next picture in our lineup, a painting known as the Grafton, after the Duke of Grafton, who was said to have owned it in the 1700s. The Grafton became public in the mid-1880s, when it was in the possession of a family in northern England. It shows a long-faced, romantic young man in clothing suitable for a young Elizabethan poet. The argument in its favour hinged on two crucial inscriptions. The front of the painting bears the marks "Æ SVÆ•24 1•5•8•8," giving the sitter's age as twenty-four and the year as 1588. The back is inscribed "W + S."

William Shakespeare was indeed twenty-four in 1588. But at that tender age he had not yet written any of the works for which he is now known, and in fact he may well have been toiling as an apprentice glover in his father's shop in Stratford. He certainly was not well-enough known to have his portrait painted in rich clothes.

Next we pause before the Felton, so named because a Samuel Felton of Shropshire purchased it for five guineas in May 1792. Felton, who was on a visit to London at the time, was doubtless impressed by the painting's helpful inscription ("Guil. Shakespeare, 1597. R.N.") and the suitably soulful and romantic rendering of the poet. The sitter is thin and pale, his eyes sunken, his hairline receded all the way back to the middle of his head.

Two years after Felton bought it, in 1794, the Shakespeare scholar George Steevens confidently declared it the sole surviving portrait of William Shakespeare, the very original from which Martin Droeshout worked. The portrait passed among various owners until the collector Henry Clay Folger bought it in 1922, planning to include it in his museum. Through those years it was defended by Steevens's supporters and derided—as, for example, "a snuff-taking German"—by his rivals.

Certainly the Felton does bear some resemblance to the First Folio engraving, but modern art historical analysis has dismissed its claim. There is evidence of extensive overpainting, although the features remain essentially as they were in the original. But the head is too different to have been painted from the Droeshout original, and the sitter's collar has been extensively altered to resemble the large flat collars of 1597. The Felton is now decisively dismissed as a work of the eighteenth century—either an outright forgery or an alteration of an existing portrait.

The next in the row is the Janssen, a picture that, like the Felton, was deliberately altered with the intent to deceive. This picture was first claimed as Shakespeare when a collector acquired it in 1770. It takes its name from Cornelis Janssen—originally Cornelius Johnson—an English-born artist of Dutch descent who worked in London in the first half of the seventeenth century, to whom it was once attributed. For many years, the Janssen and the Chandos portrait were the only two serious contenders for the life-portrait title.

Like the Zuccaro, the Janssen Shakespeare has the refined elegance that an eighteenth-century audience wanted from Shakespeare. The sitter has fine features and a smooth forehead and he wears an elaborate lace-trimmed collar. This portrait, too, has a helpful inscription, this one in the upper-left corner: "Aete 46/ 1610" (the sitter is forty-six in 1610).

Art historians did not seriously challenge the Janssen's claim until the 1940s, when research showed that the young Cornelis Janssen was but a teenager in 1610 and went to Holland to study as a young man. He did not begin to work in London until about 1618, so he could not have painted this image from life. Thus the portrait lacks an artist. The sitter's dress is also troubling—his lace collar and rich doublet mark him as a courtier or nobleman, not a middle-class playwright—although, as we shall see, this may not be an insurmountable problem. Most damning, however, are X-rays that suggest the date in the upper-left-hand corner has been altered. And finally, restoration revealed that the sitter's hairline was retouched to form a suitably broad Shakespearean expanse. Today the portrait is believed to be of the sixteenth-century author Sir Thomas Overbury; the sitter strongly resembles the one known portrait of Overbury.

The last of the contenders whose case can now be confidently dismissed is an oil-on-canvas portrait by an unknown artist, a picture "discovered" in 1847 by the Reverend Clement Usill Kingston, who hailed from Ashbourne in Derbyshire. When the good reverend revealed his portrait to the world, it was inscribed and dated "ÆTATIS SVÆ. 47.Ao 1611" and showed an appropriately Victorian Shakespearean, with a hairline reminiscent of the Droeshout engraving.

The Ashbourne enjoyed a long run as a life portrait—more than a hundred years. In 1937 an X-ray examination cast doubt on its authenticity by discovering an earlier portrait beneath the visible image. But not until the painting was restored in 1979 did it conclusively prove to be a deliberate reworking of the original to make it look like Shakespeare. The sitter's hairline had been forcibly moved back to resemble the Droeshout engraving and the date changed from 1612 to 1611 (the year the playwright was forty-seven). The restoration also revealed a coat of arms and a date that identified the original subject as Sir Hugh Hamersley, a contemporary of Shakespeare's and one-time Lord Mayor of London. The transformation from Hamersley to Shakespeare is believed to have been wrought by the Reverend Kingston himself, for he was known to be something of an artist. He also profited handsomely from its sale.

Near the end of the gallery hangs the first of the two pictures—apart from the Sanders—whose cases have not yet been thrown out of court. The weaker claimant is the Flower portrait, which surfaced in England in 1840. The Flower is painted in oils on an English oak panel and inscribed in the upper-left corner "Willm Shakespeare 1609." When Edgar Flower, of the wealthy Stratford brewing dynasty, acquired it, he proposed it as the life portrait on which Martin Droeshout had based his engraving. And, indeed, the resemblance is strong: the same expanse of forehead and drooping eyelids, the same skewed posture for the sitter.

While enthusiastically accepted in the mid-1800s as a life portrait, the Flower fell out of favour in the early twentieth century. Critics cited the inscription's cursive handwriting as too late to be from that era and argued that the painting transparently parroted the Droeshout, even the obvious flaws in the engraving. Then in 1966 an X-ray of the panel revealed that the portrait is painted over what appears to be a fifteenth-century Madonna and Child with St. John.

But as with the Ashbourne, the X-ray did not immediately eliminate the Flower. Artists of limited means frequently painted over old canvases or panels. The picture, which now hangs in the gallery of the Royal Shakespeare Theatre in Stratford-upon-Avon, has never undergone further scientific analysis. The best guess of curators assessing its partially restored surface is that the Shakespeare portion was painted in the seventeenth century, or possibly painted earlier and then altered in the 1800s. In 1986 a pair of American scholars suggested that it "was produced in a portrait shop in Jacobean London, with the Flemish painter and his assistant using an unmarketable religious picture for their panel,"[14] reviving the idea that it was the model from which young Martin Droeshout worked. In the case of the Flower, the jury is still out.

At last we arrive before the Chandos portrait. The painting now hangs in the National Portrait Gallery in London, which is the latest in a line of owners who have claimed it as Shakespeare since James Brydges, later the 3rd Duke of Chandos, acquired it in 1747. At the Gallery it is presented as a genuine life portrait, and it rivals the Droeshout as the most widely reproduced picture of the playwright. In the 1800s it was the model for dozens more portraits, miniatures and busts.[15]

The painting is attributed to John Taylor, who died in 1651 and had ties to the Droeshout family of engravers. Taylor held office in the Painter-Stainers Company, the artists' guild, of which Droeshout was a member, and so surely knew him. He also attended the same church as Droeshout's nephew John.[16] Thus Taylor may have had access to an original to paint his portrait.

Art scholars accept, based on the materials (oil on canvas) and the style in which it is painted, that the Chandos was created in approximately 1610. The sitter wears a dark doublet and has his shirt collar untied; costume historians say that both his dress and his hairstyle are correct for the period and appropriate for a man of letters. His gold hoop earring may have been a risqué fashion for a man of forty-six, but there is a contemporary portrait of the younger actor Nathaniel Field wearing a similar earring.[17] Scientific testing has not dismissed the Chandos. An X-ray photo of the portrait revealed coarse restoration that did not differ greatly from the original, while an infrared photograph showed only a slight retouching of the sitter's right temple, consistent with a later attempt at restoration rather than forgery. Had it not looked so different from Martin Droeshout's engraving, it might have laid claim to being the model for it.

The Chandos has been presented as a painting of William Shakespeare for over 250 years, yet the argument for its authenticity rests on the unproved tradition that it was once owned by the playwright and theatre manager Sir William Davenant, born 1606. According to John Aubrey, Shakespeare's early biographer, Davenant claimed at different times to be Shakespeare's godson, his illegitimate son or both.

Before 1747, the story of the Chandos depends on oral tradition. And by 1747, there was good reason to pass off an old picture as the now-famous playwright. Moreover, alone among the contenders, the Chandos does not look at all like the First Folio engraving or the Stratford monument. It shows a narrow-faced, black-haired man whom some nineteenth-century critics dismissed as an improbably "Jewish physiognomy." The Chandos may have the strongest case, but it is by no means solid.

So ends our tour of the chief contenders at the end of the twentieth century. And of these only the Flower and the Chandos have any claim to authenticity. Beyond these two, those who seek a certain sign of genius in the face of Shakespeare must still fall back on either the barren bust by Geraert Janssen or the unskilled engraving by Martin Droeshout.

The Sanders family portrait was thus only the latest in a long line purporting to be a life portrait of William Shakespeare.

Beyond family tradition and a label that was no longer legible, Lloyd Sullivan had nothing to prove his belief, except Anthony Crichton-Stuart's opinion that the painting dated to the seventeenth century. And so, soon after his meeting with the august Christie's expert in 1991, Lloyd decided to seek additional support from the art world.

Through his lawyer Les Bunning, he got in touch with Michael Pantazzi, then associate curator of European Art at the National Gallery of Canada in Ottawa. He told Pantazzi he had a picture, supposed to be of Shakespeare, which he would give the Gallery for exhibition on long-term loan. Pantazzi, of course, had questions. On March 1, 1991, Bunning wrote to explain that family tradition held that the ancestor "who painted the picture was a member of Shakespeare's troupe, though I presume this could never be authenticated." With his letter, he included a 1909 article from an art magazine about the painting and colour photocopies of pictures of the portrait.

Three weeks later, a cautious Pantazzi wrote back. He politely declined the offer of a loan, explaining that the gallery rarely took paintings on this basis because of the cost of insuring them. And he advised that only three portraits—the Droeshout, the Stratford monument and the Chandos—had any claims to authenticity. "As much depends on whether the picture is of Shakespeare or not, it may be good to first settle the status of the picture." He suggested Lloyd might want to try to lend it to the Agnes Etherington Art Centre in Kingston, Ontario, part of Queen's University, which has an excellent conservation program. And the National Portrait Gallery in London might be able to shed some light on the Sanders portrait, after which Christie's or Sotheby's, another respected auction house, could perhaps assess its value. With his reply, Pantazzi kindly enclosed a stack of photocopies of articles on Shakespeare portraiture. And that was it from Canada's national art museum.

Then, a year after the meeting with Lloyd, Lord Crichton-Stuart, the Christie's expert, kept his promise to send some advice on what to do with his picture, writing with details of a contact at the National Portrait Gallery in London. With fulsome apologies for his tardiness, he enclosed the name of Malcolm Rogers, the deputy director. "He should be able to help you in positively identifying whether your portrait is of Shakespeare or not." He concluded his brief note by apologizing again, saying lightly, "I am sure that you had quite forgotten our ever meeting!"

Hardly. With a sense of renewed purpose, Lloyd now had his lawyer write to Malcolm Rogers, describing the portrait that had been in his family for years. "However, documentation evidencing this only goes back to the nineteenth century. Undoubtedly the picture is very old, but I am unaware whether there are any modern scientific methods for accurately determining its age." The letter went on to say that Lloyd was interested in either lending or selling the picture but first wanted "to obtain information as to its age, value and authenticity."

On June 5, Lloyd received a succinct reply: it "seems to be a perfectly good portrait of the late sixteenth or early seventeenth century, but I can see no reason for thinking it represents Shakespeare. That is the one problem. A sale room or dealer can advise on likely value."

At the time, Lloyd did not know that as far as the Gallery is concerned, reputed portraits of the playwright are something of a plague. "We get a new Shakespeare about every eighteen months," the Gallery's Catharine MacLeod would later tell me when I interviewed her for *The Globe*. The curator of sixteenth- and seventeenth-century art went on to explain that these pictures invariably prove to be fakes of varying quality, or else nice old pictures with no verifiable claim to be Shakespeare. When Malcolm Rogers received Lloyd's letter, telling him of another "new" Shakespeare painting that had surfaced in a small city in the former colonies, he and his curatorial colleagues no doubt dismissed it without a second thought.

Lloyd had received discouraging—downright dismissive—responses from the first two art institutions he approached. But he is a stubborn man and his faith in his painting was unshaken. Instead of taking the experts at their word, he redoubled his efforts. His retirement project had moved from a pastime to a quest to prove a point of principle. He was determined to show that the Sanders portrait was not just another fudged eighteenth-century painting of a secondary noble.

But he soon discovered another obstacle. As he navigated his way through tomes on art history and biographies of Shakespeare, he ran into a persistent scholarly assertion: Shakespeare, small-town glover's son turned playwright, would never have had his picture painted. This was an idea Lloyd found hard to fathom. Is Shakespeare not the most famous writer in world? Was he not a popular playwright during his lifetime? Surely it would have been natural, inevitable, that someone would have painted his picture while he was alive. To a man living in the paparazzi era, it was unthinkable that no likeness was made of the live Shakespeare's great face. But as Lloyd learned more about Shakespeare's life and his world, he began to encounter some powerful arguments against the existence of a portrait.

The first argument hinges on Shakespeare's social class: that the playwright was not of a high enough standing to have a portrait painted in his lifetime. According to this line of reasoning, members of the English middle class began to have their pictures painted only in the last years of Shakespeare's life. Through Elizabeth's reign, it was only the wealthy, the nobility, and in particular those formally presented to the monarch, who had their pictures painted. Not actors or playwrights, denizens of the seedy South Bank of the Thames. Not even those successful enough to perform before the Queen. Shakespeare entertained at court, but he was never presented there, never formally admitted to that stratum of society. Even during the last of his London years, when his fame was greatest, it was not, so the argument went, sufficient to warrant a portrait.

Then there was a second problem: in Shakespeare's day an artist never began a painting without first getting at least partial payment for it. Portraiture was a highly skilled, professional activity. Most of its practitioners were émigré Dutchmen—the Dutch were far more adept at this art than Englishmen of the era—and they had a guild of their own. And even the plainest portrait didn't come cheap. If a client wanted anything fancy, such as a bright blue paint made with ground lapis lazuli imported from Afghanistan, well, he had to pay extra for it. Shakespeare, as his surviving financial records tell us, was rather careful with his shillings. Andrew Gurr—professor of English literature at Reading University in England and one of the directors of the restoration of Shakespeare's Globe Theatre—would later tell me that Shakespeare "was a notorious skinflint." When the playwright retired to Stratford, one of his first actions was to sue a man for the £5 borrowed from his father sixteen years before. Certainly we have no record of his doing anything that could be construed as extravagant.

If Shakespeare or a patron or an admirer did commission a portrait, there is no extant paperwork about the transaction: while many bills of sale for Italian paintings of this period survive, few British ones do. Similarly, few of the inventories post-mortem—lists of property prepared when an estate was being settled—that survive from the era say much about paintings, if any, in the deceased's possession. Nor were portraits the sort of property normally mentioned in wills. (None of Shakespeare's books or reference papers are named in his will, but rather are believed to have been accounted for in such an inventory, now lost.) Apart from the hero-worshipping Gullio, as Stanley Wells describes him, in the Parnassus play, who longs for a picture of "Sweet Master Shakespeare" in his study, nowhere in the written records do we find evidence for a portrait of Shakespeare painted during his lifetime.

And if there was a portrait of "Sweet Master Shakespeare" as early as 1599 or 1600, what has become of it? Art historians can only guess. Through the sixteenth century, most painting was done on wood; at the beginning of the seventeenth, canvas became more common. Pictures on canvas are much more vulnerable to damage and destruction. Perhaps there was an engraving made when Shakespeare was alive, mass-reproduced by a print shop—the equivalent, if you will, of a paparazzi snap. If so, it would have been printed on even-more-fragile paper. If the Parnassus picture or something like it ever existed, either it does not survive, or it still lies hidden and unacknowledged, perhaps in a musty attic or beneath a grandmother's bed.

Picturing Shakespeare in 1603

Andrew Gurr

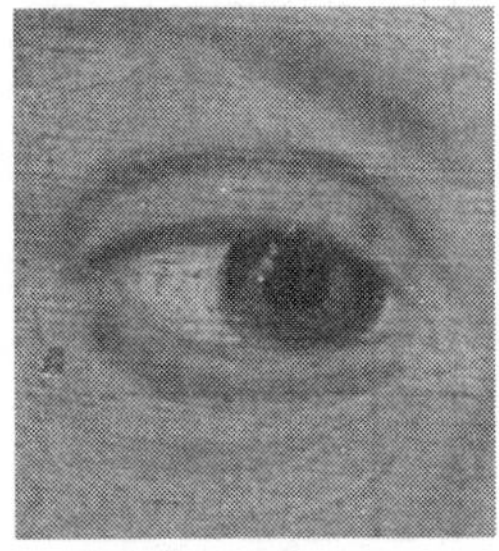

IF SHAKESPEARE EVER did have his portrait painted, no more likely year can be found than 1603. It was a confused and confusing year for the Shakespeare acting company. The dramatist Thomas Dekker later called it the "wonderful" year, because a new king came peacefully to the English throne, relieving all the doubts and fears about an old monarch with no direct heirs. But for the actors it did not begin like that. Shakespeare's company was chosen to perform the first play at court on the official opening night of the Christmas festivities, December 26, 1602, and another on February 2, 1603. But when Queen Elizabeth died on March 24, 1603, all of London's theatres were immediately closed in mourning for her. Then the bubonic plague returned, in one of the worst epidemics ever, causing the theatres to close entirely from June until April 1604. The London companies either had to leave the city, taking their plays around the country to places where the plague had not yet manifested itself, or stay at home unemployed under the risk of death from plague.

Despite these troubles, Shakespeare's company fared better than the others. For them it truly did become a wonderful year. In

May the new King made himself their patron, a unique privilege. They chose not to go on tour, instead staying in or near London in case he needed some entertainment. We have no record of their being used before December 2, 1603, when they were summoned from Mortlake to perform for the King at the Earl of Pembroke's house in Wilton. Mortlake was a safe distance upriver from the plague spots in London, a village where one of the leaders of the Shakespeare company, Augustine Phillips, had recently bought a house. After the Wilton performance, through King James's first Christmas season, they performed eight plays at Hampton Court, a palace safely upriver, and James gave them a subsidy to compensate for their long period of idleness. What Shakespeare did through that long summer of 1603 when the company was out of work, apart from completing his next play, *Measure for Measure,* we do not know. It is entirely possible that he chose to spend some of his enforced leisure having his portrait painted.

Outside London in 1603, Shakespeare was still an insignificant figure. He was famous first for the two poems he saw into print in 1593 and 1594, *Venus and Adonis* and *The Rape of Lucrece,* and only second as a popular playwright. We know that his sonnets circulated in manuscript, since the student Francis Meres in his literary commentary *Palladis Tamia, Wit's Treasury,* referred to "his sugred Sonnets among his private friends" in 1598, but they did not appear in print until 1609. The company started to publish some of his plays with his name on them in 1597. His retirement in 1610 to a quiet (and very affluent) last few years in Stratford reflects the then-minor nature of his fame. It took the next three centuries to make him into England's greatest poet; he never pushed his claims to be a poet in the way that his peers

Christopher Marlowe and Ben Jonson did. Despite his company's success in 1603, his fame seems much too limited to have prompted anyone to have commissioned an official portrait. If he did have his portrait painted in 1603, it is more likely that he commissioned it himself. But who would he have had it done for? His wife in Stratford? One of his daughters? A friend and admirer? Who paid for it, and who hung it on his or her wall? To answer such questions we need to look carefully at his personal position in 1603.

Without a doubt the biggest single constant in Elizabethan England was social rank. Your status, as a citizen of London or as a gentleman or lady, was signalled not just by your income but in your clothing. The Tudor sumptuary laws that regulated what different social ranks were entitled to wear required status to be advertized in the very cloth you wore. Common people wore jerkins or gowns of wool and were not supposed to have silk, velvet or satin garments or gold and silver thread, which were reserved for the gentry. Only the higher nobility could wear gold and cloth of gold. Only gentlemen and above wore swords. In Philip Massinger's *New Way to Pay Old Debts* (1625), Lord Lovell shows the way cloth and colour signalled status by declaring that as a lord he would never marry a citizen's daughter, "and so leave my issue / Made up of several pieces, one part scarlet, / And the other London blue" (4.1.224–5). The courtier's scarlet could not be set alongside the blue of a serving man. In that light, we can see why Shakespeare's low social status in London, where he was not even a freeman of the City, must have bothered him. His sonnets tell us that clearly. In 1596 he renewed an old application by his father, John Shakespeare, to acquire armigerous status (his own coat of arms) to make him an esquire and a gentleman. His application on his father's behalf to the College of Arms became notorious to his friends and enemies. It made him distinct from his fellow actors by permitting him to wear velvet in the street as well as on stage. Such self-aggrandizement became a joke to several of his fellow writers. A few years later, in 1603, they acquired a reason to sneer even more.

All the leading members of Shakespeare's acting company got a sharp rise in status when in May 1603 the new King took them on as his servants because they were the favourite entertainers at court. In the nine years since their formation in 1594 as the Lord Chamberlain's Men, they had performed thirty-three times at court compared with twenty-one by the Lord Admiral's Men, set up in London along with them to provide for Queen Elizabeth's Christmas entertainments. It was therefore no surprise that within a month of King James's arrival in London he issued a patent naming them the King's Men, the title they kept under his son and successor, Charles I, until the dissolution of all the acting companies in 1642, at the beginning of England's civil war.

Along with their new title went the special status accorded to the ten sharers who led the King's Men. As the new King's servants they, including Shakespeare, were made Grooms of the Royal Chamber. That was an unpaid rank, but it gave them the social status of courtier. They could wear the royal livery, for which they received the only money their new rank brought them. The ten were each paid to buy special cloth to make their royal liveries, and they paraded in their new garb at James's formal entry into London in April 1604. It was a unique elevation for a group of men who had previously had only the lowly rank of common player. Becoming a courtier, although unpaid, in May 1603 was the peak of Shakespeare's social climb.

Shakespeare and his company did not wear their royal livery only for James's welcome to the City of London in 1604. Their scarlet cloaks, doublets and breeches as Grooms of the Chamber were put on show again in August of that year for the eighteen-day visit of the Spanish Constable of Castile. With a large party of Spanish grandees, Castile came to London as the chief delegate to King James's great conference held to make peace and stop the long war between Protestant England and Catholic Spain. The Spaniards were put up at Somerset House, and the King's Men were ordered to attend them throughout their stay.[1] They presented no plays but were paid for their daily attendance, so they were evidently called on to be there solely for use as spare parts to display the King's livery as his courtiers before the Spanish guests. Their eighteen days of standing around looking handsome in their distinctive scarlet was a clear mark to the world of their status as the King's courtiers.

Neither step in Shakespeare's social climbing passed unnoticed by his contemporaries. In *Every Man Out of His Humour*, written in 1599 to be performed by the Shakespeare company, Ben Jonson used the company's actors, including Shakespeare himself, to mock his new coat of arms and its motto. He made one of the characters boast about the emblem for his own newly acquired armigerous status, which took the form of a boar's head on a plate and a crest that included a frying pan. His mockers proposed that the motto should be Not without Mustard. That was a derisive echo of the emblematic spear on the Shakespeare shield and a perversion of the ambiguous motto Shakespeare had secured for his father, *Non sans droict*, Not without Right.

This jibe started a long process of derisive exchanges between Jonson and the company and an even longer one between the two poets. In 1601 the company staged Thomas Dekker's *Satiromastix*, a complex satire attacking Jonson, and shortly after Shakespeare is thought to have parodied him as Ajax in *Troilus and Cressida*. Jonson was a Londoner, stepson of a bricklayer, who went on paying his dues as a citizen-bricklayer and therefore a freeman of the City even after he was taken up and patronized by various lords and gentry and paid large sums for writing poems dedicated to them. Once he had noble patrons, he never repeated his early mockery of his colleague's social climbing. Shakespeare's only known patron, who received the dedication of his two long poems in 1593 and 1594, was the 3rd Earl of Southampton. How close Shakespeare's relationship was with him we cannot know, unless he truly was the "lord of my love" to whom the first 126 of the sonnets were addressed. The trouble was that it did little credit to any lord to give his patronage to a professional player rather than to a poet, and only one is ever known to have done so.[2]

The second sharp jibe at the final step in Shakespeare's ascent was by a friend of Jonson's. It made a precise comment on his social pretensions that seems never to have registered with students of his life until now. Its existence strengthens the likelihood that Shakespeare had good reason to want his portrait painted in the year he became a courtier. Six years after *Every Man Out of His Humour*, in 1605, Francis Beaumont, Jonson's young friend and follower, produced a sneer about Shakespeare even more severe than the earlier one. In *The Woman Hater*, printed in 1606, he used John Shakespeare's lowly career as a whittawer (dresser of light-coloured leathers) and glover to mock the social climbing of his son as a King's man, Groom of the Royal Chamber and thus a new courtier.

In Beaumont's play, a character making a speech condemning social climbing at court says, "You shall see many legges [i.e., making a leg, or bowing low] too; amongst the rest you shall behould one payre, the feete of which, were in times past sockelesse, but are now through the change of time (that alters all thinges) very strangely become the legges of a Knight and a Courtier: *another payre you shall see, that were heire apparent legges to a Glover, these legges hope shortly to bee honourable*; when they passe by they will bowe, and the mouth to these legges, will seeme to offer you some Courtship" (italics mine).[3] The allusion to a glover, the trade of Shakespeare's father, together with the pun on "sockelesse," not wearing the classical comedian's "soc" or light shoe, is too direct to be accidental or incidental. Such men were once so poor they had no footwear, but now they can make a courtier's "leg," especially the one who went from being a mere player of comedies to a courtier. The identification, however gratuitous, of the glover's son as a new courtier was clearly a grievance for ambitious young gentlemen like Beaumont who were not getting any such rise in status themselves.

The term "gentle" for Shakespeare has become famous since 1623 because of its use in Ben Jonson's epitaph for him printed with the First Folio. In fact, and most intriguingly, it seems to have been used first in 1603. Through the 1590s the Elizabethan commentators on Shakespeare's reputation (in the Cambridge plays 2 and 3 *Return from Parnassus*) called him "sweet" and "honey-tongued." That applied to his poems, not to his personality. The term "gentle" was a much more pointed description of his personality, since it claimed that his character, if not his social status, was that of a gentleman. It was first used in the year 1603 in a poem by John Davies of Hereford. Addressed to the two leading names of the Shakespeare company, Richard Burbage and Shakespeare, painter and poet, each identified by his initials in the margin (the reference to "painting" is a clear allusion to Burbage's well-known hobby as a painter), it declared

> *Players*, I love yee, and your *Qualitie*,
> As ye are Men, that pass time not abus'd:
> And some I love for *painting, poesie*,
> And say fell *Fortune* cannot be excus'd,
> That hath for better *uses* you refus'd:
> *Wit, Courage, good shape, good partes*, and all good,
> As long as these *goods* are no *worse* us'd,
> And though the *stage* doth staine pure gentle *bloud*,
> Yet generous yee are in *minde* and *moode*.[4]

The poem makes what was evidently a familiar link between the poet (Shakespeare) and the player (Burbage) in their best roles. Its final couplet puns on the linkage of "gentle" with the Latin "generosus," which means "noble," playing on the counterfeit nobility of Shakespeare's stage creations as opposed to the true nobility of his mind. Even more suggestively, Davies seems to be echoing Shakespeare's later sonnets to the young man, about the player being stained like the dyer's hand by his occupation. It is striking that it should be 1603 when Davies chose to emphasize Shakespeare's "gentle blood."

As a description of the man's character, the term "gentle Shakespeare" was obviously never made in the early accounts without a load of social innuendo. Jonson made the word famous with his description of the Droeshout portrait in the First Folio:

This Figure, that thou here seest put,
It was for gentle Shakespeare cut.

That epitaph, composed in 1623 by a man who claimed to be his friend, is a cogent summary of what people thought of his character. But it also had a complex undertone that indicates a more complicated attitude than the one usually attributed to Jonson. Modern scholars read the word "gentle" as a joke about a poet who unlike most of his contemporaries was technically not a gentleman. Jonson was made a gentleman in 1619, when Oxford University gave him an honorary degree (all graduates were designated as gentlemen).[5] Jonson had started the mockery of Shakespeare's struggle to gentrify himself in 1599. It is easy to read the descriptive word he chose for the preliminary papers in the Shakespeare Folio as a nudge to remind readers of that earlier joke. The fact that Davies had used it first shows what was in some people's minds in 1603.

Davies made an evidently familiar link between the poet and the player of his best roles. Another indication of interest in painting among the players is the commission that the Earl of Rutland handed to Burbage and Shakespeare to design and make his *impresa*, or shield, for the tilts on the King's Accession Day, March 24, 1613. The accounts of the 6th Earl note "Item, 31 Martii, to Mr Shakspeare in gold about my Lorde's impreso, xliiijs;

to Richard Burbage for paynting and making yt, in gold xliiijs.—iiijli. viijs."[6] Each of them received two pounds four shillings ("li" signified pounds and "s" shillings, of which there were twenty to a pound of the old English currency) for Shakespeare to design and Burbage to make the shield with its special blazon for the occasion. This record confirms, if nothing else, that Burbage was known to be a painter as well as an actor, and might help to justify the idea that painting portraits of actors became a fashion in Jacobean times. The "Character . . . of an Excellent Actor," published in 1615, noted that "[h]ee is much affected to painting, and tis a question whether that make him an excellent Plaier, or his painting an exquisite painter."[7] The author of this "character" was most likely John Webster, then writing for the Shakespeare company, and it was Burbage whom he was exemplifying in his "character." He does not, however, call Burbage a gentleman, because actors were not expected to have such an elevated social status. That was part of Shakespeare's complaint in the Sonnets.

Nor was Shakespeare alone in trying to climb above the level of common player. As the company's status grew, so did that of its leading shareholders, along with their affluence. Three other sharer players in the King's company followed Shakespeare by acquiring coats of arms: Robert Armin, Augustine Phillips and John Heminges. It was evidently an attractive upward move for Grooms of the Chamber. Phillips died in 1605, Armin in 1615, Shakespeare in 1616 and Heminges in 1630. In his will Heminges did declare that he was still a citizen of London, but that may have been to enable him to keep up the fiction that he could employ a number of young "apprentices" as boy players. Whether these steps up the social ladder were simple consequences of the sharers' new affluence in the country's most eminent acting company, with the King himself as their patron, it is impossible to say. Shakespeare got there first with his bid to the College of Arms for higher social status in 1596. His father's death in 1601 had already passed that rank on to him, even though the grant to John Shakespeare, along with others made by William Dethick as Garter King of Arms, had been challenged.[8] Beyond that, it makes sense that in the year of his highest ascent, 1603, a class-sensitive man from Warwickshire should be proud enough of his new livery and his role as a Groom of the Chamber to get himself immortalized in paint.

Perhaps he did not feel sufficiently self-important to wear his new livery in the picture, but he might well have felt that his quality and his face in paint should be a reminder for his wife and children at home of their absent provider. In 1603 he not only had courtier status but the secure role in the acting company and the playhouse that was filling his pockets. His career as a King's Man now promised to be even more richly profitable than the enterprise that had built the Globe. Already his profits were being sent back to Stratford for investment. He had bought New Place, the second-largest house in Stratford, and was making the investments in land around Stratford that secured his local status and future income. The small size of the Sanders portrait not only fits Shakespeare's notorious habit of doing things cheaply and hoarding his money but would have seemed suitable to hang back home in the large house his family now lived in next to the grammar school in Stratford's main street. New Place had been his earliest investment in Stratford, a comfortable and substantial dwelling for his family, and a striking mark of his new wealth to show the locals. He well knew the value of his money, and the small picture would have exactly suited his need to make a modest show to Stratford of his new status.

These are plausible circumstances for a decision in 1603 to have his portrait painted, but the strongest testimony for the idea is really in the sonnets. The long sequence of love poems written to the rich young aristocrat, the "lovely boy" as he called him, are the only direct evidence we have for the state of his mind around this time. They were written over at least three years, on the evidence of Sonnet 104 ("Three winters cold . . . Three beautious springs . . . Since first I saw you fresh"), though their composition can only be said to have happened several years before their publication in 1609. The reference to "his sugred Sonnets among his private friends" dates from 1598. In the sequence to the young man, the author makes a lot both of his humble social status and his shameful occupation, playing Falstaff to the young man's Prince Hal. He laments the ill fortune "That did not better for my life provide / Than public means which public manners breeds." He worked for the "public" theatre, "And almost thence my nature is subdued / To what it works in, like a dyer's hand."[9] His work stains his hands indelibly. He has "gone here and there, / And made myself a motley to the view," travelling with his playing company, and wearing the multicoloured costume of a clown or fool. He declares he is ashamed of the work he does because it lowers his social status so intolerably. Some of the earliest sonnets, those from 27 to 37, lament how his kind of work and the travels it sends him away on, along with the low social rank of his work, distance him from the grandeur and the riches of the "sovereign" youth's society. The youth cannot afford to shame himself by openly associating with such an inferior person.

That was the poet's state of mind before 1603. Such an outlook could explain his application in 1596 to raise his father to the rank of esquire and his own joy at his subsequent elevation to courtier status. It is hardly surprising that such a socially sensitive figure should turn to the new fashion for portraiture in paint, one being practised by Richard Burbage, as a proud expression of his newly gained social quality.

Probably the best surviving pieces of tangible evidence about actors having their portraits painted at this first stage of their fame survives in a special collection, where one painting is said to be by Burbage himself and one is thought to be of him: the Dulwich Picture Gallery. This collection began as a part of the renowned actor Edward Alleyn's foundation given to Dulwich College in south London, along with the famous papers and theatre diary of Alleyn's father-in-law, Philip Henslowe, from his years running the Rose, the Fortune and the Bear Garden theatres in Elizabethan London. These papers are a unique record of theatre life in Shakespeare's time, and Dulwich College is rich in contemporary material that its founder left to it.

By the time Alleyn founded the College in the early 1620s, his social status and wealth were both outstanding. His new wife (his third) was a daughter of the Dean of St. Paul's, the poet John Donne. His generosity in founding the College was the sort of personal memorial that only the most eminent city magnates were accustomed to set up. His bequest to the College included a small collection of pictures, some of which now form part of the Gallery's collection. One of them was a full-length portrait of Alleyn himself, and the portraits of other actors, including that of Burbage, may have been part of his personal collection. Unfortunately, the surviving records do not readily allow Alleyn's pictures to be differentiated from those in what is now known as the Cartwright collection, a group put together quite a few years later and bequeathed to the College in the 1680s.[10]

William Cartwright was also an actor, working in London theatre both before and after the long closure between 1642 and 1660. By the time of his death in 1686 he had acquired 239 paintings, of which 76 were portraits.[11] Seventy-seven pictures from the Cartwright collection are in the Dulwich Gallery. Which of them derives from Alleyn's original bequest and which were Cartwright's own is not always clear—the Cartwright inventory is incomplete—but the combined collection does include at least one of another Shakespeare company actor, Nathan Field. Its likely date is 1610, six years before Field joined the King's Men, when he was first emerging from the boy companies as an adult actor. Like the portrait of Burbage, Field's is most likely by Marcus Gheeraerts the Younger, since the style and the shirt resemble one he painted in 1594 of Capt. Thomas Lee. The Dulwich collection certainly reinforces the likelihood that portraits of actors by professional artists were becoming fashionable in the early years of the seventeenth century.

For Shakespeare, a portrait may have had a more private justification. During the more than twenty years while he was absent from Stratford working in London, from the late 1580s until 1610, he had little chance to spend time at home with his wife and children. The company performed in London daily, and he was a sharer actor in those daily performances. The only time of year when plays were banned in London, apart from plague epidemics, was the forty days of Lent up to Easter each year. Even then, the three or four days it took to get from London to Stratford and back by horse would have bitten into his family time. His series of investments in Stratford make it clear that he always intended to retire there, once he had made his fortune. In 1603, after nearly fifteen years away, following the death of his father and his only son, and with his social standing now assured, it would have seemed logical to have his image resting at home to remind his wife and two daughters of his existence.

So there could have been a good reason why Shakespeare might have wanted his portrait done in 1603. But if we believe that he would have commissioned a small and inexpensive portrait so that his family could have a memento of him when he was away in London, where might the Sanders family have come in? How could such a portrait have found its way into the hands of the Sanderses? Can we believe that someone named John Sanders knew Shakespeare well enough to paint his picture but never gave it to him, perhaps painted it as a memento for himself of someone he admired?

While in London, besides his fellow players Shakespeare seems to have most closely associated himself with the community of French Protestant exiles, known as Huguenots. Richard Field, also from Stratford, who published his two long poems in 1593 and 1594, was married to a Huguenot, Jacqueline Vautrollier, who must have introduced him to the Huguenot Mountjoys at whose house he lodged for some years. But no Sanders appears in the list of his Stratford or his London contacts. A man named William Sanders worked for the King's Men in 1624, when he was listed as one of the company's hired men who had to be exempted from arrest on December 27, 1624, by the Master of the Revels.[12] Nothing else is known of this Sanders, though, and he does not seem to have been more than a walk-on player, or possibly one of the consort of musicians who entertained the audience during the plays at the Blackfriars playhouse. Given the date that William appears as a member of Shakespeare's old company, he might conceivably have been a son of the Sanders who acquired the portrait. But so far, there is nothing to give William Sanders any link with the company in Shakespeare's own time.

Another possible connection was closer to home. A man called Sanders or Saunders, with the same first name as the London player of 1624, can be identified around Stratford in the decade before 1603. This otherwise unknown "William Sawnders" was an attendant and probably a secretary to Thomas Bushell, a country gentleman resident near Stratford, in 1593.[13] Bushell's daughter married Adrian Quiney, son of the Stratford neighbour of Shakespeare's who wrote to him on a visit to London when doing business for Bushell in 1598. The younger Adrian Quiney was a cousin of Thomas Quiney, who married Shakespeare's younger daughter, Judith. This Sawnders may conceivably have had a relative called John who decided to go to London with Shakespeare's youngest brother, Edmund, born in 1580, who joined his elder brother as a player in or before 1606 (he had a son born in Southwark in 1607). The family tradition that a young John Sanders arrived in London from Worcestershire in 1603 or a little earlier, intending to make his fortune, does not fit this reading. Nor does the fact that the portrait stayed in the hands of the Sanders generations living in Worcestershire.

Stratford was within the Bishop of Worcester's diocese, but the county is some distance from Warwickshire.

So there are possible connections of the Shakespeares with the Sanders name. They are not, however, substantial evidence. The best key to the Sanders portrait is the date 1603. The Chandos portrait, supposedly of Shakespeare, belongs in the later Cartwright tradition of acquiring portraits of actors. Once owned by Thomas Betterton, the greatest of Shakespearean actors at the end of the century, the Chandos portrait is of a figure identified too late in the century for us to have much confidence in its being Shakespeare. But its existence, like the portrait allegedly of Marlowe at Corpus Christi College, Cambridge, affirms the popularity of the fashion, and it may well portray an actor/poet from Shakespeare's own time. The same is probably true of the Sanders portrait. But no stronger affirmation can be made with any confidence. The most persuasive evidence is its very precise date, and the coincidence of Shakespeare's elevation in that year. Identifying the Sanders portrait as a painting of the new King's courtier poet done specifically in 1603—whether or not it was subsequently transported to Stratford and so evaded the new London enthusiasm for collecting portraits of actors, or stayed in London with John Sanders, its young actor owner, and was passed down through his family, I think must be accepted as simply a very strong likelihood.

In Search of Master Shakespeare

ANDREW GURR PAINTS a vivid picture of Shakespeare's life in London in 1603. But he does it, in large part, from his extensive study of the theatrical world, because as Lloyd Sullivan quickly discovered, Shakespeare himself left us few clues. Even in the best-documented years of his life, much remains in the shadows. And when it comes to Shakespeare's life before London, we know almost nothing for certain. We know precious little of his childhood, even less of his travels, his loves and his losses. Shakespeare had no contemporary biographer, no Boswell who dogged his steps and recorded his witticisms. For a man who made his living from words, he left a shockingly thin written record. He left no journal and not a single letter. There are hints of him to be found on a few property records and in some exceedingly dull testimony in someone else's lawsuit. There is a vague flash of personality in his last will and testament, in which he snubs his daughter Judith's ne'er-do-well husband. And there are hints of the man in the plays and the sonnets, but it is dangerous business trying to read character into his characters. In the late eighteenth century, the formidable

Shakespeare scholar George Steevens summed up the maddening elusiveness of Shakespeare's life: "All that is known with any degree of certainty concerning him, is, that he was born at Stratford-upon-Avon; married, and had children there; went to London, where he commenced actor [*sic*], and wrote poems and plays; returned to Stratford, made his will, died and was buried."[1]

Given the paucity of verifiable facts, Lloyd soon realized he would get little help from the evidence provided by Shakespeare's biographers. Did Shakespeare ever share the stage of a theatre with someone named John Sanders? Would he have spent the money on a portrait? Were there men around him who sought to preserve his likeness for posterity? He would find no answers in the published record.

In some ways, we now feel we know rather less about Shakespeare's life than we did a hundred years ago. The antiquarian John Aubrey's notes for a biography of the playwright were published in 1813, and lives of Shakespeare have come fast and furious ever since. But those written before the midpoint of the twentieth century were works of romance as much as fact. The early biographers were content to relay the legends right along with the recorded facts. And while their accounts offered portraits of the man, it was the heroic, passionate genius people then thought him to be.

There are many good tales that have little but four hundred years of repetition to support them. Among these is the story of how Shakespeare was forced to flee Stratford as a young man because he was caught poaching a deer on a nobleman's estate. Another describes how he passed out under a crab tree after carousing with a gang of hard-drinking local lads in the village of Bidford near Stratford. There is an enduring story that he died of a horrendous hangover—a "fever" suffered after a night of drinking with Ben Jonson and his fellow Warwickshire poet Michael Drayton.

But in the middle of the twentieth century, a new breed of Shakespeareans undertook to weed out what the American scholar Samuel Schoenbaum called the "speculative elaboration or romantic indulgence,"[2] the Shakespeare mythos, from the documentary record. In his exhaustive *William Shakespeare: A Compact Documentary Life*, Schoenbaum tested the legends against the evidence. Most of the very best tales, the ones that breathe life into the character, failed the test. Conjecture, fantasy, wishful thinking: little of it had roots in the facts that could be deciphered from surviving scraps of Elizabethan rag paper. "Infuriatingly, whenever Shakespeare does something other than buy a lease or write a play, history shuts her jaws with a snap," the twentieth-century novelist Anthony Burgess grumbled in his Shakespeare biography.[3]

Consequently, we remain today as hungry to know the playwright as were his fans in the 1700s. And so evidence-based scholarship produces arid studies from the documentary records, with scholars debating each other in the very thin margins, these records leave open for speculation, other recent biographers invent his thoughts and emotions. And even among the scholars, there is disagreement on questions such as where and for how long Shakespeare went to school, whether he was generous with the poor or kept a miser's grip on his purse and whether he was a negligent husband.

On the year and place of his birth, at least, there is agreement, and for Lloyd this would become critical in his continuing investigations, as the age of the sitter appears to be fixed by the date on the painting as 1603. The parish register of Holy Trinity Church in Stratford-upon-Avon records, in the column for baptisms, one *Gulielmus, filius Johannes Shakspere* (William, son of John Shakespeare), christened on April 26, 1564. Birthdates were not recorded in Elizabethan England. In the 1770s, George Steevens wrote to the curate at Holy Trinity inquiring about the baptismal record and was told that the boy William was born on April 23, three days before his christening. Steevens duly reported the curate's guess as fact, and the fact entered the tradition, reinforced by the convenient coincidence that April 23 was also the day of Shakespeare's death and the feast of England's patron saint, George. We can conclude that William must have been born on or before April 23, because the monument on his grave tells us he was fifty-two when he died and thus had entered his fifty-third year. But April 21 or 22 are also plausible birthdates; Elizabethan children were normally baptized within a few days of birth.

The Shakespeares came from Warwickshire, in the geographic heart of England. (Shakespeare is the accepted modern spelling of a surname written a bewildering variety of ways—Shakspere, Shakyspere, Shaxpere, Shackespeare, Shagspere or any of a dozen others—an orthographic anarchy typical in Tudor England.) We can trace the Shakespeare family back to William's grandfather, Richard Shakespeare, a tenant farmer living in the village of Snitterfield, three and one-half miles northeast of Stratford-upon-Avon, during the reign of King

Henry VIII. This was flat, rich farmland fed by the Avon River and close to Stratford, with its weekly markets and several large annual fairs.

Warwickshire in Richard Shakespeare's adult years was a relatively peaceful county in a time of troubles. King Henry's defiant divorce and marriage to Ann Boleyn and his break from Rome launched a long period of civil and religious turmoil; at the same time, his country was under almost constant threat of invasion by Spain and France. Warwickshire may have escaped the worst of the civil conflict because the new official faith was neither widely understood nor strongly enforced, and because the half-educated clergy clung to many of the rituals of Catholicism that a man such as Richard would have grown up with.

When we first hear of Richard in 1529—he is likely in his twenties—he is a tenant farmer on the land of the Earl of Warwick. The local records show him paying a two-pence fine for failing to maintain his hedgerows rather than fight the charge in the twice-yearly manorial court, six miles away at Warwick. Richard's two sons, Henry and John, grew up not far from the Earl's manor house. Henry, the elder, seems to have been something of a wastrel. The surviving records show him fined for fighting and imprisoned for bad debts. But John leaves every sign of having been a man of considerable ambition.

Sometime in the 1550s, a twenty-something John Shakespeare moved to Stratford to take up the trade of glover and whittawer. (As a glover, he tanned the hides of deer, horses, goats and sheep and then made and sold purses, aprons and other soft leather goods.) Like his father, John first enters the historical record with a fine, this one paid to the town of Stratford in April of 1552 for keeping an unauthorized rubbish heap. The town records of that year also show him selling gloves from a house on Henley Street, a timbered Tudor dwelling that still stands.

In the middle of the sixteenth century, Stratford was a town of about a dozen streets and perhaps two thousand people. To modern ears this sounds quite small, but it was a good-size Tudor town. Because the roads were poor and modes of transport both limited and expensive, most people did not travel far from home; Stratford was the trading hub for all the surrounding villages and so a busy place.

First as an apprentice, then as a master glover, John slowly made his way up the social and economic ladder; he must have been a craftsman of some skill. In 1556 he purchased a property in town with house and garden, and let it. Then he bought the house adjacent to his residence on Henley Street. Eventually he also bought title to the half he rented, and the two were joined together into a single building, both shop and family home. Flourishing, he looked for a wife and in about 1557 married one Mary Arden, likely ten years his junior. The Ardens were respected people—if not gentry, then high-placed yeomen, the freehold farmers who ranked one rung below the gentry. Mary's father was a prosperous yeoman, and it seems she was her father's favourite (he left Mary his most valuable property) and also a bright young woman. Although she was no more than seventeen or eighteen when her father drew up his will, he named her one of its two executors, a rare distinction for a woman at the time.

John and Mary's first child, a daughter they christened Joan, was born in September 1558. A second daughter, Margaret, followed in December of 1562, and William was born eighteen months later. Precious as this first-born son must have been for Mary Shakespeare, we can infer considerable anxiety as she nursed the baby: three months after William's arrival was recorded in the baptismal rolls, the parish register burial column reads *hic incepit pestis* ("here begins the plague"). This was the bubonic plague, one of three outbreaks of the ferocious contagion in Shakespeare's lifetime. The germs were carried from the fetid alleys of London to the clean air of the market towns, and this outbreak killed some 250 people in Stratford, about an eighth of the population. The disease spread through Stratford, and fear spread with it. Infant William likely spent the first summer of his life in a house where the windows were sealed and the doors closed to visitors, while fires, believed to banish the poisoned air, burned in the street.

Despite such precautions, William's two older sisters may have been among the casualties of the plague, for neither survived childhood—and if not the plague, then one of myriad other childhood perils, for infant mortality was high in Elizabethan England: an estimated twelve of every hundred children died before the age of one. Life expectancy at birth was only about forty years, although anyone who made it through the first thirty years was likely to live for another thirty. Shakespeare's younger brother Gilbert was born in 1566 (he would grow up to be a glover too); a second Joan was christened in 1569, confirming that the first had died before the age of seven. A daughter Ann was baptized in 1571 and died before she turned eight; Richard was christened in 1574 and Edmund, who would one day follow his brother William to London and seek work as an actor, in 1580. Of John and Mary Shakespeare's eight offspring, the second Joan was the only daughter to survive childhood. Only she and William are known to have married.

When William was a child, his father John Shakespeare continued to gain wealth and status. He entered the wool trade and acted as a moneylender; he invested in properties, both land and houses that he let for income. In 1556 he was appointed a taster of ale and bread for the town council, with the responsibility of ensuring bakers were selling full-weight loaves and brewers vending decent ale in sealed pots. He was made one of the town's four constables in 1558, charged with stopping quarrels, divesting angry men of weapons, supervising fire prevention and guarding public morality (reporting those who gambled during Lent, for example). He soon rose to serve as alderman on the town council, and in 1568 he was chosen as bailiff, a role that saw him don fur-trimmed robes to preside over the town as the Elizabethan equivalent of mayor.

Through William's early childhood, his father prospered along with his town, which boasted wealthy and well-educated citizens, some fine houses for the gentry and an elegant stone church. The town's population grew, and these newcomers provided more customers for its artisans and shopkeepers. So it seems that the boy Will Shakespeare knew security and even considerable comfort in a bustling provincial town.

Was it in this bourgeois milieu that the young Shakespeare discovered his passion for the stage? Stratford, like other established English towns of the era, had a strong tradition of dramatic and civic pageantry and wealthy citizens who nourished the arts.

Biographers since the late 1700s have been tempted to believe that Shakespeare's love of drama was born and nurtured young, but the case is circumstantial. We do know that as bailiff his father authorized payment for both local and visiting players, and they performed in the Guild Hall, just a few hundred feet from the family home in Henley Street. Did Shakespeare stand between his seated father's knees at a performance of the Queen's Men during their visit to Stratford in 1569? In the same era, a youth in Gloucester recorded just such an excursion, so it is reasonable to imagine the bailiff taking his place of honour at such a performance and bringing with him his young son.

In 1575 Queen Elizabeth visited Warwickshire on a "Progress," a royal tour, that included performances and spectacles. She went to stay at Kenilworth Castle, just twelve miles from Stratford, where she was entertained with theatrics, singing, even fireworks. Perhaps the twelve-year-old Will was among the curious throng who watched the festivities.

The greatest question about Shakespeare's childhood concerns the circumstances of his education. There is some debate about whether the parents of the great playwright could themselves read or write, for only their marks, not their full signatures, survive. But there is a strong argument that John must have learned to read, given the public offices to which he was elected. Many people in the Tudor age mastered reading but not the more formal skill of writing, and we know that other literate Elizabethans chose to sign documents with a mark. A friend would later leave John Shakespeare all his books, an odd bequest to an illiterate man. And while Mary Shakespeare is more of a mystery, minute scrutiny of documents that bear her mark has led some scholars to suggest that the smooth flow of the ink indicates more than passing familiarity with a quill; she once left what appears to be the backward-written letters M. S. on a land deed.

But surely Shakespeare, our greatest writer, was well educated? We assume so. Stratford had what was known as a grammar school—quite a good school for boys, according to contemporary references. Although we have no school records to prove the Shakespeare boys were enrolled, young William's father was a man of considerable standing in the town and would surely have sent his eldest son to this school, which was free for the sons of burgesses.

Most scholars agree that William likely began his formal education at the age of four or five at the local petty school, a sort of pre-school. Contemporary accounts tell us the boys at petty school spent serious days learning the alphabet and the catechisms of the Book of Common Prayer. At age seven, they moved up to the local grammar school.

For Shakespeare, who turned seven in 1571, that would have meant the lower school of King's New School, where lessons lasted from six or seven in the morning to five or six in the evening, six days a week, almost all year long. Boys learned both Latin and English grammar, memorized the Latin dictionary, studied the ancient Greek fables of Aesop and read Latin literature. All learning was done by rote. Each morning a class of some forty boys gathered under a schoolmaster and his assistant to be taught a lesson they were expected to repeat "perfectlie" by memory the next day.

In the upper school, from about the age of ten, they learned rhetoric and logic, made declamations and orations, read the

Roman writers Ovid, Virgil, Seneca and Horace and likely the Bible in an early translation into English. No surviving curriculum, however, suggests that the boys learned anything about modern history, politics, the human body, agriculture, the trades or their own town or country. Shakespeare's later heavy reliance on the classics—on Ovid's *Metamorphoses*, for example—gives weight to the very logical argument that he received the advantages of this grammar school education.

About the time young William would have moved to the upper school, his father's financial fortunes began to decline, possibly as a result of an economic recession that affected the whole region. John Shakespeare was fined for usury and illegal practices in his wool dealings. Soon we find him mortgaging for ready money the property his wife had inherited. By 1576 he no longer showed up regularly for town meetings; the council records show that his colleagues kindly exempted him from taxes and levies for poor relief.

We can only guess how much his father's changed circumstances affected the young Will and his family. Boys typically left the grammar school by fifteen—in William's case that would be 1579—although biographers have long conjectured that as the eldest son he was withdrawn early so that he could aid his father in the shop or bring some extra shillings home by taking outside work.

Shakespeare's next appearance in the documentary record—the first since his birth—has spawned endless speculation. In November 1582, "William Shagspere" wed "Anne Hathaway of Stratford in the Dioces of worcester maiden." Shakespeare was just eighteen, while his bride was twenty-six. She lived in the nearby village of Shottery and was a woman of some means, having inherited a small amount of property from her father.

William and Anne were issued their marriage licence in haste, after only one reading of the banns instead of the customary three. The marriage was insured by friends of Anne's father with an unusually large bond of £40, exempting the bishop from liability lest the union somehow prove "irregular." William and Anne's first child, Susanna, was christened on May 26, 1583—and so likely conceived in early September, two months before her parents' formal union.

These details suggest that while shotgun weddings were not unknown in Tudor Stratford, they could still be sources of unpleasant gossip. Some scholars argue, however, that the tradition of plighting a troth allowed "fleshly meddling" before formal sanctification by the vicar. Did Anne and William make an oral contract to wed the previous summer? Did a dalliance at a summer festival have unintended consequences, obliging young Shakespeare to do the honourable thing? Or was theirs an unconventional love match? With only the stark parish register record of the marriage, we are left with conjecture.

The marriage of Will Shakespeare and Anne Hathaway affords one of the finer examples of extrapolation about the life from the work. Some find in *Twelfth Night* evidence of his bitterness at a forced union, as when Duke Orsino says, "Then let thy love be younger than thyself, / Or thy affection cannot hold the bent; / For women are as roses, whose fair flow'r / Being once display'd doth fall that very hour.") But Andrew Gurr suggests that a disguised tribute to Anne can be found in one of the early sonnets: "'I hate' from 'hate' away she threw/ And saved my life, saying 'not you,'" with Hate-away a pun on Hathaway (one that rhymed rather better in the pronunciation of the Tudor Midlands).

Around the time Will got married, his father's decline became a collapse. John Shakespeare was sued for debts, placed mortgages on more properties and had completely ceased to attend council. In 1586 a new alderman was elected to replace him, for, as the council record tells us, "Mr. Shaxspere doth not come to the halls when they be warned, nor hath not done of long time." In 1592 John was fined for failure to attend church—taken by some as evidence to support the theory that he was a recusant or a secret Catholic. More likely he was simply lying low to avoid his creditors. If nothing else, his son's marriage to Anne Hathaway and the birth of their daughter brought two more hungry mouths into the struggling Shakespeare household. And by marrying, Shakespeare forever closed the door on attendance at university or formal apprenticeship in a trade, for these were open only to bachelors. He was left, we suppose, to aid his father in his work as glover, perhaps to accompany him on his journeys trading wool.

Most scholars assume that Shakespeare stayed close to home from the time of his marriage in 1582 until February 1585, two months before his twenty-first birthday. That February Anne Hathaway Shakespeare gave birth to twins, Judith and Hamnet. It is tempting to imagine the young Shakespeare at the kitchen table in an ill-heated timber house, surrounded by squalling infants, watching his father worry over the accounts and brooding on how, failed glover's son though he might be, he was meant for greater things.

But now the documentary trail goes completely cold, furnishing great fodder to those who continue to argue that the man named William Shakespeare could not have written the plays so long attributed to him. The next seven years are known as the "lost years": from 1585 to 1592, when William went from age twenty-one to twenty-eight—the prime of an Elizabethan life—there is no record. Shakespeare will next turn up in the London theatre, but we have no true sense of the path he took from Stratford to Southwark.

Theories abound. Some are wild: that he joined Sir Francis Drake to circumnavigate the globe, or that he served as a soldier. More logically he assisted his struggling father at his trade and in his business dealings. Some scholars, noting the firm grasp of legal matters that informs the plays, have suggested that the young Shakespeare worked in a law office. But surely, then, his name would endure on a will or deed he witnessed?

Many make the enticing argument that the young Shakespeare spent some time as a schoolmaster. His earliest biographer was the first to say so, and John Aubrey had living sources of information, including William Beeston, the son of Christopher, one of Shakespeare's colleagues in the Lord Chamberlain's Men. Aubrey reported that the playwright knew Latin "pretty well" because "he had been in his younger yeares a Schoolmaster in the Countrey." Some have inferred from this that Aubrey meant, in fact, the years before his marriage, while others think Shakespeare would not have been given such a job much before the age of eighteen. Certainly his plays show both student's and teacher's knowledge of the classroom. There is no record that he earned the licence a schoolmaster required, and the masters in the grammar schools were for the most part Oxbridge educated. But he might have taught in the petty school, perhaps the one he himself attended.

Others favour the theory that the young William served as a tutor in a noble home. The Hoghton family of Lancashire has a long oral tradition that Shakespeare lived and taught with them, and a "William Shakeshafte" is listed on the household retinue from the period—Shakeshafte being a not uncommon variation on Shakespeare. This theory gets tangled up with an even more seductive speculation that while living in the Hoghton household William made his first acquaintance with the theatrical life. Sir Alexander Hoghton's will of 1581 links Shakeshafte and a fellow servant named Folke Gillom with a stock of players' clothes; these are to go to Hoghton's brother, unless he won't keep a company of players, in which case they go to Thomas Hesketh, Hoghton's good friend. The will directs Hesketh "to be ffrendlye unto" Shakeshafte and Gillom. And Hesketh was a friend of, and had visits from, Lord Strange, who had a company of players that Shakespeare may have joined.

Another plausible theory holds that the young Shakespeare joined the performing retinue of a nobleman such as the Earl of Leicester. Connections made through a noble household would help to explain how he made his entrée into London's tight-knit theatrical world. And he might have ventured as far as continental Europe with the household of his noble master, travels that would help explain his precise use of maritime terms—referring, for example, to "the waist of the ship"—or the acquaintance with Italy that colours such plays as *The Merchant of Venice* and *Romeo and Juliet*. Yet such knowledge might also have come from the books that Shakespeare read so hungrily; we know he drew his plots from a host of texts. Connections made through a noble household would also help to explain how he made his entrée into London's tight-knit theatrical world.

There is one final theatrical theory: that he ran away to join a company of players. In 1587 the hugely popular Queen's Men visited Stratford. That same year, in Thame, Oxfordshire, an actor called William Knell drew his sword and assaulted his colleague John Towne. Cornered, Towne plunged his own sword into Knell's neck. A coroner's inquest found that Towne had acted in self-defence, but with one man dead and one arrested, the Queen's Men now lacked two actors. Did they spy a young man of promise named Will Shakespeare and enlist him for the rest of their tour? Corroborating evidence is sorely lacking.

After the birth of his twins in Stratford in 1585, the next firm sign of Shakespeare's existence comes in the form of a reference to a play we know he wrote because it was later included in the First Folio. On March 3, 1592, the account books of a London theatre called the Rose show that the play *Harry the Sixth* drew the highest takings of the season. Precisely when he left home, and why, remain open questions, but by 1592 Shakespeare must have long since left his wife and family in Stratford and immersed himself in the theatrical world in London, putting in several years as a hired man with a company before penning *Harry*.

Poor as he was, he almost certainly made his journey from Stratford on foot, walking for several days, to the gates of the teeming, plague-ridden metropolis. London was then the biggest city on earth, with 150,000 people overflowing its stone walls, where stately mansions with elegant gardens pressed up against crowded mud-and-timber tenements and where jutting second storeys blocked out the sunlight and rubbish cast from windows clogged the laneways. The neighbourhood of the theatres was rife with alehouses, brothels, gaming houses and unlicensed barber-surgeons. Its streets were crowded with beggars, prostitutes and their soldier clientele—and theatregoers.

Shakespeare inhabited this teeming demimonde during years of political unrest and economic trouble. In 1587 Elizabeth ordered the execution of her cousin Mary, Queen of Scots for plotting to kill her. The next year, England defeated the Spanish Armada, but the country continued to wage a costly war with Spain. From 1593 to 1599, the pound was at its worst buying value for seven centuries, after six successive failed harvests, famine and riots over prices. And though Elizabeth chose a moderate course on religious matters, many of her subjects remembered the violent civil wars of "Bloody Mary's" reign, when King Henry's Catholic daughter had restored the Roman Church and burned heretics who did not follow her.

Yet these were very good years for the arts. London boasted three permanent theatres, including the newly opened Rose, and the Theatre, established by James Burbage in 1576. Demand for theatrical entertainment was growing as the city's population swelled; for a penny, soldiers and apprentices and serving girls could be relieved of their drudgery for an afternoon. The gentry attended too, and the young courtiers and law students made for an audience of reasonable sophistication. A crowd of young gentlemen known as the University Wits was writing real plays, not morality skits or performances by acrobats, but comedies and dramas. Among them was Christopher Marlowe, the author of the great plays *Dr. Faustus*, *Tamburlaine* and *The Jew of Malta*. And the Queen had even taken a company of players under her patronage as the Queen's Men.

Somehow the small-town boy from Stratford found theatre work, possibly taking advantage of connections forged years earlier. Between 1585 and 1592, he may have joined Lord Strange's Men, the best of a handful of struggling actors' companies. In 1574, an Order of the City Council had threatened to punish players as vagabonds; they could protect themselves by putting themselves under the patronage of a nobleman such as Lord Strange. His men competed with a half-dozen acting companies for the right to perform in a handful of venues around the city.

References to *Titus Andronicus* and *Henry VI*, two of Shakespeare's earliest plays, tell us they were first performed by Lord Strange's Men, which suggests Shakespeare was then in the company's employ. From what we know of the workings of the theatrical world at the time, we can surmise that whatever company or companies he worked for, he began as a hireling (an actor who worked for a small salary, not a full member of the company) and was obliged to keep an estimated thirty parts straight in his head. The companies spent a great deal of time touring in the countryside, an arduous and ill-paid life of performing and trudging between towns. When in London, a company performed a different play every single afternoon except Sundays and the forty days of Lent.

With such a relentless schedule, the companies were always hungry for scripts. Shakespeare probably worked his way into playwriting by first repairing and tidying other writers' drafts. He must have learned fast, for we know he soon graduated from hireling to full-fledged playwright. Before he had left his twenties, Shakespeare had written a series of historical dramas, including the *Henry VI* trilogy, *Richard III* and a number of other crowd pleasers: *The Comedy of Errors*, *Love's Labour's Lost* and the bloody *Titus Andronicus*. From evidence such as the books of the various London theatres, scholars have pieced together a rough chronology of composition for Shakespeare's surviving works.

From 1592 to 1594 Shakespeare and his fellow players had little work in London. There was another savage outbreak of the plague—14 per cent of the population of the capital died. The playhouses, viewed as incubators of contagion as well as moral cesspools, were forced to close. Desperate for income, the companies went on tour, a much less lucrative pursuit.

What did Shakespeare do in this two-year hiatus? He likely travelled with his company during at least part of that period. He may have performed before a hometown crowd in Stratford and perhaps even stayed behind to spend some time with his wife and children. With little market for new plays, he wrote and published *Venus and Adonis* and *The Rape of Lucrece*, a pair of long narrative erotic poems that he dedicated to a generous patron, Henry Wriothesley, the 3rd Earl of Southampton. Both poems proved popular and went through many printings; Shakespeare made no money from royalties, a concept that did not exist, but in a payment from the publisher and possibly in a gift from his pleased patron.

Shakespeare was twenty-nine the year the first of the poems

was published. The Earl of Southampton was a decade his junior, a wild young noble recklessly tearing through his inheritance. Supporting an up-and-coming young poet appears to have appealed to the flamboyant young playboy; it was a fashionable thing to do. But there may have been more to their relationship than that of a writer on the make and an aristocrat who fancied a dabble in the arts.

Some scholars have recently speculated that Shakespeare and Southhampton's was a romantic, even sexual, relationship. As evidence, they cite not only the emotional language of the second of Shakespeare's dedications—"The love I dedicate to your Lordship is without end"—which is not in itself so unusual, but also contemporary accounts that suggest the Earl enjoyed same-sex amours. One writer says of his relationship with another nobleman, that the Earl "would clip and hug him in his arms and play wantonly with him." And he was known to make "rewards and preferments" to his male favourites—including, perhaps, an actor somewhat older and from a much lower social class. Some argue Southampton is the "fair youth" of Shakespeare's first 126 sonnets—it makes excellent fodder for speculation.

Shakespeare resurfaces in the theatre world during the festive Christmas season of 1594. That year at the palace at Greenwich, William Shakespeare, Richard Burbage and William Kempe, "servants of the Lord Chamberlain," performed two plays before Her Majesty. (The Accounts of the Treasurer of the Queen's Chamber list them as joint payees.) It is the first direct mention of Shakespeare as a man of the theatre and implies that he, Burbage and Kempe were now business partners.

Shakespeare had by now thrown in his lot with the Lord Chamberlain's Men, the company set up in May 1594. He would remain with the company for the rest of his life.

Four years later, in 1598, the men found themselves without a theatre. The lease held by James Burbage, Richard's father, on the Theatre, where the company then played, had expired. Instead of renewing the lease, the landlord, sniffing at the debauchery of the players' world, resolved to demolish it and put the timber to some "better use." The Burbages had a better idea.

On December 28, under cover of darkness, the Burbage sons, a few friends and a dozen workmen pulled down the theatre building—theirs in the lease—and hauled the timbers across the Thames—either on ice frozen solid in a freakish cold snap, or by the more predictable bridge. On the south shore, near the site of the Rose, they built the finest theatre London had ever seen and called it the Globe. The Lord Chamberlain's Men now had a permanent home. A visitor to London in the autumn of 1599, one Thomas Platter of Basle, records seeing the "tragedy of the first Emperor Julius Caesar, very pleasantly performed with approximately fifteen characters,"[4] the first recorded performance at the Globe. The play, of course, was written by Shakespeare.

Shakespeare was one of eight men in the company who formed a syndicate to lease the Globe site, build the theatre and operate it; he was now a sharer in its profits. While the surviving financial records give us no proof of his earnings for the average of about two plays a year he produced in this period or from his share in the company, the best current reckoning is about £200 a year, or ten times the annual wage of an Elizabethan schoolmaster. It was this increasing prosperity that had allowed Shakespeare to restore his father's fortunes and his social standing, including the much satirized coat of arms that Andrew Gurr describes.

Throughout his London years, Shakespeare kept up his ties to Stratford. Convention holds that he made at least an annual visit home, perhaps in the summer when the theatres were shut. It seems almost certain that he returned home in August 1596, when his eleven-year-old son, Hamnet, died of unknown cause, ending the male line of Shakespeares. Though Shakespeare cannot have been close to his children, having lived away from home almost since their birth, some critics mark a new depth in his writing after Hamnet's death. *King John*, for example, may date from that year and contains the lament "Grief fills the room up of my absent child."

Anne and William had no children after the twins, evidence perhaps that Anne's reproductive health was impaired by the delivery of the twins—or that the often absent Will shunned his wife for London paramours. There is no shortage of speculation about his extramarital liaisons, including possible homosexual ones. There is the Dark Lady who incites his passion in the sonnets and whose identity is the subject of endless debate, and Jennet Davenant, whose son William appears to have been Shakespeare's godson and who would one day be the reputed owner of the Chandos portrait. Jennet was said to be witty and "very beautiful," but the idea of her entangled with the playwright lies only in oral tradition (including hints from the younger William himself, when drinking, that he was not godson but illegitimate son).

In 1603 King James took the throne and adopted Shakespeare's company as the King's Men, placing the partners at the top of their profession. As the company's "ordinary poet"—their playwright-in-residence—Shakespeare wrote *King Lear*, *Othello* and *Macbeth* between 1603 and his retirement to Stratford about 1610.

Plague again closed the theatres in 1608 and all of 1609, and it is assumed Shakespeare spent the bulk of that time in Stratford, writing his last great works. In 1611, according to the Royal Accounts, *The Tempest* was performed for the Court at Whitehall. (It was his last unaided play, or at least the last that survives.) Scholars assume Shakespeare attended the performance. He may have spent much of the next year in London, for he now began to collaborate with John Fletcher, the young writer who would replace him in supplying the King's Men with playbooks; this is taken as a sign that he was withdrawing from the theatrical world.

In June 1613 the Globe went up in flames when the firing of a cannon in *Henry VIII* set the thatch of the roof on fire. Although the theatre was crowded, everyone escaped without injury, but the building burned to the ground. The theatre was rebuilt, but Shakespeare sold his shares and bore no part in the cost of rebuilding. He did buy a house in Blackfriars in London that year, a pied-à-terre close to the theatre, but he seems to have spent little time there. He was just forty-eight, and there is no sign that he was in ill health; he had settled in with his wife and children, who were living in New Place, which Shakespeare had purchased in 1597. New Place had five gables, three storeys and ten fireplaces (then a taxable luxury), two gardens, an orchard and two barns.

Over the years he had kept up his ties to Stratford. He was a shrewd investor in local grain dealings and acquired a number of Stratford properties in addition to his new house. When his father died in 1601, William had inherited the two houses in Henley Street. In 1605 he invested the vast sum of £440 in the Stratford tithes. With rising Puritanism in the town, there is some speculation that he sought to buy himself respectability not normally accorded to a player.

Once more a Stratford local, he soon faced domestic worries. His quick-witted elder daughter, Susanna, had married the town doctor, John Hall, but his younger daughter, Judith, was betrothed to Thomas Quiney, a wine merchant of dubious morals. (Thomas was found to have impregnated a woman who died in childbirth a month after he married Judith, a scandal that scholars assume chagrined the playwright in the last months of his life.) As for his relationship with his wife in these final years, it is as much of a puzzle as it was at the time of their marriage.

William Shakespeare died, we think, in his bed at New Place on April 23, 1616, at the age of fifty-two. His will is suitably oblique. With nary a word of affection, he famously left Anne only his "second-best bed." He willed his clothing to his sister Joan; a sword to his friend Thomas Russell; £10 to the poor (some scholars see this as generous and others stingy); the great bulk of his estate to his daughter Susanna and her doctor husband, and a mere £150 to Judith.

He also left a pile of manuscripts, perhaps stacked in the storeroom of the Globe Theatre. These were the plays his friends would publish seven years later, edited and corrected from the Quarto copies in circulation and finally collected for the First Folio.

And there it is: the bones of the documentary life as we know it today. There is enough evidence to track Shakespeare's major movements, and we know enough about life in pastoral Stratford and theatrical London to draw a fairly detailed picture of his days in each place. Yet the gaps in the record remain troubling—the lost years, in particular. We have no idea how the humble glover's son made his way into the world of the London theatre. We can agree that he must have been well-educated and well-read, even ambitious. We know he was shrewd in financial matters. None of this much helps us know the man.

In the same way that biographers of the 1700s embroidered where the documentary cloth was thin, many today seek to flesh out the evidentiary bones. The Oxford professor Katherine Duncan-Jones has worked from the legal and financial records to construct a mean, misogynist Shakespeare, an avaricious social climber who nonetheless spent plenty of time in taverns drinking with his playwright buddies, caroused with brothel keepers and possibly died of syphilis. Park Honan, professor at the University of Leeds, has postulated a cautious, astute fellow who was easily roused to emotion and chronically eager to please. Others have reached more wildly, among them the poet and biographer Garry O'Connor, who has brought twentieth-century ideas about the psychosexual to his subject: in his book *William Shakespeare: A Popular Life*, Shakespeare is a man with a highly developed feminine side—womb envy, even.

But so great are the holes in the documentary record that they leave room for honest speculation about these kinds of questions—and about the greatest mystery of all: did Shakespeare write his plays?

Scenes from the Birth of a Myth and the Death of a Dramatist

Jonathan Bate

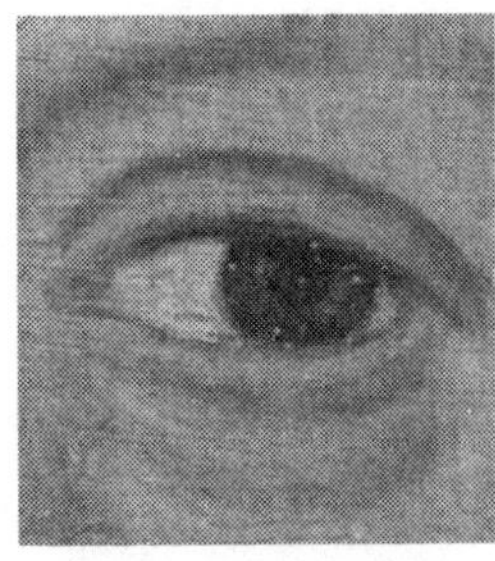

WHY SHOULD THE "discovery" of what might be a portrait of William Shakespeare make it to the front page of the newspapers? Because, the answer will come, Shakespeare was the greatest writer in the history of the world. "After God," proclaimed the nineteenth-century French author Alexandre Dumas, "Shakespeare created most." Shakespeare has become the supreme deity not just of poetry or drama but of high culture itself.

The technical term for the transformation of a mere mortal into a deity is "apotheosis." In myth and religion, apotheosis happens in an instant. The hero dies, and the next thing you know he has ascended into the heavens and become a star. In history, the process is slower. Even a hundred years after his death, William Shakespeare was regarded as a great dramatist but not a unique genius. His apotheosis was the work of the eighteenth century. His contemporary Ben Jonson admired him "on this side Idolatry." In 1769, by contrast, David Garrick's commemorative Shakespeare Jubilee proclaimed him "the God of our Idolatry." With Garrick, serious Bardolatry was born.

There was, however, a downside to the apotheosis. Gods have an unfortunate propensity for attracting wild-eyed extremists and earnest cranks. A few years after Garrick's Jubilee, a retired Oxford don, the Reverend James Wilmot, went poking around Stratford-upon-Avon in pursuit of relics and reminiscences of the divine William. Disappointed by the paucity of what he found, he became the first person to consider the possibility that the plays might really have been written by someone else. He did not, however, publish his theory.

Fast forward to the mid-nineteenth century. Bardolatry and the British Empire are in their heyday. It is 1852. An unsigned article in an Edinburgh magazine asks for the first time the question over which so much ink would be needlessly spilled in the next century and a half: "Who wrote Shakespeare?" The author found it hard to reconcile our knowledge of Shakespeare's life—his mealy-mouthed business dealings, his churlish will (that second-best bed)—with the glories of his plays. Maybe Shakespeare hired someone else to do his writing for him?

Within a few years, a favoured candidate emerged: Francis Bacon, one of the most learned authors of the age. The Baconian argument came to prominence through a book titled *The Philosophy of the Plays of Shakspere Unfolded* (1857). Its author was one Delia Bacon, who was born in a log cabin in Ohio and was eventually committed to a lunatic asylum near Stratford-upon-Avon. Late in life, she claimed personal descent from Lord Bacon and attempted to locate certain hieroglyphic communications from him that she believed were hidden near Shakespeare's grave.

Delia and her many followers were driven by the belief that the wisdom of the plays was so profound that they could only have been written by a great philosopher. Bacon was the greatest English philosopher of the age, therefore he must have been the author of the plays. The ignorant actor from Stratford was but a front man. It did not seem to matter that Bacon's two distinctive modes of thinking—arcane Neoplatonic symbolism on the one hand and radically modern empirical inquiry on the other—represented an altogether different species of learning from that in the plays, which was derived from a combination of classical sources readily available in the grammar school curriculum (such as Ovid and Seneca) and middle-brow vernacular texts (such as Holinshed's historical *Chronicles*, Sir Thomas North's English versions of Plutarch's lives of the heroes of antiquity and a host of popular novellas, plays and romances).

Bacon was an extremely busy politician. His own efforts at drama were distinctly wooden: he had no interest in the professional theatre. Partly for these reasons, he fell out of favour in the twentieth century and a new candidate found vociferous support: Edward de Vere, the 17th Earl of Oxford. The case for his authorship was first put forward in 1920 by an elderly schoolmaster called Thomas Looney. Convinced that the plays evinced an aristocratic sensibility, Looney happened on some lyric poems by the Earl of Oxford and decided that they sounded similar to Shakespeare's *Venus and Adonis*. Knowing little of the conventions of Elizabethan literature—the tendency of lyric poems to recycle stock images—he failed to see that similar parallels could have been found in dozens of other poets of the period, both amateur and professional, aristocratic and low-ranking.

The Oxfordian argument goes something like this. The plays were clearly written by a learned man, whereas Shakespeare came from an illiterate household in an ignorant backwater. The plays reveal an intimate knowledge of Elizabethan high politics and court intrigue, whereas Shakespeare was a humble player. The plays are stamped with the genius of a great human spirit, whereas the documentary records of Shakespeare of Stratford concern such low business as tax evasion and money-grubbing land deals. The Oxfordians have, of course, been so busy pointing to the mote in the eye of Stratford William that they have neglected the beam in that of Earl Edward. But we will return to the specifics of the case against him. For now, let us leave him in the company of other claimants to the authorship of Shakespeare's play—candidates who represent a multitude of the best and brightest of the age: at various times, more than a dozen aristocrats have been put forward, as have Queen Elizabeth, King James, John Florio the Anglo-Italian dictionary maker and Christopher Marlowe (a case that involves the fantasy that he was not killed in the summer of 1593 in a brawl over a bill in Deptford but was spirited away to Italy, whence he despatched his masterworks back to England). The key point to grasp about all these contenders is that their names—every one of them—only entered the frame *after* the apotheosis of Shakespeare from accomplished dramatist to god of our idolatry.

The Shakespeare authorship controversy is an epiphenomenon, a secondary symptom, a consequence of the extraordinary elevation of the dramatist's status that occurred in the eighteenth century. Before this, the conditions simply did not exist for a controversy. The idea of Shakespeare as the greatest artistic genius of all time has now taken such a powerful hold that we are surprised by things that should not surprise us. Why, for instance, ask the anti-Stratfordians, was there no great public reaction to his death? To answer such questions as this we need to suppress the instinct to think of Shakespeare as unique and supreme. We need to return to the age before Bardolatry and to recover the perceptions of Shakespeare's own time.

Spring 1616. The most brilliant dramatic talent of the age is no more. A man who came to youthful fame with a witty and erotic narrative poem taken from the classical mythology of Ovid. Who wrote occasional verse but found his true vocation in the theatre. Whose gifts were such that even the prodigiously learned Ben Jonson deferred to him in the art of playmaking. He has written for the leading acting company of the age, the King's Men, the actors who bore the livery of James himself and played at court more than any other company.

There is only one place to lay such a man to rest: in Westminster Abbey, close to the tombs of Geoffrey Chaucer, father of English verse, and Edmund Spenser, greatest poet of the Elizabethan age. For the first time in the nation's history, a man of the theatre is acknowledged as equal to the makers of courtly verse. Move over, Chaucer and Spenser. The triumvirate of English genius is complete. Make room for the fallen star, cut off in the prime of his thirty-third year: Francis Beaumont is dead.

Spring 1616, take two. It is three weeks after Beaumont's death. Master William Shakespeare has for some time been retired in his hometown of Stratford-upon-Avon. Now he is redrafting his will. Maybe he knows he is dying. His daughter Judith has finally married, but within weeks of the ceremony she has endured the humiliation of her new husband's being publicly accused of "incontinence" with another woman, who has just died as a result of giving birth to his illegitimate child. Shakespeare must change the terms of the will in order to protect his daughter's interests. He also takes the opportunity to add in a bequest of money for the purchase of memorial rings to "my fellows John Hemynnges Richard Burbage & Henry Cundell." They were fellows in more than one sense: friends, but also fellow actors and fellow shareholders in a highly successful business venture dating back over twenty years. That venture was of course the theatre company, established on a joint stock basis in 1594 as the Lord Chamberlain's Men and upgraded to the title of King's Men, courtesy of James I on his accession to the English throne in 1603.

A month later, Shakespeare is dead. We do not know the cause, though tradition speaks of the unfortunate aftereffects of a drinking bout on the occasion of a visit from the dramatist Ben Jonson and the poet Michael Drayton. The latter was a local man, a patient of Shakespeare's son-in-law the highly reputable Dr. John Hall.

The town's most famous son is buried in the parish church. A monument is erected (the most likely commissioner of it is Dr. Hall). It shows Shakespeare holding a quill pen in his right hand and a piece of paper in the left. For a desk, he has a tasselled cushion. Beneath, there is an inscription that tells of how "Quick Nature died" with him but "Living Art" remains in the pages that manifest his "wit." A Latin motto compares him to the very greatest geniuses of antiquity: he had the wisdom of the philosopher Socrates, the literary skill of the poet Virgil and the good judgment of the legendary Nestor. This would be a very strange set of claims if the man in question were anything but an author.

News travels slowly between the provinces and London. We do not know when the theatre world hears of the master's end. Certainly not in time to arrange for a burial in Westminster Abbey. Such is the unfortunate fate of the man who dies away from the capital. And besides, theatre is a fickle business. Shakespeare is yesterday's news. It is the death of Beaumont, so young and still in the prime of his writing, that has captured the imagination of the court and the literary world. Even to contemplate bringing the body of yesterday's man up from the country would take the shine off Beaumont's glory.

Less familiar than Beaumont's burying place is his opinion of the older playwright who died so soon after him. Sometime before his untimely end, Beaumont wrote two verse epistles from the country. The two letters share the same easygoing style and the same addressee (Ben Jonson). One of them is nostalgic for literary company and "full Mermaid wine,"* while the other includes an account of the art of their fellow dramatist William Shakespeare. It was an art that concealed art:

Here I would let slip
(If I had any in me) scholarship,
And from all learning keep these lines as clear
As Shakespeare's best are, which our heirs shall hear
Preachers apt to their auditors to show
How far sometimes a mortal man may go
By the dim light of Nature.

* In March 1613 William Shakespeare was in the city, completing the purchase of a gatehouse in the theatre district of Blackfriars. Shakespeare put up the money, but it was actually a co-purchase in company with three other men, one of whom was John Heminges. Another was William Johnson, landlord of the nearby Mermaid tavern. Although the story of Shakespeare and Ben Jonson engaging in wit combats at the Mermaid is probably apocryphal, landlord Johnson's part in the gatehouse purchase shows that Shakespeare was a Mermaid man and lends credibility to the claim that he and Ben Jonson were drinking companions within its walls.

Jonson himself would later reiterate this characterization. He too knew that Shakespeare had outshone his predecessors (Marlowe, Kyd, Lyly) so far that his plays rivalled those of the ancients (Aeschylus, Euripides, Sophocles, Seneca), despite the fact that the writer of them had "small Latin and less Greek." We must not forget, though, that Ben Jonson liked to show off his own prodigious learning in the classical languages. Small Latin by his standards may well be great by ours.

It is regrettable that Beaumont's letter remained unpublished for three hundred years. Here is another dramatist and drinker saying that the distinctive feature of Shakespeare's writing is its lack of learning. And yet one of the main causes of the authorship controversy has been—what was it now? oh, yes—the supposed irreconcilability between Shakespeare's writing and his lack of learning.

Let us here and now put to rest for good the image of Shakespeare as an ill-educated country bumpkin. As witnesses for Will's defence, I call upon his Stratford friends the Quineys. There is a surviving letter from Richard Quiney, the town bailiff, to Shakespeare, addressing him as "good friend" and "loving countryman." Quiney's roguish son Thomas was the man who married Judith Shakespeare. But a glance at his eldest son gives us a revealing picture of the level of learning common in Shakespeare's Stratford. At the age of just eleven, Richard Quiney Jr. wrote a letter to his father requesting new schoolbooks. Nothing unusual about that, except that the letter was written in perfect Latin. Elizabethan England was not a place where ordinary people were ignorant and wealthy aristocrats were learned. On the contrary: the eleven-year-old Stratford boy Quiney had, as we shall see, much better Latin than the mighty Earl of Oxford!

The myth of Stratford as a backwater devoid of all learning was born in the eighteenth century as another incidental consequence of the apotheosis of Shakespeare. It was a fiction that allowed people to believe that Shakespeare's genius was a freak of nature. It gave Romantic spirits the opportunity to gasp at the miracle of such a man coming from such a place.

The consensus in the immediate aftermath of Shakespeare's death was that he had been a great dramatist but no freak of nature. Soon after 1616, a minor Oxford poet called William Basse made the pilgrimage to Stratford, saw the monument to the playwright's memory, noted the month and year of his death and wrote these lines:

> Renowned Spenser, lie a thought more nye [near]
> To learned Chaucer, and rare Beaumont lie
> A little nearer Spenser to make room
> For Shakespeare in your threefold fourfold tomb.
> To lodge all four in one bed make a shift
> Until Doomsday, for hardly will be a fifth
> Betwixt this day and that by fate be slain
> For whom your curtains may be drawn again.
> If your precedency in death doth bar
> A fourth place in your sacred sepulchre,
> Under this carved marble of thine own
> Sleep rare tragedian Shakespeare, sleep alone
> Thy unmolested peace, unshared cave
> Possess as lord not tenant of thy grave,
>   That unto us and others it may be
>   Honor hereafter to be laid by thee.

This moving little poem circulated in numerous manuscripts in the seventeenth century, testimony to the admiration in which Shakespeare was still held in the immediate aftermath of his death, despite the fact that he had written nothing in the last few years of his life. For Basse, the trinity was not enough: Shakespeare was as good as Chaucer, Spenser and Beaumont. The four of them made up sufficient English genius to last until the crack of doom. Still, however, Shakespeare is one among others. He may be *rare* but he is not *unique*. At this moment, then, there was no need to attribute the writing of the plays to someone else. If anything, one would have expected someone to come forward and ask why Beaumont wrote so brilliantly about the life of the court, given that he was not a courtier.

The master's life now over, Shakespeare's surviving business partners—led by Richard Burbage, foremost player of the King's Men, and John Heminges and Henry Condell, the company's sharpest businessmen—have to decide what to do with his work. It is in their interest to keep as much as possible in manuscript as their own exclusive property. Once a play is disseminated in print, control of it is lost (copyright in its modern sense has not yet been invented). The demand in the literary marketplace for Shakespeare's writing is such that by one means or another, about half his plays have already found their way to the press, sometimes in the form of what Heminges and Condell call "stolen and surreptitious copies." For a while, it seems best to keep the written text of the other works out of the public domain.

Then in 1619 a London publisher named Thomas Pavier, who has already laid his hands on a number of the plays, appears to be moving toward the production of what will advertise itself as a complete Shakespeare. Burbage dies that year, so it is left to Heminges and Condell to act. They set about blocking Pavier's plans and launching their own. The time is right to immortalize their colleague by way of an authoritative collected edition of the plays.

It is a formidable task to gather together all the texts and transform them from working theatre scripts to coherently and consistently presented printed works that will stand the test of time. Even once the copy is prepared, it will still take a long time to print the book: each individual letter of type has to be set on the press by hand. Heminges and Condell initially have thirty-five plays in their possession. At a late stage in the process, they make room for a thirty-sixth, *Troilus and Cressida*. They decide to exclude *The Two Noble Kinsmen* and *Cardenio*, two of Shakespeare's three final plays, written in collaboration with John Fletcher. (Fletcher is also believed to have helped write *Henry VIII*.) The latter had achieved fame as Beaumont's collaborator and then taken over from Shakespeare as "in-house" playwright for the King's Men. To have included work that was partially Fletcher's in the Shakespeare Folio would have added to the lustre of the dead dramatist at the expense of the living one. *The Two Noble Kinsmen* was eventually published in 1634 with a title page describing it as the joint work of Shakespeare and Fletcher. *The History of Cardenio by Mr Fletcher and Shakespeare* was registered for publication in 1653 but is now lost. There is, however, ample evidence that it was a collaboration between the two dramatists, undertaken shortly after the publication in 1612 of the English translation of Cervantes' *Don Quixote*.

By 1623 the great book is finally ready. It is printed in large paper double-columned "folio" format. A consortium of publishers, headed by William and Isaac Jaggard, has joined together in the publication of *Mr William Shakespeares Comedies, Histories, & Tragedies. Published according to the True Originall Copies.* That latter phrase proclaims the accuracy of these texts, in contrast to the unauthorized earlier editions of individual plays, which Heminges and Condell dismiss in their prefatory address to the reader as "maimed and deformed by the frauds and stealthes of injurious impostors." In the 1623 Folio (known as the "first," to distinguish it from later editions that appeared in 1632, 1663 and 1685), Shakespeare's two friends and colleagues have left us not only a priceless record of his work but the strongest evidence of his authorship.

The title page of the First Folio is adorned with Martin Droeshout's famous engraving of the dramatist, his forehead domed like the Globe, as if to gesture toward the name of his theatre and the fecundity of his art. Opposite the "cut" is the brief poem by Ben Jonson, attesting to the authenticity of the image but telling the reader that the works matter more than the face. Heminges and Condell contribute both their address to the reader and a dedicatory epistle to the Pembroke brothers, two noble earls who assisted in the blocking of the Pavier edition. The actors praise their friend and colleague for his extraordinary verbal facility: "His mind and hand went together: And what he thought, he uttered with that easinesse, that wee have scarce received from him a blot in his papers."

The preliminary pages of the First Folio also include four commendatory poems. One of these, by a poet identified only by the initials "I. M.," makes witty play on the dual identity of "Master William Shake-speare"* as both actor and writer. But pride of place in the Folio's front matter is given to Ben Jonson's magnificent tribute, "To the memory of my beloved, the Author Mr William Shakespeare: and what he hath left us." In this poem, Jonson responds to William Basse's complaint that Shakespeare lacked an appropriate physical memorial. It does not matter that Shakespeare lies beneath the ground in Warwickshire. There is no need to build him a monument beside those of Chaucer, Spenser and Beaumont in the Abbey. His monument is his book. This book. The Folio itself:

> My Shakespeare, rise; I will not lodge thee by
> Chaucer, or Spenser, or bid Beaumont lie
> A little further, to make thee a room:
> Thou art a monument without a tomb,
> And art alive still, while thy book doth live,
> And we have wits to read and praise to give.

William Shakespeare of Stratford, an actor who lacked a university education, and Ben Jonson of London, an actor (and sometime bricklayer) who lacked a university education, were intimate friends and friendly rivals. In the first years of the seventeenth century—before the advent of Beaumont and Fletcher—they were regarded as indisputably the nation's two greatest living dramatists. The best response to skeptics who doubt that the Stratford man could have written his plays on the foundation of

* Several occurrences of the dramatist's name in the preliminary matter to the First Folio are hyphenated, but most are not. The presence or absence of a hyphen is quite arbitrary—a printer's vagary, not the momentous matter supposed by anti-Stratfordians.

nothing more than a grammar school education is an invitation to read the complete plays of Ben Jonson. They are vastly more academic than Shakespeare's, yet they too were written on the foundation of nothing more than a grammar school education. The thing is, Elizabethan grammar schools were very good. They put our high schools to deep shame.

Jonson knew perfectly well who wrote the plays that were now being properly published for the first time. In the First Folio poem to the memory of his beloved friend, he praised Shakespeare's plays to the skies and referred to him as the "Sweet Swan of Avon." Jonson knew the dramatist intimately in the context of the London theatre world but also linked him to the Avon, the river that runs through Shakespeare's hometown.

And there is more. Shakespeare acted in Jonson's plays. There is strong testimony that he was godfather to one of Jonson's children. In his private notebook, Jonson remarked on Shakespeare's extraordinary verbal facility and the speed of his writing. He spoke about him with affectionate mockery in his conversations with the Scottish poet William Drummond. As for Heminges and Condell, they are remembered with affection in the will of the Stratford man and they were editors of the First Folio. These links ought to be evidence enough to lay to rest all claims that Shakespeare's plays were really written by someone else.

But if all this is still insufficient to satisfy the doubter, there is a fascinating series of further links to consider, a chain that connects the First Folio and Shakespeare's London world to his Stratford world. This chain begins with another poem printed in the Folio's preliminary pages, opposite the "Catalogue of the severall Comedies, Histories, and Tragedies contained in this Volume." It was written by one Leonard Digges, an Oxford-educated poet and literary translator, and is titled "To the Memorie of the deceased Authour Maister W. Shakespeare." Digges's verses refer both to the stone of the author's tomb and to "thy *Stratford* Moniment." Digges, then, knew that "the deceased Authour" lay beneath a stone in the aisle of Holy Trinity Church, Stratford-upon-Avon, and that there was a monument to him and his work on the adjacent wall.

Here we have the first link in the chain. For Digges had a Stratford-upon-Avon connection: his stepfather was Thomas Russell, a local Stratford gentleman who served as overseer of Shakespeare's will. (Shakespeare was sufficiently fond of Russell to bequeath him his ceremonial sword.) Digges was proud of his stepfather's acquaintance with the great writer. On a visit to Spain, he wrote an inscription in a book sent to a friend, noting that Lope de Vega was admired as both a poet and a dramatist just as "our Will Shakespeare" was admired back in England for both his plays and his sonnets. The combination of that intimate "Will" and the proudly proprietorial "our" speaks volumes. As with Jonson's private notebook, a personal note of this kind is a very special sort of evidence. Digges knew Shakespeare well enough to call him "Will," and he had no doubts about the authorship of the plays.

Thomas Russell leads us to the second link in the chain, for he has some other very interesting connections. In 1591 his name was joined in a legal bond to that of his friend Henry Willoughby of Wiltshire. Russell and Willoughby were connected by marriage: the previous year Russell had married one of a pair of sisters and Willoughby's elder son had wed the other. Then in 1594 Willoughby's younger son, an Oxford student, published an enigmatic poem called "Willobie his Avisa." Among the characters in this work of about three thousand lines is one H. W. (the poet himself?), who has a "familiar friend W. S." whose profession is "player." There is a strong probability that "W. S." stands for William Shakespeare.

In the poem of the younger Willoughby (or Willobie) there is a dialogue between W. S. and H. W in which W. S. says, "She is no saint, she is no nun, / I think in time she may be won," a couplet remarkably similar to lines found in three of Shakespeare's early plays (*1 Henry VI*, *Titus Andronicus* and *Richard III*). Scholars have long supposed that there may be some connection between "Willobie his Avisa" and the tangled love matter of Shakespeare's sonnets, in which the poet veers between his worship of a beautiful male youth and his desire for a dark female temptress. The commendatory verses prefixed to "Willobie" include an allusion to Shakespeare's poem *The Rape of Lucrece*, which was hot off the press at the time Willoughby's poem was written.

The Rape of Lucrece, together with *Venus and Adonis*, belongs to the period in 1593 and 1594 when the theatres were closed because of plague and Shakespeare was trying to make his way as a non-dramatic poet by gaining the patronage of the 3rd Earl of Southampton—whose family home at Titchfield was not far from Willoughby's in Wiltshire. The character of "H. W." may denote Henry Willoughby himself, but it may alternatively (or additionally) be a coded representation of Southampton, Henry Wriothesley. Thus Thomas Russell provides the link to Henry Willoughby, whose poem may just provide us with a link to Shakespeare's patron—and possible lover?—and thus back to Shakespeare himself.

Thomas Russell also links Shakespeare's country origins to his city world. He turns up in the London theatre district toward the end of the 1590s, when he was arrested as surety for another friend, with whom he had been "bound to go on a sea of voyage"—a misadventure that has the whiff of Antonio, Bassanio and Shylock's bond in *The Merchant of Venice*. It was at this time that Russell was wooing the widow Digges, Leonard's mother. She lived in Philip Lane in the Aldermanbury district of London, an address close to those of Heminges, Condell and Shakespeare himself, who was lodging in nearby Silver Street. All this makes for a fascinating and highly suggestive set of relationships and interconnections.

The gap between Shakespeare's Stratford world and his London one was not nearly so great as is sometimes assumed. Whereas Leonard Digges went from London to Stratford, others moved as Shakespeare did in the opposite direction: from Stratford to London. Thomas Greene, the Stratford-upon-Avon town clerk, was Shakespeare's kinsman. He named his children Anne and William, which suggests that the Shakespeares stood as godparents for him. It was customary to name children after their godparents: thus Shakespeare's twins Hamnet and Judith were named after his friends Hamlet and Judith Sadler—Hamnet and Hamlet being alternative spellings of the same name. Greene and his children lodged with Shakespeare's family in New Place for about two years (1609–11) while waiting to move into a house of their own. Greene had earlier ventured to London for his legal training. In the capital he moved in the same circle as John Marston and John Manningham, clever young lawyers and writers who were familiar with Shakespeare and his works (Manningham attended an early performance of *Twelfth*

Night and recorded a note in his diary about one of Shakespeare's extramarital sexual escapades, recounted earlier by Stanley Wells.)

The path from Stratford to London was also followed by Richard Field, a boy slightly older than Shakespeare. In London he became a printer, and it was to him that Shakespeare turned for the publication of his poems *Venus and Adonis* and *The Rape of Lucrece*. Field also printed high-quality classical texts, thus revealing what a good education had been available to him at the grammar school in Stratford-upon-Avon, which Shakespeare had been entitled to attend free, as a result of his father's position on the town council.

The force of the "anti-Stratfordian" myth in the popular imagination has become so powerful that it is necessary to present all this minute evidence in order to reiterate a simple fact that was quite evident to Shakespeare's contemporaries: it was perfectly possible for a boy from a "small trade" background in the provincial town of Stratford-upon-Avon to enter the London theatre world and write some very accomplished plays.

Shakespeare's place of origin was a matter of chance. Original genius is always the result of some freak combination of genes and circumstances. Thomas Greene had some of the same genes. Richard Field and eleven-year-old Richard Quiney Jr., who could write a letter to his father in perfect Latin, shared the same educational circumstances. There is no intrinsic reason why one of these men should not have become a dramatist rather than a lawyer (and amateur poet) or a printer. It so happened that the hand of chance chose William Shakespeare.

Plays are the most impersonal of literary forms, so it is only with the greatest degree of caution that we may draw inferences about the life from the work, but it is to the work itself that I will turn for the final evidence on Shakespeare's behalf. His last plays do seem to echo the doings of the man who claimed to have written them. They hint at a settling of accounts, a contemplation of retirement and of mortality. In *The Winter's Tale* a man asks for a fresh start with his wife, some sixteen years after he has wronged her. When Shakespeare writes these lines, he has spent much of the past sixteen years away from his wife. And there is strong evidence that he was not always sexually faithful to her. In *The Tempest* a man of "potent art," who has acted out the role of a dramatist, speaks of his retirement. And in both plays there is much harping on daughters and their marriages—Shakespeare had two daughters, one of whom was not yet married, despite being in her mid-twenties.

For stronger proof, read the First Folio from cover to cover. You will be filled with wonder at the sheer range and variety of Shakespeare's style and vocabulary. The courtly language may make you think he must have been a courtier. But then the country language will make you think he must have been a countryman. In establishing the author's identity, what you need to look for are the quirky things. Courtly language may be learned by imitation—it is the sort of thing you find in books (or observe when your theatre company is invited to perform at court).

The small, seemingly inconsequential details are what constitute the unique fingerprint. The plays ascribed to William Shakespeare were written by a man who knew of a fat alewife called Marian Hacket in the village of Wincot near Stratford-upon-Avon (she is mentioned in the induction to *The Taming of the Shrew* and parish records reveal the historical reality of the

Hackets of Wincot). The plays ascribed to William Shakespeare were written by someone who refers to many different kinds of animal hide and to the technicalities of leather manufacture. Sounds like the son of a glover, not the son of a lord. All non-Stratfordian, non-glover pretenders to the title of author of these plays suffer from the same debilitating deficiency: they have no way of proving their knowledge of Marian Hacket or the distinction between "neat's leather" (used for shoes) and sheep's leather (for bridles).

Sometimes it takes a creative eye to identify the fingerprint. Thus the novelist Robert Nye in *The Late Mr Shakespeare*, a biographical "faction" of 1998, draws attention to a particular watery detail:

> If you stand on the eighteenth arch of Clopton Bridge (the one nearest the point where the road goes to London), and if you watch the River Avon below when it is in flood, you will see a curious thing that Shakespeare saw.
>
> The force of the current under the adjoining arches, coupled with the curve there is at that strait in the riverbank, produces a very queer and swirling eddy. What happens is that the bounding water is forced *back* through the arch in an exactly contrary direction.
>
> I have seen sticks and straws, which I have just watched swirling downstream through the arch, brought back again as swiftly against the flood.
>
> The boy Will saw this too. Here's how he describes it:
>
> *As through an arch the violent roaring tide*
> *Outruns the eye that doth behold his haste,*

Yet in the eddy boundeth in his pride
Back to the strait that forc'd him on so fast,
In rage sent out, recall'd in rage, being past:
Even so his sighs, his sorrows, make a saw,
To push grief on and back the same grief draw.

That's from *The Rape of Lucrece*, lines 1667–73. How many times must he have watched it, perhaps with tears in his bright eyes?

Next time you meet members of the anti-Will brigade, ask them on how many occasions their candidate stood on the eighteenth arch of Clopton Bridge in Stratford-upon-Avon and watched the eddying movement of the water.

In one of his loveliest songs, the dramatist writes, "Golden lads and girls all must, / As chimney-sweepers, come to dust." In Warwickshire vernacular dialect, a dandelion is a "golden lad" when in flower, a "chimney-sweeper" when ready to be blown to the wind. This is no lord's memory. It belongs to a local country boy in a Warwickshire field.

Having laid out the powerful, one might say overwhelming, evidence that the plays attributed to Shakespeare were written by the man from Stratford-upon-Avon, we must return to the chief among his current rivals and to the very strong case against Edward de Vere, Earl of Oxford. It is a case, I would submit, to which the Oxfordians can make no adequate answer.

The plays were clearly written by a man reasonably well versed in Latin, whereas Oxford's surviving letters reveal that he was hopeless at Latin. The plays reveal an intimate knowledge of

Jacobean high politics and court intrigue, whereas Oxford was on his deathbed at the time of King James's accession to the English throne. Oxford died in June 1604, whereas many of Shakespeare's plays were written after this. So, for instance, works such as *King Lear* and *Cymbeline* engage with the idea of "Britain" (whereas the Elizabethan plays always refer to "England") at exactly the time when King James was attempting to unify England and Scotland into a single British nation. And, of course, Oxfordians are strangely silent about their man's ability to co-write plays with John Fletcher some eight years after his own death.

The plays reveal an intimate knowledge of the grammar school curriculum, leatherwork and professional stagecraft, whereas Oxford did not go to grammar school, join the leather trade or work backstage with a theatre company. And, allowing for the sake of argument the very dubious assumption that it takes a good man to produce a good work of art: the plays are stamped with the genius of a great human spirit, whereas the documentary records of Oxford concern such low business as casual killing and pedophilia. All this will be revealed in a forthcoming biography of Edward de Vere by Alan Nelson of the University of California, Berkeley, who has tracked down every extant piece of writing by, and reference to, the wretched Earl. Thanks to Nelson's researches, the case for Oxford as Shakespeare will die in the early twenty-first century, just as that for Bacon died in the early twentieth. But it is a certain bet that another candidate will emerge.

On this occasion, truth is, alas, less strange than fiction. There was no conspiracy, no dashing lord in disguise. Just a very clever boy called Will—but there were other clever boys in Stratford, who were lucky enough to benefit from the newly established grammar school there. This one grew into a very talented dramatist called Shakespeare—but there were other very talented dramatists in London, who were his friends, rivals and co-authors. It was not until over a hundred years after his death that people began putting him in an altogether different league from Beaumont, Fletcher and Jonson.

Once that happened, though, Pandora's box was opened. When Shakespeare became God, some of his more ardent admirers started finding his life too dull and provincial. They set about the hunt for a mystery, the search for a suitably glamorous alternative candidate. Others, meanwhile, started finding his *image* too dull and provincial: dissatisfied with the portly figure on the Stratford monument, they set about the hunt for a lost portrait, the search for a suitably glamorous alternative face. We'll never find an alternative candidate for the authorship, since the plain fact of the matter is that Shakespeare did write the plays. We just might, however, find an authentic alternative for the image. But we must be wary: for who, the Bible reminds us, can look upon the face of God and live?

Family Traces

SO SHAKESPEARE wrote Shakespeare. While Jonathan Bate crushes the cases of the other candidates in one fell swoop, Lloyd Sullivan had much more laboriously reached the same conclusion. The debates about the Earl of Oxford and Francis Bacon struck him as either lunatic conspiracy theories or academic self-indulgence. His engineer's brain weighed the evidence, and his money was on the glover's son from Stratford.

And anyway, he had more than enough on his hands trying to prove his portrait was genuine. By 1993 he had Anthony Crichton-Stuart's encouraging but inconclusive opinion, and he was beginning to understand just how complicated—and expensive—it could be to authenticate a work of art. There are two parts to the process of proving that a painting actually is what it claims to be. One part requires proof of a painting's "provenance," the art historian's term for the ownership history. The second is forensic: showing that a painting is genuinely from the place and time it claims and that it has not been altered since it was first created. This step requires both scientific tests and the assessment of art historians.

To determine the provenance of the portrait, Lloyd needed to be able to tell its life story all the way back to the Sanders who painted it. He needed to be able to lay out the evidence for any critic to examine. And that meant he needed documents: wills, letters, anything that could prove the painting had belonged to his family since 1603. Best of all would be a letter, a will, a receipt that showed the first John Sanders giving a portrait of his friend William Shakespeare to his son. When Lloyd began this part of the project—now far more than a pastime—he possessed a few relatively recent documents that linked the painting to his family. But others, if they existed at all, resided in parish records or civic archives dating back four hundred years.

Charting a painting's provenance involves telling its life story backward, just as people trace their family trees by starting with their parents and going back in time. Normally a provenance will rely heavily on the records of auctions and art sales to chart how a work changed hands from the time it was created. But the painting in question, so Lloyd believed, had never left his family.

The first part of his painting's backward story was the easiest, for he knew it first-hand. This chapter took him and Willy Shake back to 1940, when he was seven years old. That year, his maternal grandmother, Agnes Hales-Sanders, and his aunt Mary Agnes (affectionately known as Auntie Uggie) moved in with Lloyd's family so that his mother, Kathleen, could help Uggie look after Agnes, who had become unwell. Agnes mostly kept to her bed. Sometimes Lloyd took his invalid nanny tea, for which he was handsomely rewarded with a nickel. Once in a while he would crouch down to peer at the great mass of treasures she kept stored under her bed in boxes and trunks. One of them was a brown-paper-wrapped parcel that Agnes always warned him not to touch, for it was very valuable: it contained a portrait of William Shakespeare. On special occasions, his mother would get the parcel out from under the bed, unwrap it and they would all look at the man in the picture. The seven-year-old boy didn't have any idea who Shakespeare was, except that he was the subject of a great stack of dusty books that Nanny also kept under her bed. But the portrait was impressive, mostly because everyone handled it so reverently. His father, a bit of a fanatic for neatness, would occasionally get riled up and threaten to toss out the whole mess under the bed—the books, pictures, old china tea set, even that darn portrait. Agnes would furiously rally to its defence, Lloyd's mother would placate his father, and the tempest would subside.

Agnes Hales-Sanders died in 1943, leaving no will. Most of her possessions automatically went to her eldest son, Frederic, then a buyer for Henry Morgan and Company, a Montreal department store that catered to the "carriage trade." But the portrait of Shakespeare already belonged to Auntie Uggie, who had been given it by her mother many years before. Uggie never married and had no children, so on her death in 1959 the picture passed to Freddie. He had long since left Morgan's and retired from a job with the electric company, though even in his seventies he kept busy with real estate around town, mowing the lawns and shovelling snow.

When Freddie died in 1971, his widow, Marguerite, became the owner, but she felt strongly that it should stay within the Sanders clan. Marguerite was francophone and, so the story goes, had often felt ill at ease as part of the sprawling English family into which she had married. But her sister-in-law Kathleen, born after her parents immigrated to Canada and educated at Montreal's Marguerite Bourgeoys College, was fluently bilingual. Kathleen and her small family lived just across the street from Marguerite in Notre-Dame-de-Grace, and she alone of the sisters could communicate easily with her, welcoming Marguerite at the noisy Thanksgiving dinners and Easter parties. So it was to Kathleen that Marguerite gave the painting, and on Kathleen's death it went to Lloyd.

In his lifetime, he had seen the painting passed from his grandmother to his aunt to his uncle to his mother and finally to him. His grandmother's death in 1943 thus marked the furthest back he could go in retracing his painting's life story from personal memory. To go earlier than that, he needed family documents.

He knew from his grandmother that she had inherited the painting on the death of her husband, Aloysius—Louie to his friends and family—in Montreal in 1919. Agnes and Louie were the immigrant generation, the branch of the Hales-Sanders clan who came to Canada. Both Agnes, born Agnes Helen Briggs, and her future husband, Aloysius Joseph James Hales-Sanders, grew up in England. When they married in the simply named Catholic church in Croydon, near London, in 1887, Louie was a young schoolmaster just starting his career. Over the next six years they had five children, two of whom died before they reached the age of five. Sometime in 1894, Louie and Agnes gathered up their three surviving offspring and boarded a ship for Montreal.

The 1901 Canadian census shows them settled in Montreal, where Aloysius founded Blinkbonnie Academy, a boys' school in the English enclave of Notre-Dame-de-Grace. He taught math and served as its principal for many years. Later, he helped to start two Catholic high schools, where he also served as principal. And in his spare time, he painted—as had his father and grandfather, both members of one of Britain's leading art societies, the Royal Institute of Painters in Water Colours. Louie had also been accepted into the society and occasionally sent his work to England for exhibitions. He and Agnes had eight more children, seven of whom survived. Apart from one son, who ran away in his early teens and never rejoined the family, they lived a conventional life in middle-class anglo Montreal. Louie's educational innovations won him some recognition, and A. J. Hales-Sanders is noted in the 1912 edition of *The Canadian Men and Women of the Time*, a precursor to *Who's Who*, as "a successful and efficient principal."

Louie was comfortably ensconced on the other side of the Atlantic Ocean when his father, Thomas Hales-Sanders Jr.—Lloyd's great-grandfather—died in England in 1915. This Thomas Hales-Sanders was a London banker, who was born in Worcester in 1830 but moved as a young man to the capital. Still a teenager, he began as a clerk at the National Provincial Bank of England and worked there all his life. In his spare time he painted soft watercolour scenes from the busy docks along the Thames in London, and he exhibited with the Royal Academy for twenty years. He had inherited the Shakespeare picture from his father, Thomas Sr., who got it from his half brother, John. In 1909 the younger Thomas told an assessor with whom he discussed the portrait that he could "remember it for between sixty and seventy years," in other words, as far back as the time of his uncle John, when he was a young boy in the early 1800s.

Louie was Thomas Jr.'s fourth child, but his eldest son. In a will written December 14, 1915, Thomas directed his wife and children to each "select three pictures" from among the works in his studio. The rest were to be sold "towards the support and education of poor orphan children." Next, the will reads, "I give to my son Aloysius Joseph James Hales-Sanders my reputed portrait of Shakespeare dated 1603." This is the earliest reference to the Sanders portrait in a family document.

In March 1919, six months after the end of the war in Europe, Louie died suddenly of a heart attack, just short of his fifty-fifth birthday. Because of the war, he never collected his inheritance, so it fell to his wife, Agnes, to go home to England and settle the estate. In the fall of 1919, a year after the war ended, she made the trip with several of her children. They arrived in London just in time for the armistice parade; they saw swaggering American troops with huge signs reading "We Won the War," and, at the back of the procession, a contingent of Canadian soldiers whose small signs read "And We Helped Too." When they returned to Canada the following spring, they brought back with them the "reputed portrait of Shakespeare" along with the allowed-for three of Thomas's own paintings. They must have brought others, as well, for eventually Louie's children found themselves with a trove of almost three hundred paintings, some by him and some by his father. Today these pictures are spread among his descendants in both Britain and North America. Lloyd Sullivan has one, a large watercolour done in 1856, that depicts schooners docked along the Thames with London Bridge in the background.

The Shakespeare painting's Canadian ownership was thus well established and fully documented as far back as 1915, the year the owner's grandfather Aloysius Hales-Sanders—Louie—inherited it from his father. But documenting the story of the portrait in the country of its creation proved far more challenging. A chasm of more than three hundred years stretched from 1915 to 1603, the year it was supposedly painted.

For the next piece of detective work, Lloyd turned to that staple of genealogy, the family Bible. The flyleaf of a huge, heavy Bible he inherited from his mother lists each generation of the Sanders family dating back to 1790. Its earliest entry, recorded in faded ink and spidery handwriting, is for Thomas Hales-Sanders (Sr.), born on February 3, 1790. The last entry includes the thirteen children of Aloysius and Agnes, among them Lloyd's mother, Kathleen, who as the youngest is barely squeezed onto the crowded page. Genealogists put considerable stock in family Bibles, especially if the entries begin around the time of publication—that is, they have been added by each successive generation, not reconstructed by a later family historian working back several generations. The Hales-Sanders Bible shows evidence of several people's handwriting and has a publication date of 1822; Mary Griffiths, who joined the family in 1829 and is part of its earliest entry, may have begun the family tree. The Bible thus provided documentary proof of Lloyd's descent from Thomas Sr., the last Sanders on record as having known the painting in his family.

But a family Bible is not a will. It may document each branch of a family tree, but it makes no mention of the family's possessions. In no family document dating earlier than the Thomas Hales-Sanders will of 1915 is there an explicit reference to the

Shakespeare portrait. From 1915 to 1603, the history of the portrait's ownership was still unproved. But provenance is a slippery concept. Few paintings as old as the Sanders portrait have left an uninterrupted paper trail from their original owner. And, in a major difference from most of the other contenders, including the front-runner, the Chandos, the Sanders had a claim to having been owned by the same family from the day it was painted until now. To bolster this claim, however, Lloyd needed to document each generation of the Sanders family going back to the one he believed had painted the portrait in 1603.

As many amateur genealogists do, he went first to the International Genealogy Index (IGI) maintained by the Church of Jesus Christ of Latter Day Saints, the Mormons. The Mormons promote genealogical research because they believe a person can make a "covenant with God" from beyond the grave and so be saved posthumously. Their index is available on-line and in the Mormons' many Family Research Centres around the world and contains more than 240 million entries. The most recent records are from a hundred years ago—no living person is listed, to protect privacy. The entries are drawn from original source material—wills, tax rolls, military rosters and immigration records—compiled by Mormon researchers. (Because the Mormons believe people do not die when their physical bodies expire, the IGI contains no death records.) The indices for the British Isles, a major source of immigration to the United States, where the Mormon Church was founded, are particularly comprehensive.

In late 1993 Lloyd began to make his painstaking way through the records at the nearest Family Research Centre, which was not far from his home in Ottawa. First he sought the man who had painted the picture, a Sanders born in Worcester, England, who would have been the right age to have known Shakespeare at the start of the seventeenth century. After a lot of hunting, he hit gold: three Sanders babies, christened at All Saints Church in Worcester in the late 1570s, the children of a Thomas Sanders who was likely born about 1550, although Lloyd could find no record of Thomas's christening. Here, in the only Sanders family in the records from Worcester at this time, he found the man he believed he was looking for: John Sanders, the eldest of Thomas's children, born in 1576. This was the name his mother had passed on to him as the painter of the portrait. But John's younger brother Thomas, born 1579, could also have gone up to London in about 1600, and it was always possible that Thomas had painted the picture, then perhaps given it to his brother John. And then no more Sanderses.

Now the most difficult part of the search began, the hunt for the missing generations that would link the original John Sanders with the first entry in the family Bible, the 1790 birth of Thomas Hales-Sanders Sr. That meant Lloyd had to fill in a gap of more than two hundred years. After several false starts, he enlisted the help of a female cousin who had been working on a history of the Sanders family and who had mastered the cherished tool of the family historian: the Internet.

The cousin decided to work back from their mutual great-great-grandfather, Thomas Hales-Sanders Sr. After a great deal of hunting, she came across Thomas's father, Richard Sanders, christened April 21, 1744. Richard and his first wife, Sarah Harris, had a son, John (the uncle who would give the portrait to his half brother Thomas Hales-Sanders). But then it seems Sarah died. In

1789, at St. Peter's Church in Worcester, Richard married a widow named Elizabeth Owen, with whom he had six children, including the Thomas from whom Lloyd was descended. And the widow's maiden name was Hales, marking the entry of the portmanteau name Hales-Sanders into the family.

Then the trail went stone cold. The Sanders family records either were not in the index or Lloyd and his cousin did not know how to find them. There seemed no alternative but to go to the source, the county records office in Worcester, England, a town where Sanders descendants still reside. Lloyd says he never considered going there himself. He was then busy supplementing his pension with contract work for Bell, he did not have money to spend on a lark in England, and he knew he would feel like a fool shuffling around in records he didn't understand. Besides, he wondered whether it was even worth the trouble. What were the odds of finding records going all the way back to 1603? Nonetheless, he wrote a letter to the town of Worcester and quite promptly he received a most encouraging reply: yes, the county had records covering the years he was interested in—had some, in fact, that dated all the way back to 1400.

The actual records (as I would subsequently learn on my own visit to Worcester) are carefully preserved in a temperature-controlled archive in the shiny new County Record Office. But most are duplicated on microfiches—flat sheets of film that each contain many microphotographs of document pages—stacked in orderly rows in dozens of cabinets. Half the public research room, about the size of a school classroom, is given over to computer terminals with Internet access, the other to about forty bulky microfiche readers. The registers and wills are indexed by name in all the various permutations of spelling. The records Lloyd needed might be under Sanders, Sander, Saunders, Saunder, Sawnders, or Sawnder. The index suggests which microfiche to explore for each name and date a researcher is seeking.

As far back as about 1700, the Worcester records are quite logical and straightforward. Before that, the films are filled with pages covered with ink-spotted, haphazard, indecipherable or simply missing entries. The older records are in Latin, Middle English or French and impenetrable for a layperson. Even were Lloyd to scrape together the money to go to England, he knew he wouldn't get far. He needed help. At the advice of the Worcester records office, he hired himself an expert, a retired county archivist named Susan Campbell.

Campbell does the slow and meticulous research craved by the Canadians and Americans and Australians caught up in the craze for genealogy. She hunts through the parish registries, running her trained eye down the columns for baptisms, weddings and burials. Sometimes these dry records include wonderfully humanizing details, such as the weather at the time of a child's birth or a newborn's bastard status. Campbell also searches wills. Many of those that survive from the early 1600s are lengthy and florid. For example, one Katherine Sampson who died in 1682 distributes her warming pans, which held coals to warm sheets before bedtime, the best to her eldest sister, the second best to her next sister and so on through four pans and four sisters.

Lloyd did not tell Susan Campbell why he was looking for his ancestors, only that he wanted to trace the Sanders family back to the 1500s. The archivist soon confirmed that he had been on the right trail with Richard Sanders and Elizabeth Owen, née

Hales. She found Richard's father, William, born in about 1714, who married Mary Hawkes in 1737, when they were both twenty-two years old. And she found an earlier William Sanders who might have been William's father. He first appears in the marriage records for 1703, marrying one Rebecca Perkins. But without a baptismal record indicating that the earlier William was the younger William's father, the connection is simply a good guess.

And Campbell was not optimistic about finding the generations before William and Rebecca, to bridge the gap between William Sr.'s marriage in 1703 and 1576, the year John Sanders—the man Lloyd believed had painted the portrait—was born. (Genealogists define a generation as normally spanning about twenty-five years.) These missing generations included the particularly chaotic period in English history known as the Interregnum. From 1649, the year King Charles I was executed by Puritan rebels, until 1660, the year the dead King's son was brought back to England and "restored" to the throne as Charles II, the country was ruled by a fundamentalist Protestant regime known as the Protectorate, under Oliver Cromwell. And in the years immediately before the King's overthrow, the country was embroiled in a bloody civil war. The keeping of parish registers was largely suspended during this period. Many existing record books were lost, some in looting and burning, others destroyed by those keen to hide their religious affiliation. Among these, perhaps, were the parents of William Sanders.

Campbell did find some precious shreds of information about the early Sanders family. The John Sanders born in 1576 later became a clothier. He married Winifred Haw on February 22, 1605, two years after the date on the Sanders portrait.

Clothiers were members of guilds, just as were candlemakers, silversmiths, glovers and indeed painters—part of what was essentially a middle class—so the Sanders family likely had a comparatively comfortable life.

But the gaping hole in the genealogical record remained. There was nothing solid to tie the William Sanders of 1714 to the John Sanders who married in 1605, leaving 109 years unaccounted for. It is probable that the Sanders family that baptized its babies in Worcester in the Catholic All Saints in the early 1700s is the same one that did so in the 1570s. Worcester was a small city, in those days people stayed put, and the records of the same families move down through the years. To date, however, Lloyd has found nothing to prove it.

And no entry in the parish records even hints at a connection between John, or Thomas, Sanders and William Shakespeare. As support for this crucial link Lloyd had found but one fleeting reference in a Victorian volume called *Fleay's History of London Stages*, that identifies a "J. Sanders" as a London actor in Shakespeare's era.[1] But modern scholars question *Fleay's History* as the work of an unreliable if enthusiastic amateur. It certainly did not tell Lloyd what a humble Worcester clothier was doing in faraway London in 1603. There were other places to hunt for clues—in inventories post-mortem, for example, which might list the possessions of a John Sanders deceased sometime in the first half of the seventeenth century, or in London parish registers, which might have made mention of a John or Thomas Sanders during their London years. But Lloyd did not yet know enough to try these scholarly routes.

Did the young Sanders, like the young Shakespeare, leave

home at an early age to seek his fortune in the theatre world? Perhaps he, unlike Shakespeare, found the going too tough and returned home to take up his father's trade. These questions were as troubling as the gaps between the generations. Unless someone somewhere could find a link between John Sanders and William Shakespeare, the painting's claim would remain speculative at best.

There was another, very different, history of the Sanders portrait that Lloyd began to uncover at the same time as he was tracing the painting's ownership: the record of previous attempts to authenticate it. This story begins, as far as he can tell, with his great-grandfather Thomas Hales-Sanders Jr., the banker and Sunday painter who died near the start of the First World War and left his portrait of Shakespeare to his eldest son, who was by then living in Canada.

One day in 1908, when Thomas was almost eighty, he parcelled up the painting and placed it in the hands of the man who was then the world's great expert on such work, Marion Henry Spielmann. Then in his fifties and solidly established as a critic of renown, Spielmann was a connoisseur of art and literature, a poet, the editor of *The Magazine of Art*, a contributor to *Punch* and a man with a particular interest in the iconography of Shakespeare, that is, the representations of the great writer. The Victorians had a rejuvenated interest in the playwright, and it was to Spielmann that hopeful owners brought their putative pictures of the poet for authentication.

He seemed to relish these weighings-in and pronounced with great authority on many of the key "Shakespeare" portraits of his time. Spielmann published his investigations of their provenance in a book titled *Portraits of Shakespeare* in 1907. He dismissed the Flower portrait as copied from the Droeshout and said of the Chandos, "in every important physiognomical particular, and in face-measurement, it is contradicted by the Stratford bust and the Droeshout print."[2] He was a man with the most exacting standards, and not one portrait, sculpture or miniature won his unguarded approval. But he was always willing to examine another.

Thomas Sanders told Spielmann the picture had come to him through his father, by way of an uncle called John Sanders, a man in the wool trade in Worcester. But Spielmann would later quote him as having said the picture "had been for nearly a century in the possession of his relations."

The painting Spielmann examined in 1908 was identical to the one that Lloyd showed me in the spring of 2001 in all but one respect: in 1908 the label on the back was still legible. In old-fashioned script, it bore these words: "Shakspere / "Born April 23 = 1564 / Died April 23—1616 / Aged 52 / This Likeness taken 1603 / Age at that time 39 ys."

To Spielmann's critical eye, the picture had some merit: a reasonably well painted portrait of a young man with keen blue eyes, slightly smiling lips and fluffy auburn hair, wearing a simple blue quilted doublet, typical of the Jacobean period. The work was unsigned, but this was not unusual for portraits from the era. It looked slightly off centre; in his opinion, it had been trimmed, likely to fit in a frame. (Someone, probably Spielmann, left a small vellum label, edged in red, on the back of the picture; it reads "panel might be enlarged this side about half an inch. / M. H." —the initials may represent his names, Marion Henry, and refer to what he believed to be the trimmed portion.)

Spielmann held on to the Sanders portrait for some time, and a year later, he discussed it at length in an article in *The Connoisseur*, a richly illustrated magazine "for collectors."[3] Spielmann often chose it as his medium to pronounce on both historical and newly emerged contenders for the life-portrait title. In the article, Spielmann first addressed the Grafton portrait, then in the possession of a pair of sisters, the Misses Ludgate. After examining a photograph and considering the Grafton's history, he observes that it appears to be of the period, notes that "the painting of [the doublet] and of the gauze collar are vastly inferior in merit to the head" and that "the nose is thick, especially towards the end, without the marked *columna nasi* common to the Stratford bust and the other leading portraits of repute," then politely expresses skepticism at its provenance. He concludes by doubting the picture is of Shakespeare. (Modern science, of course, has proved the Grafton to be a clever forgery.)

Having dispensed with the Grafton, Spielmann turns his attention to the Sanders portrait, first hastening to assure his audience that the picture is not the handiwork of the well-known nineteenth-century forgers Holder or Zincke. "I am far from suggesting Mr. Hale [*sic*] Sanders' portrait is a fake," he continues, then adds, "although the date upon it could not be accepted as otherwise than [a] relatively modern [addition], even if it fitted with Shakespeare's age, which it does not." There were, in Spielmann's opinion, some points in favour of the portrait as a likeness of the playwright. He notes that the face is painted in "a delicate manner characteristic of seventeenth-century portraiture" and says it is "pure, and a good example of the period." The face, eyes, brows, hint of moustache and "attachment of the ear" all match the Droeshout engraving.

But, but. The hair is too fluffy. The collar and coat are, he is certain, additions of much later date than the face: "they are painted with a hand as hard and inflexible as the head is executed by one sympathetic and tender. They suggest the unmitigated precision of an engineering diagram or a ticket-writer's decoration. The embroidered tunic, of white, grey, and black, is surmounted by a grey collar, apparently of steel plate, which betrays the stupidity of the faker." The collar pleats are wrong—made to stand up like the ruff in the Droeshout. "Now, in the ordinary 'falling collar' pleats are not only unnecessary but, I believe impossible." And crucially, Spielmann opines that the paper label on the back is only fifty or sixty years old.

Though Marion Henry Spielmann declines to use the word "fake," he is clearly suggesting that the Sanders is an existing Jacobean portrait that has been altered to give it a collar and jacket like the Droeshout, and that a falsely aged label—and quite likely the date 1603 on the painting itself—were added by the forger. Given the plethora of altered portraits (the Holder and Zincke specials) that he examined regularly, Spielmann sees absolutely no reason to credit the idea that the portrait might be Shakespeare.

But perhaps Spielmann's paramount objection to the Sanders portrait is one he only hints at: the man in the picture did not look the way William Shakespeare was supposed to look. At thirty-nine, the poet was a man whose lone son, a child of eleven, had recently died; who was estranged from his wife; who made his living in the unstable and demanding world of the theatre; who had struggled to resolve his father's insolvency and win his family gentle status. But the portrait shows us the face of an insouciant young-looking man. "Yet this is the man Shakespeare, we are asked to believe, at the age of 39!—for in the top right-hand corner is painted the date—AN° 1603." Two years later, in the 1911 edition of the *Encyclopaedia Britannica*, Spielmann wrote a lengthy entry about Shakespeare portraits, at the end of which he dismisses the Sanders as belonging to "the class of capital paintings representing some one other than Shakespeare." In the years that followed, this seems to have become the received opinion.

Thomas Hales-Sanders Jr. did not accept the expert's judgment. His faith that his portrait was of Shakespeare remained unshaken—his children often heard him say so—but in 1908, there was no gainsaying M. H. Spielmann. And there the matter rested until long after the death of Thomas's son, Aloysius, whose widow, Agnes, had carried the painting across the ocean to Canada in 1919. For almost a decade, as Agnes's young family grew up, the painting rested quietly.

Sometime in the late 1920s, Agnes Hales-Sanders's one unmarried daughter (the maiden aunt Lloyd knew as Auntie Uggie) took an interest in the heirloom portrait. Uggie must have suspected there was money to be made on the family Shakespeare. And as it happened, she spent some time in Manhattan in the later 1920s, working as a nanny for friends of the family. She took this opportunity to arrange for the portrait to be put on public display, apparently for the first time in its long life.

On Friday, October 19, 1928, *The New York Times* reported without a breath of skepticism that the day before at Stern

Brothers, an elegant department store with top-hatted doormen, a portrait of William Shakespeare painted in 1603 had gone on public exhibit. The portrait was owned, the paper said, by one Miss Mary Hales-Sanders, a direct descendant of the artist, and she believed it to be worth $100,000. "Thousands" of people were said to have attended the opening of the exhibit. "Miss Sanders . . . said that Shakespeare and Sanders were supposed to have been close friends and that their names are to be seen together in an old visitors' book kept at Swansea Inn, London." (A lovely story, that, but one without any factual evidence to support it—there is no record of a Swansea Inn in the period, and there is no Shakespeare signature in any guest book yet discovered; guest books, in fact, were hardly in use in the Jacobean age.)

The Times added that "Shakespeare's name is on the back of the painting, on which is also written 'Likeness at this time—age 39'" and described the painting's quiet fame. "During her grandfather's lifetime he had been approached many times by Shakespearean societies and individuals who wished to purchase the Sanders portrait, but he always refused to part with it, as he considered it his most treasured possession and did not want it to leave the family to which it had always belonged." His granddaughter, the newspaper went on to explain, "is selling the portrait because she is alone and has given up her home in London."

This rather bizarre explanation of Uggie's motives may have been the result of journalistic sloppiness—a reporter not bothering to check the details of a story—or, more plausibly, a case of a respectable woman entering middle age, disinclined to explain to the reading public that she had a host of siblings waiting to hear how much the sale of the family heirloom might bring them.

Perhaps those same siblings now objected to her selling it. Perhaps she received no offers she felt high enough. Regardless, the painting returned with her to Montreal, when she came home to look after her ailing mother.

Soon after Aunt Uggie's return, the portrait became her official property. On July 16, 1929, Agnes Hales-Sanders took a sharp nib to a small piece of paper and formally gave her portrait, reputed to be of William Shakespeare, to her daughter Mary Agnes. She signed the deed, with a flourish, Agnes Briggs, Widow of Aloysius Hales-Sanders. Agnes's descendants are not sure why, thirteen years before her death, she took up her fountain pen specifically to bequeath the portrait. Lloyd speculates that his grandmother foresaw squabbling over the painting and felt it was best left to her cautious and practical eldest daughter.

Exactly what Uggie did next with her new possession is far from clear, but there is an intriguing piece of evidence to suggest that in the early 1930s she wrote to the Folger Shakespeare Library in Washington, D.C. The library, which opened its doors in 1932, was the legacy of the twentieth century's great collector of Shakespeariana, Henry Clay Folger, chairman of the board of Standard Oil Company (later Mobil Oil) of New York. He and his wife, Emily, built a collection that eventually included seventy-nine copies of the First Folio and 204 Quartos, including the sole surviving Quarto copy of *Titus Andronicus* printed in 1594, and amassed, through almost offhand purchases, what would prove to be the world's greatest trove of Shakespearean-era art. The Folger owns pictures of David Garrick and other great actors of Shakespeare's day; illustrations of scenes from the plays; and many portraits of Shakespeare, including the Ashbourne (purchased in 1931) and the Janssen (acquired in 1932).

In the early 1930s, the Folger was the obvious place to look for a buyer, and that may well be exactly what Aunt Uggie did. Circumstantial evidence for this possibility turned up during my own research, in the form of a memorandum unearthed by Erin Blake, the current curator of art for the Folger Library. The memo, dated 1933, came from the desk of Joseph Quincy Adams, the Folger's first supervisor of research. It was addressed to the library's first director, William Adams Slade:

> Mr. M. H. Spielmann discusses the "Sanders" portrait in *The Connoisseur*, February, 1909. He writes: "Although I never for a moment believed the picture to have been intended for Shakespeare, I was at once attracted by it"; and he praises the delicacy with which the face is executed. The face he regards as genuine seventeenth-century workmanship; the costume, he is sure, was done by a crude forger later in the eighteenth century; and the date "1603," he declares, was "undoubtedly added" at a more recent date. Mr. Spielmann, it should be said, is a very conservative [this word replaces "destructive," crossed out] critic, unwilling, one feels, to accept any oil portrait as a genuine representation of the poet. In his caution, he leans backward, it seems to me, to the point of danger. For reasons that I need not cite here, I believe the Sanders portrait to have *very decided* Shakespearean interest; and I should be glad to have it placed on exhibition in the Folger Library along with the Felton, the Zuccaro, the Janssen, the Ashbourne, and the Lumley.
>
> With respect to the question about Richard Burbage [Shakespeare's friend and acting colleague] as the possible painter of the Sanders portrait: Burbage was, it is true, a painter of portraits in oil. I have made a careful examination of the originals known to

> have been painted by him, and am able to say with assurance that his heavy and rather wooden style is entirely different from the delicate and exquisite work revealed in the face of the Sanders portrait. The Felton portrait, now in the Folger Library, has the initials "R.B.," and has been attributed to Burbage; two other portraits in the Folger have likewise been tentatively attributed to Burbage. The truth is, whenever the artist is unknown, persons suggest Burbage. But the Sanders portrait can not possibly have been painted by Burbage.

This memo makes for an intriguing clue, for Slade clearly gave the Sanders portrait more credence than did Spielmann, and he was a man with considerable knowledge of Shakespearean art. He carefully uses the phrase "Shakespearean interest," allowing for the fact that certain portraits were interesting because they were thought to be Shakespeare as much as for their claim to be authentic. But he groups the Sanders together with other images that were then thought to have quite credible claims to being life portraits. He even questions the objectivity of Spielmann, the authority who had so decisively demolished the painting's claims almost twenty-five years earlier.

The memo Erin Blake found may have been spurred by an inquiry from one Mary Agnes Hales-Sanders of Montreal, though no such inquiry survives. Perhaps, soon after the Library opened, Slade was instructed to draw up a list of potential art acquisitions and put the Sanders on his agenda. Regardless, the portrait did not make it onto the Folger Library shopping list in the 1930s. Blake notes that the library stopped acquiring art, as its resources were increasingly strained after the 1929 stock-market crash and Mr. Folger's death a year later.

The first hard evidence of an attempt to sell the Sanders portrait to the Folger appears a year after Uggie's death in the form of a letter written in 1960 by her younger sister Alice. The painting was once again being thought of as communal property, shared among the surviving siblings. Alice was acting on behalf of her three brothers and three sisters, who had decided it was time to sell the portrait—and profitably. Lloyd remembers a period of several years, when he was a teenager, when the question of whether to sell the painting preoccupied his aunts and uncles. "Saturday nights when I was a kid, they'd all be in my mother's kitchen; there were almost a dozen of them, all the aunts and uncles," he recalls. "And they'd be saying, keep it, sell it, keep it."

Sometime during that year Alice took the portrait to Montreal's Museum of Fine Arts for evaluation. The museum's curators pronounced it interesting but advised her to look elsewhere for a buyer. Accordingly, she wrote to the Folger Shakespeare Library in September.

She told the curators at the Folger that she wanted their advice on how to go about selling her portrait of William Shakespeare, executed in 1603. In fact, Alice wondered if there was even a market for such an oil painting. She told the Folger that her family had possessed the portrait for many years and had always believed it to be of William Shakespeare, though she had "no way of proving my claim." She explained the painting's provenance by saying that the family believed it was a gift from Shakespeare himself to one of their ancestors. And she noted that M. H. Spielmann's article in the eleventh edition of the Encyclopedia Britannica cited the Sanders portrait as one of the many paintings purporting to be of Shakespeare. Alice went on to say that she was willing to have any appropriate expert examine the painting to establish its authenticity—but she told the Folger that art dealers in both North America and England had already looked at it and "the best that can be said for sure" is that it appeared to have been painted in the early 1600s.

Alice's version of how the painting came to be in the family's possession mimics the 1909 Spielmann article but differs from what Lloyd was always told. He is at a loss to explain the discrepancy, except to speculate that Alice was keeping her cards close to her chest. Regardless, the new curator of the Folger, James McManaway, displayed much less enthusiasm about the portrait than had the former director. In his reply to Alice, he seems to accept Spielmann's verdict without question:

> All that appears to be known of the Sanders portrait of Shakespeare is contained in the words of M. H. Spielmann in the fourteenth edition of the Encyclopaedia Britannica, p. 451: "The 'Rendelsham' and 'Crooks' portraits also belong to the class of capital paintings representing some one other than Shakespeare; and the same may be said of the 'Grafton' or 'Winston' portrait, the 'Sanders' . . . and others."
>
> I cannot presume to advise you about the sale of the painting. Perhaps the Canadian Shakespeare Festival people at Stratford, Ontario, might be interested; or Mr. Levi Fox, Director of the [Shakespeare] Birthplace Trust, Stratford-Upon-Avon. On the other hand, you might dispose of the picture profitably by auction.
>
> If you have a photographic print you can spare, we should be glad to have it to add to our collection of materials for the study of Shakespeare portraiture.

It was not until the spring of 1964 that the Kitchen Council again decided to take a stab at selling the portrait. By this time, Alice had died and the painting had passed to her brother Freddie. With an eye for publicity perhaps sharpened during his days in the department store business, he decided to first put the picture on display.

Once again, the venue was a department store—this time the flagship Eaton's store on St. Catherine Street in downtown Montreal. The Sanders portrait went on display in the store's Sixth Floor Picture Gallery, where it was placed behind velvet ropes and protected by round-the-clock guards. Once again, it was insured for $100,000 (though the sum meant rather less in 1964 than it had in 1928). Eaton's paid the cost of mounting the exhibit; its gallery would get a commission on any sale.

As it had in New York City, the painting attracted the attention of the press. *The Montreal Star* called it a "controversial portrait," one of five or six "interesting possibilities" for an authentic life portrait of Shakespeare. *The Star* noted Spielmann's objections and said the picture showed a man much too young to be thirty-nine. The Montreal *Gazette* cited Spielmann too, but called the portrait "a most engaging work." Glib Freddie told the papers that if the painting sold, he would use the money to finance a trip around the world—a declaration that won him no favours with the siblings back at the kitchen table. Freddie also said he wanted to sell because he had no children to whom to leave it and that his only surviving brother was also over seventy—his four surviving sisters and their children having apparently slipped his mind.

With the portrait now garnering plenty of publicity, Freddie took up his pen to compose a most serious letter. On January 31, 1966, he wrote to Prime Minister Lester B. Pearson. In the letter he drew the prime minister's attention to a local convent that he and others in the neighbourhood wanted turned into a museum. Then he discreetly brought up the subject of the painting.

In his small, crabbed handwriting, he told the prime minister that he was descended from an old English family, and happened to possess an antique portrait of William Shakespeare on a wooden panel—possibly the sole portrait of the playwright, painted in 1603. He was getting on in years, Freddie wrote, and so had "decided to dispose of the painting for the benefit of the family." The picture gallery at Eaton's department store in Montreal had the portrait, he said, and its general manager, Mr. A. E. Bates, would deal with enquiries from anyone who might be interested in buying it. Unstated, but clearly implied, was Freddie's hope that the Canadian government would purchase the Sanders portrait.

Two weeks later the Prime Minister's Office replied to Freddie's letter, informing him "that the matter of preserving Villa Maria convent as a historical monument has already been referred to the Historical Site Division of the Department of Northern Affairs and National Resources. Mr. Pearson has also asked me to inform the director of the National Gallery of the availability of the old picture of Shakespeare which you own."

On February 22, 1966, William Dale, then acting director of the Gallery, wrote to express interest: "If you care to send us a photograph, together with particulars as to size, price, known history, etc., we shall be very glad to consider it for possible acquisition."

On May 13, 1966, Freddie wrote to William Dale asking whether the National Gallery was still considering the painting.

He offered to pay Dale a visit in Ottawa to discuss the matter, and promised to await his comments before contacting any other art galleries. Five days later, Freddie received a curt reply from Willem Blom, the Gallery's research curator: "Your letter of May 13th to Dr. Dale was handed to me. . . . After due consideration of your portrait the National Gallery will not be interested in this painting. May I thank you for bringing it to our attention." In a letter to Eaton's, thanking them for early assistance in supplying details of the portrait, Blom hinted at the reason for the sudden change of tune: "Our reference material has revealed nothing to connect this painting with Shakespeare's meager iconography."

That "reference material" seems to have included the experts in Tudor portraiture at London's National Portrait Gallery. In the National Gallery of Canada's "Sanders file" can still be found a memo, dated May 4, 1966, from Alan Wilkinson, in the curatorial department, to his boss, William Dale. "I have spoken to Roy Strong about this portrait, as you suggested. In his opinion, without a pedigree there is no point even considering the portrait. It could be of anyone he said and we have no way of knowing." Roy Strong was then the keeper of sixteenth-and seventeenth-century portraiture at the National Portrait Gallery and the acknowledged authority on the subject. He is one of the experts to whom I would turn thirty-five years later, when first I learned about the portrait.

Freddie had been betting on a big sale to the country's premier art museum. Now he had to settle for the one offer that had come out of the Eaton's show. It was from a local art dealer, who was willing to pay $100,000 for the Sanders portrait. The tangible prospect of $100,000 ignited fierce family debate.

In the end, it was Lloyd's mother, Kathleen, always the peacemaker, who prevailed, convincing her siblings the painting should stay in the family. And there the matter rested until the 1990s, when Lloyd began his own quest to authenticate the painting.

These, then, are the two life stories of the Sanders portrait as I have been able to reconstruct them. The more crucial story—of the painting's provenance—is full of gaps and inconsistencies. Why, for example, did the Sanders portrait never surface before M. H. Spielmann wrote his article for *The Connoisseur* in 1909—especially given the Victorian craze for all things Shakespearean? Why is it not mentioned in any of the surveys of existing portraits written in the 1800s? Why did none of the antiquarians of the eighteenth and nineteenth centuries, who wrote voluminously about the artifacts they saw or heard tell of, ever record even a mention of the portrait? Worcester was off the beaten track, certainly. But Thomas Hales-Sanders Jr. was a cultured man, familiar with the art world—why did he not have the portrait exhibited or at least submit it for examination by the early iconographers? The Sanders family seems to have been comfortably off over the years but never wealthy. How is it that none of the painting's previous owners ever tried to avail themselves of the riches the portrait might have brought them?

Lloyd was frustrated by these gaps and ambiguities. He was sure people would want certain proof from any new portrait of Shakespeare. He never imagined that for some scholars and even some of the playwright's most devout fans, the unanswered questions simply added a layer to the portrait's appeal. It seems that what a modern audience sees in the Sanders portrait says as much about us as it does about it.

Looking the Part

Marjorie Garber

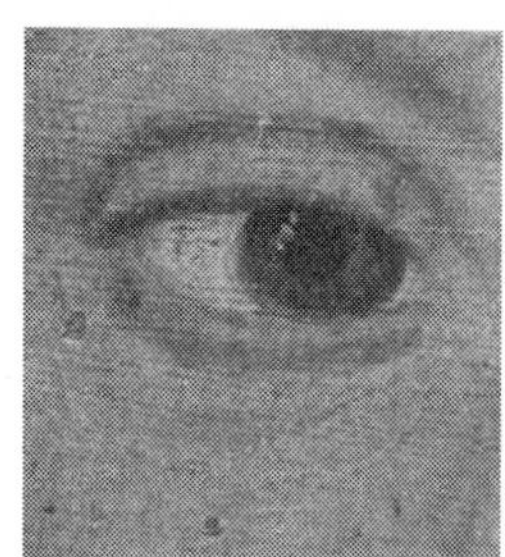

Painting in England was not any great shakes at this time.

—Catherine Johnston, Curator of European and American Collections at the National Gallery of Canada, Ottawa, speaking of the Sanders portrait

Was this face the face . . . ?

—Shakespeare, *Richard II* 4.1.281

"What a striking face! Do tell me who he is," says the narrator of Henry James's tour de force of a novella *The Aspern Papers,* as he fondles a small oval portrait with "fingers of which I could only hope that they didn't betray the intensity of their clutch." He is determined not to mention the name of the portrait's subject, the Romantic poet Jeffrey Aspern, although he longs to acquire the poet's unpublished letters. The person he is speaking to, the niece of Aspern's former mistress, replies that "critic and historian though you are," it is possible he will not recognize the name, since "the world goes fast and one generation forgets another," and all the while the narrator is afraid she will name a price that is too high. "The face comes back to me, it torments me," he remarks, with all the casualness he can summon. "You expressed doubt of this generation's having heard of the gentleman, but he strikes me for all the world as a celebrity. Now who is he? I can't put my finger on him—I can't give him a label. Wasn't he a writer? Surely he's a poet."[1]

James's story is loosely based on the life of Lord Byron, not of Shakespeare, but the same attention is always directed toward what purports to be Shakespeare's face. At a time when the discovery of a "new Shakespeare portrait" has intrigued both critics and historians and the general public, it is worth remembering other moments of literary lionization and the way they have tended to turn on images and relics. Of course, the use of portraits as evidence of character, personality, honour and sympathy—not to mention Shakespeare's vaunted "genius"—has a history as long as Shakespeare himself. What *is* it, though, that we seek in a face, whether it is the face of Shakespeare or another? What counts as evidence—and, most important, what might it be evidence *of*?

It is generally assumed that there is no point in gazing into Shakespeare's face and asking deep questions of it if his portrait turns out to be a forgery. Hence, a great deal of effort goes into the modes of authentication: dates, watermarks, carbon, uninterrupted provenance. But while authentication can eliminate anachronism and forgery, can it give us the "authentic" Shakespeare? Can there be evidence of real historical existence to ground an individual in certainty, in the absence of any reliable point of comparison? What can tell us—beyond a reasonable doubt—that this is the real historical Shakespeare? And even if we knew for sure that this was what a certain man from Stratford really looked like on a certain day in a certain year, do we have any way of verifying that this man is the author of the plays and sonnets that are, after all, the real objects of our emotional investment?

In an essay written several years ago called "Shakespeare's Ghost Writers," and in a more recent article for *Harper's* magazine, I looked at the so-called Shakespeare authorship controversy as a cultural symptom, noting that writers, in particular, have preferred the mystery about the author of the plays to any "answer" that would locate Shakespearean genius in a mere mortal, with personal quirks, a family history, a set of ambitions and wishes and failings—and a face. The less clear we are about "who wrote Shakespeare," the more "Shakespeare" can be idealized and indeed idolized. "Shakespeare is the only biographer of Shakespeare," wrote Ralph Waldo Emerson, and Charles Dickens summed up the views of many when he wrote, "The life of Shakespeare is a fine mystery, and I tremble every day lest something should turn up."

Those who have actively, even aggressively, sought to identify the author of the plays, and especially to identify him/her as someone *other* than William Shakespeare of Stratford, have also been motivated by a strong set of personal concerns, ranging from something like cultural *schadenfreude*—a delight in watching the conventional scholars squirm—to concerns of status and class, to more pragmatic issues having to do with the huge economic investment in the Shakespeare business, from publishing to tourism to T-shirts, and the sheer pleasure of investigative reporting against the grain. Just as "man bites dog" is a more eye-catching headline than "dog bites man," so "Oxford is Shakespeare" makes a better story than "Shakespeare is Shakespeare"—at least in some quarters. The brouhaha about any portrait is beside the point if the subject of the portrait didn't write the plays. The "historical Shakespeare" has all the fascination and power of the "historical Jesus"—in fact, as we shall see, looking "too Jewish" or "too foreign" haunts them both.

Similarly, it seems to me, the way that each fresh image of William Shakespeare is received reveals a cultural symptom, a clue to understanding the place and time of the portrait's celebrity. What, then, is the cultural meaning of the Sanders portrait—or of any portrait of Shakespeare that for a while is taken seriously as an authentic image of the great writer? The philosopher and cultural critic Michel Foucault established precepts for what he called the "author-function" in his influential essay "What Is an Author?" The historical concept of the author, Foucault argued, permitted a way of organizing and categorizing texts, of ascribing a certain coherence to a body of work and a literary style, and of according prestige. Noting that authors were not particularly important, valued or even known in Western literature before 1500, when anonymous texts were the norm, Foucault explored the role the author had played in the recent past and might play in the future.

Rather than beginning with the "originating subject" (in the case of Shakespeare, the "author" of the plays and poems published under that name), the author-function described the way literary reputation was conveyed and provided the back story that could be told about the "author" by and through a historical consideration of "his" (or "her") works. It is therefore evident why Foucault cites Shakespeare as an example of how the name of an author works. "The disclosure that Shakespeare was not born in the house that tourists now visit would not modify the functioning of the author's name, but if it were proved that he had not written the sonnets that we attribute to him, this would constitute a significant change and affect the manner in which the author's name functions. Moreover, if we establish that Shakespeare wrote Bacon's *Organon* and that the same author was responsible for both the works of Shakespeare and those of Bacon, we would have introduced a . . . type of alteration which completely modifies the functioning of the author's name. Consequently, the name of an author is not precisely a proper name among others."

I want now to propose a variation on Foucault's provocative title question and equally provocative phrase, in order to speak directly to our present concerns. Suppose that we asked the question, What is a portrait? And that we tried to elaborate a theory of the "portrait-function" both for Shakespeare's time and for our own?

We can begin to understand the portrait-function of the Sanders portrait when we recall some of the history of the Shakespeare portraits that have gone before and the way they have been received. The nineteenth and twentieth centuries produced myriad works on this fascinating topic, from *Shakespeare's Portraits Phrenologically Considered* (1875)[2] to *A New Portrait of Shakespeare: The Case of the Ely Palace Painting as against that of the so-called Droeshout Original* (1903),[3] to Leslie Hotson's *Shakespeare by Hilliard: A Portrait Deciphered* (1977)[4]—which begins, "Consider for a moment the opening of a hunt in real life for a Wanted Man"—to *Changing the Face of Shakespeare* (1996),[5] a posthumous, privately printed monograph by an American schoolteacher who had worked as a cryptographer in the Second World War and helped to break the Japanese code. In many if not most of these accounts, the attempt is to read the man in the portrait, and, not infrequently, to read the man *into* the portrait or, conversely, to cast doubt on the authenticity of the portrait because it does not seem to match the Man.

Thus, for example, the author of *The Droeshout Portrait of William Shakespeare, An Experiment in Identification* (1911) demonstrates to his own satisfaction that the portrait is in fact that of Francis Bacon, whose authorship of the plays he had shown, "in two books [which have been] in some quarters misunderstood, and consequently misrepresented and ridiculed, but which neither ha[ve] been nor can be refuted." [6] In his previous books he had detected Bacon's signatures cunningly hidden in the "Shakespeare" text, some in acrostics. Using a method of identification he compares to fingerprinting or to the Bertillon measurements—a system of bodily measurements and cataloguing of characteristics used in the late nineteenth century for the "scientific" identification of criminals—he finds that "the portrait of the poet, used as a frontispiece to the plays in which Bacon's structural signature is found," matches up precisely with the physical features in a contemporary portrait of Bacon.

In a similarly cryptographic vein, the author of a book called *The Bacon-Shakespearean Mystery*, which had claimed to prove that Anthony Bacon, Francis's older brother, was the real author of the plays, weighed in six years later with *The Shakespearean Portraits and Other Addenda* (1964, revised 1966), in which she disclosed that Anthony Bacon's initials could be read on the collar of the Droeshout engraving. (She was able to discern this, she said, by putting a piece of tracing paper over a copy of the Kökeritz facsimile of the Yale University copy of the First Folio.)[7]

But even when the object is not to prove that someone else wrote the "Shakespeare" plays, the degree of critical energy and ingenuity applied to the portraits cannot really be disentangled from cultural fantasy. *A New Portrait of Shakespeare* makes a claim for the authenticity of the so-called Ely Palace portrait, which came into the possession of the Bishop of Ely in 1846, having previously languished in "an obscure broker's shop." Cleaning of the portrait disclosed the words "Aet. 39, 1603," the supposed age of Shakespeare in that year. The author is especially impressed with the suitability of the portrait's image: "It gives the impression of representing a real person, a sentient human being.... The eyes, in spite of the error in drawing, have a very distinct and interesting expression—a disquiet vacancy that often denotes a deeply troubled mind. The mouth is both sensuous and sensitive, and the seriousness of the lower part of the face indicates dignity, even elevation of character."

Since the supposed date of the Ely portrait, 1603, was the very time in Shakespeare's life that "critics have generally taken as marking some sudden change in the underlying mood of Shakespeare's mind," leading to the writing of *Measure for Measure* and the great tragedies, the portrait supports the theory of a crisis in spiritual development. "If now the Ely Palace portrait may be taken as authentic, it distinctly confirms the theory. The expression of the disquiet, indwelling eyes, and the dignified, serious face, is what one would naturally expect at the period of *Hamlet*."[8] Thus assumptions or projections about Shakespeare's spiritual life and his character are brought to bear on the question of authenticity; although visual evidence and issues of provenance are part of the argument, the clincher is that this portrait looks like

Shakespeare. Or at least like the Shakespeare that critics were thinking and writing about at the time.

If psychology, emotion and affect were not convincing, there was science to be consulted—for example, the late-nineteenth-century practice of phrenology, whose adherents believed that they could read a person's character and intellect from the size and shape of the skull. As Dickens wrote of Shakespeare, "If he had had a Boswell, society wouldn't have respected his grave, but would calmly have had his skull in the phrenological shop-windows."[9] The questions raised by *Shakespeare's Portraits Phrenologically Considered* are those of what was regarded in the latter half of the nineteenth century as a certain kind of cutting-edge science. Only "within the present century," writes the author, has the discovery been made that "special characteristics are connected with particular portions of the head, and that mental greatness mainly depends on the size, form and condition of the brain."[10] The head of a "mere mathematician" will differ from that of a musician, and both from the linguist, "while the universal genius must possess a well-balanced and finely constituted nervous organization."

According to the author's phrenological analysis, the Stratford bust fails the universal genius test. It "presents the appearance of a stout unintellectual figure." Admittedly "it has a jovial, cheerful, life-like look," but "the features are not those indicative of sensibility and refinement." Especially disturbing to the phrenologist is the fact that the head is broadest at its base, evidence of "destructiveness, secretiveness, alimentiveness, and acquisitiveness," while "ideality and wit are scarcely indicated." This, in short, cannot be Shakespeare. "I have examined many thousands of heads, and never met with such a heavy-looking figure associated with a man of capacity, culture, and mental power." What is likely is that the image is just a monumental effigy, and not an exact likeness, and that the "tombmaker" Geraert Janssen "left details to be executed by his assistants."[11]

The Droeshout engraving comes out better; from the shape of the head it seems that "there is an ample endowment of the higher sentiments. The imaginative and imitative faculties are represented as very large," as are "ideality, wonder, wit, imitation, benevolence, and veneration." This is a much more appropriate phrenology for Shakespeare: "his large benevolence, veneration and ideality, and his small destructiveness and acquisitiveness leading to his control over his feelings and generous sympathy with others." All this can be read in the Droeshout portrait. It is worth noting that the phrenologist is not daunted by the wide variety of representations in the "various portraits" of Shakespeare: if they are all to be believed, his eyes "must have been at the same time black, brown, and blue," the nose "at once Roman, Grecian, aquiline and snub," and so on. But what emerges, nonetheless, is a clear sense of Shakespeare's "temperament, which was evidently a combination of the mental, the nervous, and sanguine, imparting great susceptibility, activity, quickness and love of action."[12] "Evidently," says the author with confidence. From the evidence of the portraits and the shape of the skull.

So strong, in fact, was this fascination with Shakespeare's skull that J. Parker Norris, an American keenly interested in Shakespeare portraits, encouraged disinterring the body. In a book published in 1876, he wrote, "If we could even get a photograph of Shakespeare's skull, it would be a great thing, and would help us to make a better portrait of him than we now possess."[13] As Norris observes serenely, "It is strange how differently people look at the same object." Thus, for example, nineteenth-century opinions on the Stratford bust varied from J. O. Halliwell-Phillipps's assessment, that "to those who can bring themselves to believe that, notwithstanding his unrivaled genius, Shakespeare was a realization of existence, and, in his daily career, much as other men were, the bust at Stratford will convey very nearly all that is desirable to know of his outward form"[14] to the very different ideas of the distinguished lawyer and Shakespearean C. M. Ingleby.

To Ingleby, the Stratford bust was "coarse and clownish, suggesting to the beholder a countryman crunching a sour apple or struck with amazement at some unpleasant spectacle."[15] Professor J. S. Hart had similar doubts. "The skull has the smoothness and roundness of a boy's marble, and about as much individuality or expression," wrote Hart in *Scribner's Monthly*. "The cheeks are puffy and spiritless; the mustaches are curled up in a manner never found except on some city exquisite; . . . finally, the expression of the eyes, so far as they have any, is simply that of easy, rollicking good nature, not overburdened with sense or intellect."[16] On the other hand, the portrait painter Abraham Wivell, author of yet another study, *An Inquiry into the History, Authenticity, and Characteristics of the Shakespeare Portraits*,[17] admired the bust's nose and forehead and thought that if the space between the nose and mouth were just a little shorter, "the face would be remarkably handsome." He also thought this portrait "has much less the look of a Jew than most of them," since the beard was fashionably trimmed. A century later, the Shakespeare biographer Samuel Schoenbaum added his own judiciously acerbic commentary: "Can this be a true likeness of the Bard? Surely not—this must be some affluent burgher of Stratford confronting us with his sleek, well-fed, middle-aged prosperity. . . . Supposedly we are to conceive of the poet as declaiming verses he has just composed, but he appears for all the world to be struggling with indigestion."[18]

Coarse and clownish, dyspeptic, remarkably handsome, not very intellectual, not like a Jew. A similarly Rashomon-like panoply of views can be marshalled for virtually any of the Shakespeare portraits currently in the running, as well as for works once described as portraits of Shakespeare and now fallen out of favour. Thus the Droeshout engraving in the First Folio was described by nineteenth-century Shakespeare buffs as everything from a "monstrosity" (C. M. Ingleby) to a figure of "calm benevolence and tender thought" (James Boaden). In point of fact, no one has much wanted Shakespeare—their Shakespeare—to look like either the Stratford bust or the Droeshout engraving. For a time, the Chandos portrait fared much better, despite the serious doubts about its claim. Schoenbaum notes that "it has always been the favorite likeness of Shakespeare—if it is of Shakespeare."[19] In the late 1880s, when J. Parker Norris was writing in the journal *Shakesperiana*, the Chandos portrait, with its pointed beard, lace collar and earring, was "the most familiar to the large mass of people,"[20] and the "popularly accepted representation of Shakespeare."*

* Here I cannot resist quoting the epigraph to this interesting journal, in which the editor performs a delightful sex-change on Enobarbus's praise of Cleopatra. Under the large-print title *Shakesperiana*, and above the date and the portrait image, runs the line from *Antony and Cleopatra*, "Age cannot wither nor custom stale his infinite variety." Through the blithe replacement of one possessive adjective with another, *her infinite variety* becomes *his*, and the quotation-out-of-context praises Shakespeare's art rather than Cleopatra's erotic power.

Yet this portrait, of much more doubtful "authenticity" than the bust or the engraving, has been consistently criticized over the years for not being English enough, or for looking too "Jewish." The eighteenth-century editor George Steevens disputed its authority on the grounds that "our author exhibits the complexion of a Jew, or rather of a chimney-sweeper in the jaundice."[21] A mid-century Victorian, J. Hain Friswell, found it disappointing at first glance, because the person depicted looked foreign, and—again—too much like a Jew: "One cannot readily imagine our essentially English Shakespeare to have been a dark, heavy man, with a foreign expression, of a decidedly Jewish physiognomy, thin curly hair, a somewhat lubricious mouth, red-edged eyes, wanton lips, with a coarse expression, and his ears tricked out with earrings."[22] J. Parker Norris agreed: "very Jewish," "foreign," "most disappointing." Though some Englishmen did wear earrings in Shakespeare's day, the rings, he thought, contributed to the "foreign look." (Critics today who cast doubt on Chandos because of its un-English appearance tend to call this look "Italianate"[23] rather than "Jewish.")

The lack of similarity between this portrait and the more fully authorized versions, the bust and the Droeshout engraving, led some scholars to dispute its genuineness. (The irrepressible Steevens, noting the many hands through which it had passed, called it the "Davenantico-Bettertono-Barryan-Keckian-Nicolsian-Chandosan" portrait.) But the real issue remained cultural, political and aesthetic: was this the way Shakespeare, our Shakespeare, *should* look? Or, to take up my variation on Foucault, did the Chandos serve its proper portrait-function? Did it show us the image we needed to construct?

Were we to make our way, one by one, through the succession of proposed "portraits" and likenesses of Shakespeare that have attracted attention over the years, we would be able to notice the same pattern again and again. Assessment of the portrait appears at first to depend on technical questions like the age of the wood and the paint, the provenance or history of ownership, the clothing, hairstyles and so on, but what is always really at stake is the question of whether the image fits the man. If it doesn't, the fault may be said to lie in the artist (too unskilled for his task), the medium (intractable stone, clumsy engraving tools) or the occasion (funerary monuments all looked alike); alternatively, a competing aesthetic could be called into play, discovering that what one beholder found stolid or vapid or monstrous, another could find emblematic of wisdom, wide experience, imagination and sympathy. Here we have a lesson, displayed for all to see, in the limits of both historical and interpretative criticism. When read backward, beginning from a supposed goal (is this really an image of Shakespeare?), these purportedly neutral elements become materials for conscious fiction making.

Thus (just to emphasize this point) the author and critic John Dover Wilson chose the so-called Grafton portrait, an attractive small painting in the style of Holbein or Nicholas Hilliard that had come to light in the early years of the twentieth century, as the frontispiece for his *Essential Shakespeare*, first published in 1932, even though it had small claim to authenticity, because he simply liked it better than the "pudding-faced effigy" of the Droeshout engraving or the "self-satisfied pork-butcher" depicted in the putative Janssen portrait.

In his introduction to *The Essential Shakespeare*, Dover Wilson cites a "learned essay by Mr. M. H. Spielmann," the same Spielmann who so confidently dismissed the Sanders portrait when he examined it in 1908, in which he characterizes the Stratford bust as having a "wooden appearance and vapid expression," staring eyes "set too close together," a nose "too small for the face." Dover Wilson notes that Spielmann's essay "also draws attention to the extraordinary upper lip, the hanging lower lip, and the general air of stupid and self-complacent prosperity. All this," writes the author of *The Essential Shakespeare*, "might suit well enough with an affluent and retired butcher, but does gross wrong to the dead poet." In short, "this Shakespeare simply will not do." People don't want their Shakespeare to look like this.

So inadequate is the Stratford bust, in fact, that Dover Wilson holds it largely responsible for "the campaign against 'the man from Stratford' and the attempts to dethrone him in favor of Lord Bacon, the Earl of Derby, the Earl of Oxford, or whatever coroneted pretender may be in vogue at the present moment." His own explanation for the problem is a familiar one: the artist was not up to the task. "The proportions are admirable, and the architectural design, with its pillars and canopy, its mantled shield, and its twin cherubs, is quite beautiful. But one thing was clearly beyond the workman's scope—the human face, the face that happened to be Shakespeare's!"

Ah yes, that elusive "face that happened to be Shakespeare's." For reasons he is admirably clear about, Dover Wilson prefers a fantasy to the possibly real, but palpably disappointing, historical monument. For him the "beautiful" Grafton portrait, inscribed with a date that shows the sitter was Shakespeare's exact contemporary, looks much more the way Shakespeare *should* look, although, as he unblushingly acknowledges, "there is nothing whatever to connect the unknown youth of the wonderful eyes and the oval Shelley-like face with the poet who was also twenty-four years old in 1588." In other words, the Grafton portrait is a screen on which thoughts can be projected, a fantasy, a space for wish fulfillment. Another Shakespeare biographer of the time had "found in it his own idea of the youthful Shakespeare and wished it genuine," and Dover Wilson explains, in direct and explicit terms, why he has selected this image for his frontispiece: "I do not ask the reader to believe in it, or even to wish to believe in it. All I suggest is that he may find it useful in trying to frame his own image of Shakespeare. It will, at any rate, help him to forget the Stratford bust. Let him take it, if he will, as a painted cloth or arras, drawn in front of that monstrosity, and symbolizing the Essential Poet."[24]

We might draw an analogy here with the modern practice of "profiling" in law enforcement and in media marketing: in racial profiling, for example, law enforcement officers select their targets for investigation or stronger action on the basis of race, national origin or ethnicity. The word "profile," which derives from the drawing of the outline of the human face, quickly became a term for a biographical sketch or character study. In effect, what Shakespeare scholars and amateur enthusiasts have engaged in over the years is a form of what might be called "author profiling": developing an ideal image for what the author of the Shakespeare plays *ought* to look like. Indeed, Dover Wilson's word "frame" ("to frame his own image of Shakespeare") also carries an inadvertent second meaning from the world of criminal investigation. To profile Shakespeare, to frame him, in these accounts of the portrait evidence, is thus an idealized and idealizing activity that owes as much to psychology and psychological projection as it does to provenance and paint.

What, then, is the portrait-function of a picture of William Shakespeare in our own time? Trying to frame our own image of Shakespeare has become, in these post-*Shakespeare in Love* days, an increasingly respectable activity. The alleged new portrait discovered in Canada, whether it is ultimately determined to be real or fake, or to lie somewhere in the limbo occupied by the much-debated Chandos, fits into this strong history of "Shakespeare" portraits and their reception perfectly well. If the culture correspondent for *The Los Angeles Times* was moved to say, on behalf of the Hollywood film industry, that the Shakespeare of the portrait strongly resembles Joseph Fiennes, the playwright hero of *Shakespeare in Love*, are we at risk of revaluing our portraits—and our Shakespeares—yet again, to fit this year's fashions? If so, we can at least take comfort in the fact that this way of reading portraits as if they told us something about character and genius rather than about art and counterfeiting is part of a tradition as old as Shakespeare and his plays.

A commentator in the Queensland *Courier Mail* certainly saw the Sanders, which might be "the real face of William Shakespeare," in terms of its attractiveness to modern eyes. The new portrait "conflicts with the traditional image of Shakespeare having a bald head, thin brows, and humourless countenance. Instead, it suggests he was a mischievous-looking chap with fluffy red hair and blue-green eyes."[25] In *The New York Times*, Verlyn Klinkenborg editorialized that "if this is Shakespeare, it is a younger and more roguish Shakespeare than we have ever seen," and went on to argue, in a way that many literary critics have as well, that "the resemblance we see in this portrait is not a resemblance to Shakespeare," but rather "a resemblance to what we would like to imagine that Shakespeare looked like."[26] Tim Rutten in *The Los Angeles Times* was even blunter: what is "troubling to many, is how the balding, stiff, dour old man the engraving and bust portray could have created the world's most enduring body of dramatic and poetic art. It is precisely that reservation that has churned the enthusiasm for the new portrait."[27]

The authors of modern detective stories have long known about this device, of making the artist look like his or her work. Robert Barnard's mystery *The Cherry Blossom Corpse* features the murder, at a romance writers' convention, of the woman whose appearance and behaviour personify everything a writer of romance novels should be—and who turns out to be an actress hired to put a glamorous face on books ghost-written by drabber women, and men, behind the scenes. In Ngaio Marsh's *Final Curtain*, a famous actor owes his celebrity to his superbly theatrical head, which is as outsize as his ego. Despite her forebodings, the detective's wife, herself a notable painter, cannot resist the invitation to do his portrait. Both stories, it is worth noting, end in the tragic deaths of the actor-author-artist. "Looking the part" has its dangers as well as its pleasures.

There is a superb fictional analysis of the portrait-function in Josephine Tey's classic murder mystery *The Daughter of Time*, which turns on a portrait of England's Richard III. Inspector Alan Grant of Scotland Yard, hospitalized with a broken leg, is entertained by an actress friend who, knowing his "passion for faces," brings him an array of portrait images. Thumbing through images of Lucrezia Borgia, Louis XVII and the Earl of Leicester, each labelled only on the back of the sheet, Grant tries to read the story behind each face. His attention is arrested by the portrait of a man dressed in "the velvet cap and slashed doublet of the late fifteenth century," a man about thirty-five years of age, lean, clean-shaven, wearing a richly jewelled collar and caught in the act of putting a ring on his finger, and he tries to speculate about the man and his character. "A judge? A soldier? A prince? Someone used to great responsibility, and responsible in his authority. Someone too conscientious. A worrier; perhaps a perfectionist. A man at ease in a large design, but anxious over details." When he turns the picture over and reads the caption, he finds printed there the following words: "Richard the Third. From the portrait in the National Portrait Gallery. Artist Unknown."[28]

The rest of the plot consists of the inspector's quest to read the face against the reputation of the man and, ultimately, to exonerate the portrait sitter from the calumny of having murdered the princes in the tower. Inspector Grant becomes convinced that the man with the "interesting face" and the "haunted eyes" could not be a destroyer of innocence, a "synonym for villainy." The remainder of the novel puts the case, in terms at once artful and engrossing, for Henry VII, the Earl of Richmond (and Elizabeth I's grandfather), as the true author of the crime.

So successful was Tey in putting the case for Richard that her novel has become a key piece of "evidence" for members of the Richard III Society, an international organization dedicated to restoring Richard's reputation. The function of portrait evidence as a guarantor of character carries over even into the Society's Web pages. Thus the American branch of the Society, pinpointing the true villain according to its lights (and Tey's) offers a feature called "rearranging Henry Tudor's face," in which Ricardians are presented with a period portrait of the man who would become Henry VII and invited to "click and drag on Henry's face to reveal his true character (http://pobox.upenn.edu/~lblancha/alexwarp/henry7.html)." Perhaps the publishers of this book will provide a similar service for those who wish to rearrange the Sanders portrait or some other Shakespeare image.

But what, finally, are we looking for in a portrait—and especially in a new portrait of Shakespeare? Can character be read in a painted likeness, whether or not it is "rearranged" by the viewer? What's in a face? Here is what the twentieth-century philosopher Emmanuel Levinas has to say about "the face" in the context of a discussion of ethics: "I think rather that access to the face is straightaway ethical. You turn yourself toward the Other as toward an object when you see a nose, eyes, a forehead, a chin, and you can describe them. The best way of encountering the Other is not even to notice the color of his eyes! When one observes the color of the eyes one is not in social relationship with the Other. The relation with the face can surely be dominated by perception, but what is specifically the face is what cannot be reduced to that."[29]

The capital-O "Other" employed by Levinas designates a particular and idealized one-to-one relationship. This Other differs from all "others." And in the numinous world of literary-biographical fantasy, Shakespeare is clearly the Other rather than one of the "others." Matthew Arnold's famous sonnet of 1844 titled "Shakespeare" begins with this same comparison, in the form of an address to its subject:

Others abide our question. Thou art free.
We ask and ask.
Thou smilest and art still,
Out-topping knowledge.

Where "others" have biographical stories that explain them (they "abide our question"), Shakespeare is, for Arnold, unique, and the mystery of his identity is preferred to any solution. Arnold's poem ends, significantly, with an unmistakable glance at the portraits, and specifically at the high forehead of the Stratford bust and the Droeshout engraving:

All pains the immortal spirit must endure,
All weakness which impairs, all griefs which bow,
Find their sole speech in that victorious brow.

Here is another effect of the portrait-function, a speaking picture. The "victorious brow" (later to be described by Dover Wilson as a "great forehead") speaks volumes about human pain, grief and weakness, while the enigmatic Shakespeare, Mona Lisa–like, smiles and is still, refusing to explain the source of his wisdom.

Those who gaze in fascination and recognition at the Sanders portrait will not find wisdom writ large on the somewhat foxy face, even though the "great forehead" (a k a receding hairline) is again present to the viewer. Arnold's sonorous verses may sound dated to us, but the wish they express continues to be felt. Our own celebrity culture, though, pries into every personal detail, unsatisfied with mystery and with silence. When asked about the interest provoked by the Sanders portrait, the Toronto

Shakespeare scholar Alexander Leggatt nicely voiced the general dissatisfaction with the traditional authenticated images, "the engraving and the sort of lumpy statue," which "have a kind of inexpressive quality that is frustrating."[30] "Inexpressive" is the key word here, I think. These portraits do not speak to us, whereas the male minx in the Sanders image, with his knowing eyes and flirtatious, up-curved mouth, seems about to burst into words—words as witty and perhaps as improper as our current taste will permit. This is not Arnold's Victorian Shakespeare.

If this new Shakespeare looks more like Benedick than like King Lear (or Polonius), that too seems to suit the temper of our time. *Shakespeare in Love* fantasizes about the private life of the world's most celebrated and venerated author, trying to explain the inexplicable, which is how he came to write those astonishing plays, those luminous sonnets. In Tom Stoppard's screenplay for *Shakespeare in Love*, the "explanation" was the fictional Viola de Lesseps (played in the movie by Gwyneth Paltrow). In Oscar Wilde's playful work of literary detection, "The Portrait of Mr. W. H.," it was the imaginary Willie Hughes, the supposed dedicatee of Shakespeare's sonnets and "the boy-actor for whom he created Viola and Imogen, Juliet and Rosalind, Portia and Desdemona, and Cleopatra herself."[31] Boy-actor or fantasy-girl, this is a distinction without a difference. We will not find "genius," whatever it is, in any biographical detail, or in any portrait. What we will find, when we look at the portrait of Shakespeare, as Richard II does when he calls for a looking glass, and as Jaques in *As You Like It* does when he gazes into the brook, is an image of ourselves.

Is the Sanders portrait an "authentic" portrait of Shakespeare, the "real" Shakespeare? Why not think so, if you like? Every age invents its own Shakespeare, as Coleridge found "a smack of Hamlet" in himself, and Goethe too, and Freud, and just about every scholar and artist and actor who has spent time reading and performing Shakespeare's plays. The portrait-function is a reflection-effect, holding, in the case of this author above all others, the mirror up to Shakespeare, showing the very age and body of the time his form and pressure. Dover Wilson sought his "essential Shakespeare," and we seek ours. In an era where "rearranging [the] face" is as easy as dragging a cursor or turning to Photoshop, the portrait, and the portrait-function, will inevitably read very differently from the way they read in Shakespeare's time or during the lively Shakespeare-portrait debates of a century and more ago.

One thing is almost sure, though. If this portrait is judged to be genuine, or catches the media's fancy, its cultural effect will be felt in fashion circles before it is adopted by the historians of literature. The Shakespeare collar and the Shakespeare doublet—maybe even the new Shakespeare beard, in a hue dubbed "Bard red"—will appear on the runways and in the fashion magazines. It is no accident, believe me, that the first full-page reproduction of the Sanders portrait in a major periodical could be found in the December 2001 issue of *Vanity Fair*, with a bare-chested Brad Pitt on the cover and the legend "All-American Hearththrob" emblazoned there, right below the "van" of *Vanity*. This is the new mode of *vanitas* painting, replacing the two well-dressed gentlemen in Holbein's sixteenth-century *Ambassadors*, surrounded with symbols of transient wealth, power and earthly pleasure: Sanders-Shakespeare/Brad Pitt as two sides of the same, All-(North) American coin.

Forensic Revelations

FOR MARJORIE GARBER, it is enough that the Sanders portrait "looks the part." Should it prove to be a genuine image of Shakespeare, that would merely add to its multiplying cultural and historical reverberations. For Lloyd Sullivan, however, only definitive proof that the portrait came from Shakespeare's time and place would vindicate his long labours. To find this proof he turned to the reassuringly precise world of science. In the first few years of his project he had made a frustrating succession of failed attempts to authenticate the portrait, but those frustrations ended one morning in March 1993, when he walked through the doors of the Canadian Conservation Institute in Ottawa.

The Institute is an agency of the Canadian government's Department of Canadian Heritage. It was created in 1972 to do restoration and scientific work for Canada's public museums and galleries and is housed in a deceptively innocuous brown-brick building in the east end of the nation's capital. Other Institute labs (and a warehouse that houses its exhibition transportation arm) are scattered through the city, but this has been its heart since it opened for business thirty years ago.

Here, in fits and starts over the next seven years, Lloyd Sullivan submitted the Sanders portrait to the mysterious process through which science reveals the secrets of art. In the Institute's quiet laboratories, a painting ceases to be about technique, composition and expression. It becomes instead a question of chemistry, of the bonds between atoms and the structure of crystals. Science, of course, cannot say for certain what a picture is, but it can very often say what it isn't. As long as the debate centred purely on the identity of the portrait's subject, there could be no conclusive answer. But laboratory analysis could reveal evidence that the portrait was not painted in 1603 or that it had been altered from its original form—proof that it was not William Shakespeare painted from life. Then the value of the painting would plummet, but it was a gamble Lloyd had finally decided he had to take.

Since he had begun his "retirement project," various friends and friends of friends had offered him their "expert" help. Innocent and trusting, he accepted their offers and was led on more than one fool's errand and several wild-goose chases. Lloyd showed the painting to the head of a large British china company who was speaking at an Ottawa shopping mall; the teacup expert told him the portrait was a most intriguing work but could say no more than that. A friend heard that the English actress Vanessa Redgrave (an alumna of the Royal Shakespeare Company) was coming to perform in Ottawa and wrote to her manager about the picture; she expressed an interest in seeing it, but nothing happened. And one evening in spring of 1993, Lloyd and a friend slunk through the back entrance of the Ottawa Civic Hospital with the portrait in tow. After making a wrong turn into a room where a patient with a brain tumour was being examined, they finally found a hospital employee who had offered to take a furtive X-ray of the painting. He charged them $50, for which they received a negative image of the man in the picture—almost identical to the original. There did not seem to be another, different painting underneath the visible one—a common sign of a fake. "That was encouraging, I thought," Lloyd says.

Encouraging, yes. But he could hardly take an ill-gotten hospital X-ray to Christie's or Sotheby's. Ultimately he realized that the only sensible course was to consult the professionals, although he was not sure how to find them, and it would probably be a very expensive proposition. Then he heard about Patrick Legris, an art conservator who lived in the town of Carp, about an hour from Ottawa. In February 1993, Lloyd put the painting back in the suitcase and took it out to Legris' studio. The conservator listened to the peculiar story of the portrait, then agreed to take a look at it. Lloyd left the picture in his care. A few days later, Legris sent Lloyd his assessment. After a "cursory examination" under a low-power microscope and UV light, he found that "no retouchings are visible over the varnish. In spite of Spielmann's comments [in 1909] . . . the costume does not appear to be a later addition. It appears to be of the same age as the face and background and doesn't appear to cover any earlier design." Lloyd felt the first tingle of vindication. "The date," Legris went on, "painted in thick red paint in the upper right background, lies under the varnish. This means that it is not a recent addition but does not necessarily rule out its having been applied spuriously." With his small studio, this was an issue Legris could not settle. "To determine the age of the painting and authenticity of the date, more extensive chemical and microscopic analysis would have to be carried out."

And so Lloyd wound up at the doors of the Canadian Conservation Institute. One enters through a series of doors requiring punched codes and pass cards. Stairs from the entrance lead up to a mezzanine looking out over vast workrooms, each with ceilings two storeys high. Here the tables hold all kinds of museum artifacts and huge paintings in various states of undress. Around the periphery of the building's interior are a dozen smaller laboratories, cluttered with microscopes and machinery. Lloyd found the overall effect closer to science fiction than four-hundred-year-old art. "I was in awe of the place," he recalls. "It was like *2001: A Space Odyssey*—all the machines and such."

That first morning in March 1993, he was given a tour by John Taylor, a chemist who then ran the Institute's analytical research lab. Taylor, who works today with the National Research Council, does not remember much about that 1993 meeting. He received inquiries like Lloyd's quite often—even the big art fraud cases didn't get him too excited any more. "And most of the time, when people came in with paintings, it turned out to be disappointing," he now says. Nonetheless, he patiently explained to Lloyd the process involved in authenticating—or, more often, debunking—a painting. "I wanted him to know it wasn't just add water and stir," he says. "It wasn't magic, it wasn't smoke and mirrors." He also told Lloyd how much the process could cost. At $110 an hour, and requiring tests that could take a team weeks of work, the cost of reaching any firm conclusions about the Sanders portrait could be as much as $50,000, Lloyd says Taylor estimated. "I almost fainted," Lloyd recalls. Taylor also kindly added that the lab's work was generally done for other institutions, not wide-eyed innocents who walked in off the street with a portrait in an old vinyl suitcase.

Lloyd then met briefly with Marie-Claude Corbeil and Ian Wainwright, two of the laboratory's conservation scientists. They gave the painting a quick once-over. "At the time, it was just a painting for me," recalls Wainwright, a shy but affable fellow with a beard and large dark-framed glasses. "We work in a lab where we see many things that are quite extraordinary. But it was clear to me that this was an old painting, and with lots of clients who walk in off the street, that's not the case."

Marie-Claude Corbeil, a slim, stylish chemist, remembers seeing a well-preserved panel painting that looked, at a glance, quite old. "Panel paintings are not that common in private collections—they usually end up in museums. It's rare for one to stay in a family," she explains. "And for most of the things we get, people can't go far in the provenance. They may have some information, but usually not a whole lot—maybe it's something they bought at an auction. So this case was quite different, because this painting stayed in the same family, and Lloyd had done all this research—that was what made it special."

But Lloyd left the Institute a discouraged man. The cost of authentication was well beyond the means of someone living on a fixed pension. And even if he could manage to pay for the tests piecemeal over a number of years, the Institute was leery of taking on commissions from private owners.

As a courtesy, however, Corbeil wrote to Peter Klein, a professor of wood science and technology at the University of Hamburg in Germany. Klein is the world expert in using dendrochronology (the science of dating from the annual growth rings of trees) on works of art. By measuring the distance between the growth rings visible on the edge of a painted panel and comparing those rings with data drawn from a large body of other samples, he can determine precisely when a medieval lumberjack felled the tree from which a panel was cut. Through a series of calculations, he can then pinpoint a probable date when a panel was used for painting.

From the perspective of Corbeil and her colleagues at the Institute, dendrochronology was Lloyd's logical first step. If the tree was cut down later than 1603, the portrait could not have been painted in that year. In her letter, Corbeil informed the German expert that the Institute had a private client with a painting that required dendrochronological analysis and asked if he had any plans to be in North America in the next while. Klein replied that he was planning to come to Ottawa the following spring to do some work for the National Gallery of Canada and that he would be happy to extend his trip to take a look at the Sanders portrait. Corbeil passed this news along to Lloyd.

So great was Klein's reputation, and so potentially decisive the information he could reveal about the picture, that Lloyd decided to seize the opportunity. (He winced when told it would cost him about $500 to pay the scientist's fee for examining the painting and several hundred dollars more in expenses to extend his stay in Ottawa by a day or two.)

In June 1994, Peter Klein presented himself at the Canadian Conservation Institute and was ushered into one of its pristine laboratories. A dapper man in his mid-fifties, the German scientist has cornered the market in his abstruse specialty. As a student at the University of Hamburg in the 1970s, he studied wood science and technology, an interdisciplinary mix of economics, biology, physics and chemistry. Graduates of the program typically went to work in the furniture or pulp-and-paper industries. But Klein chose to do his doctorate in wood protection and preservation under Joseph Bauch, the first person to apply dendrochronology to works of art. Quite unexpectedly, Klein found himself seduced into the art world.

That June day, the Sanders portrait had been taken from the vault and placed on one of the large laboratory tables. Before the Institute scientists left him to his work, they mentioned to Klein that the sitter was possibly Shakespeare. The suggestion distracted the German expert only briefly. "I thought, This is very strange," he says, "but in different museums or from private owners, I look at panels . . ." He trails off, the polite implication being that he has heard just about everything in his twenty-five-year tour of the world's fine art collections.

While dendrochronology is a meaty mouthful of a word, the actual analytical process involved is relatively straightforward. First Klein placed the painting on a light table and swabbed the edges clean. Then he examined them for a suitable area to study. He needs about a hundred growth rings to be able to draft a dating curve. The narrower of the two pieces of board that had been joined together to make the panel was too small to analyze—it contained only forty-seven rings—but the larger piece (25 x 25 cm, or about 10 x 10 inches) provided ample material. Klein now examined the edge of the panel with a small magnifying lens, to the power of ten, which has a tiny scale set within it, measuring each tenth of a millimetre. Using only his highly trained eye and the magnification of the lens, he counted the rings in the wood—264 in total—and measured the distance between them. The whole process took a bit more than an hour.

Today, after examining more than twenty-five hundred panel paintings and compiling his findings in a vast database, Klein has accumulated an unparalleled body of knowledge. Most of his work is for museums; he is a member of the Rembrandt Research Project, a scholarly initiative begun in 1968 to identify the original works of the Dutch master, for which he has analyzed 250 putative Rembrandt works. He jokes, in his formal English, that he spends most of his time looking at the *backs* of very famous paintings. "But I have also a lot of time to turn them over—that is my advantage in comparison to an art historian: I take the painting from the wall and I can look at it in my hand without the frame. An art historian often has to look at it on the wall, behind glass, and they cannot see so much."

Klein had been able to identify the type of wood used for the Sanders panel at a glance, since it had the dark colour and distinct cell structure of oak. (Maple, beech, poplar and willow, whose anatomies are similar, are more difficult to distinguish.) Oak was the preferred choice of panel painters and furniture makers in the 1600s and 1700s, since its hard, dense wood is less susceptible to insects and rot. Oak trees grew widely in England, but by the late sixteenth century the supply was dwindling and oak began to be imported. The English traded wine and other consumer goods for oak planks and corn from Poland. Oak also grew in Spain and the Netherlands, but there it was in high demand for ships and houses; French, Dutch and English artists used Baltic oak, while the Italians of the era preferred poplar.

Klein could only complete his analysis once he had returned to his office in Hamburg. Since each area of Europe has a unique climate, its trees show distinct rings of growth each year. Klein entered the precise pattern of the 264 rings on the Sanders panel into his computer, then ran these numbers through a statistical program that looked for a match in his extensive database of European woods. The pattern of rings on the Sanders panel matched the pattern for a Baltic oak tree that first broke through the earth in 1323.

With 1323 as his starting point, he performed a series of simple calculations that would yield the most probable date range within which the Sanders portrait was painted. The first calculation added the 264 years represented by the 264 rings he had counted to the year, 1323, yielding a date of 1586. As a tree grows, it adds a ring each year. The newest rings, on the outside, are called sapwood. They are lighter in colour and contain the biological system that keeps the tree alive. Each year the eldest (innermost) of the sapwood rings turns into dark wood and a new exterior ring is added, so that there are always about a dozen sapwood rings. Klein was well aware that panel makers routinely removed the sapwood, which was susceptible to fungi and insect infestations, until they reached the more solid darker wood underneath. A minimum of nine years of sapwood would have to be removed to create a durable panel like the one he had examined in Ottawa.

Adding nine to 1586, Klein reached the earliest year the tree was felled: 1595. But no self-respecting artisan would work on freshly cut wood. The minimum seasoning time—a period when the wood is left to dry outside—is two years. If the tree were felled in 1595, the earliest possible year for the painting would be 1597. And given that wood was generally seasoned for longer than two years, 1603 began to look just about right.

It is possible that the panel sat around unused much longer.

But, as Klein explains, this rarely happened. "I very seldom find a very large time between creation and felling date—wood was expensive in this time, and panel makers did not have [much] storage room. They used the planks directly. This wood from the Baltic was imported wood, and it was transported by ships. You would have to pay also the transport. . . . It's an economy question." Similarly, it is possible that a later fraud artist trying to create a 1603 picture used an old oak panel from a church or piece of furniture—Klein can only date the wood, not the paint applied to it. But he has yet to encounter a faker who managed to get the wood date right. "Perhaps we find a fake of a fifteenth-century painting, made in the eighteenth century—the faker used wood from the seventeenth century. It's old but not old enough. But of course in the eighteenth century the faker could not tell this."

As a general rule, private owners seeking to authenticate a panel painting in their possession do not like dendrochronology because of its precision. If Klein concludes that a tree was felled in 1595, he will not be out by twenty or thirty years. The growth rings of 1323 to 1586 don't look like any other set of 264 years. "The private owners like [the more subjective] art historian analysis more, because when you process a very famous painting by wood analysis, you can prove that this is *not* a famous painting, and then there is a loss of a lot of money."

A few weeks after Klein completed his analysis, Lloyd Sullivan received his report. "The youngest heartwood ring of the panel was formed out in the year 1586," he wrote on July 1, 1994. "Regarding the sapwood statistic for Eastern Europe, an earliest felling date can be derived with the year 1595. Based on the statistical variation of oak sapwood rings, a felling date is more plausible between 1599 [and] 1605. With a minimum of a 2 years storage time, an earliest creation of the painting is possible from 1597 upwards. Under the assumption of a median of 15 sapwood rings and minimum of a 2 years storage time, a creation is plausible from 1603 upwards." According to the most accurate dating method available, the date on the painted side of the Sanders portrait was not merely plausible, it appeared to be dead-on.

For Lloyd, this was stunning news. "Klein's report was the big thing. That really turned me on. If he had said 1750 or 1850, that would have thrown it all out."

With Klein's report in hand, he went back to talk to the Institute's conservation scientists about the authentication process. Wainwright and Corbeil told him that the next logical step was to X-ray the painting, which would show what, if anything, lay beneath the surface. He already had the illicit hospital X-ray, but the CCI had the facilities to do the test properly. The X-ray could almost instantly reveal any major problem with the paint that had been applied to the board. For it remained distinctly possible that the board was of the right date but the portrait was not. "Okay, so the wood is old," explains Corbeil, "but what if the painter used an old wood panel, or reused the panel later?" Artists have often reused surfaces previously painted on by themselves or others. The portrait of Titus, Rembrandt's son, for example, is painted over another Rembrandt work, one of a Madonna with a cradle. Should a previous painting show up beneath the portrait, it would be, Corbeil says with dry understatement, "a bit suspicious." If the Sanders portrait had been painted over, it would almost certainly join the long list of Shakespeare might-have-beens, just like the Janssen, the Zuccaro and the Ashbourne.

Given that the Institute was not in the business of serving private clients, Lloyd asked if they could recommend a facility that would do the X-ray for him. They could not, for they are the only such lab in the country. Finally, Ian Wainwright, by then the manager of the analytical research lab, decided that they would make an exception to normal practice and do the X-ray themselves. One senses that the scientists had a certain sympathy for Lloyd, an obvious novice doing a lonely job on his own—and that they might have felt a slight prickle of intrigue at the possibility of discovering the face of William Shakespeare.

Accordingly, one morning in September 1995, the radiography specialist Jeremy Powell opened the heavy door of the vault on the second floor of the Institute. The shelves of the vault, lined with boxes and wrapped packages, have held some amazing treasures over the years: rare paintings; antique coins; shards of pottery from the Iron Age; stone sculptures; fragments of ancient cloth; even the eight hands from the Peace Tower clock. Powell lifted down the small, thin, rectangular package wrapped in protective plastic sheeting, then placed it on a four-wheeled trolley.

He wheeled the cart through the quiet corridors of the laboratory building, nodding a quick greeting to scientists who passed, dressed like him with a white lab coat over their street clothes. The large main room of his studio was brightly lit and crowded with tripods and lights and cameras. In the back was a small lead-lined room, empty but for a bulky X-ray machine hovering above a platform. Powell lifted the portrait out of the wrapping and set it down in the centre of the platform.

Powell has done photography and radiography work for the Institute for twenty years. He is also something of a Shakespeare fan and with his wife attends Ontario's Stratford Festival each year. So while fabulous works of art—even the occasional ancient skeleton—regularly wind up in his studio, the Sanders portrait was something special. "When I learned that it was supposed to be Shakespeare, painted while he was alive, at thirty-nine, that piqued my interest a bit," he recalls. As he held the painting in front of him, he paused for a moment to look at the face that stared impishly up at him from the small wooden panel. "I wonder," he mused.

Then he got down to work. He placed the panel on a 1 x 1.5 metre (about 1 x 1½ yard) platform, above which hung a huge gantry holding a Philips industrial X-ray machine. Lying below the portrait on the platform was a black-and-white film plate, measuring 14 x 17 inches, enclosed in a light-tight film holder. Powell lined up the edges of the portrait precisely with those of the plate. "With that picture, there was just the breadth of a hair to the edge of the film," he recalls. If the portrait had been any bigger, he would have had to shoot several images, then knit them together digitally on a computer screen to encompass the whole.

Once he was satisfied with the painting's position, he returned to the shielded control room and closed the lead-lined doors. He pressed a button on the control panel to turn on the voltage generator. For the next sixty seconds, thirty-five kilovolts of X-ray energy passed through the small piece of weathered oak board and the layers of paint that covered it.

Although this X-ray examination was performed under somewhat more stringent, professional conditions than Lloyd's surreptitious hospital trip two years earlier, the principle was the same. Radiography has been used to analyze objects such as paintings since shortly after X-rays were discovered in 1896. And in the same way that a medical X-ray reveals the bones that lie beneath skin, X-rays may reveal a painting's secrets. "It produces an image showing the physical or structural integrity of the painting," Powell explains. "X-rays will document the density and thickness of the materials used to produce the painting. Ideally, they can show the underpaint and often the preparatory work done to achieve the work of art—the things you can't see beneath the paint."

X-rays pass through the paint to the wood or canvas—and each element absorbs different amounts of the radiation, depending on its density, thickness and chemical constituents. Typically, X-rays pass through black pigments; white ones absorb the rays. Similarly, a patient's gums do not show up on a dental X-ray, because X-rays pass through them; the teeth and bone, however, stop the beam and appear white on film. X-rays (instead of light, as in a photograph) are used to expose the film. Powell uses a slower film than that used for a dental X-ray, and he exposes it for a full minute, compared with the tenth of a second in the dentist's chair.

When the minute was up, Powell came back in the room and removed the sheet of film, then carried it next door into a small darkroom. There he diluted developing solution in a five-gallon tank and lowered the exposed film into the warm, slippery bath.

With the help of his sophisticated machine, Powell was about to look through the surface of a painting. It is something he has done many times before, and he has had his share of shocks—once he X-rayed a banal portrait of a woman and found an elaborate landscape painting underneath. Frequently, the radiograph will reveal an artist's change of course during the painting process. "You will see where an eye has been shifted, or, quite often, changes in the position of the hands or fingers, because hands are quite difficult to draw."

Organic materials—canvas, varnish, dyes, woods—are virtually transparent to X-rays. But a radiograph will reveal places where the original paint has been removed and painted over, inevitably using elements with different X-ray-absorbing properties. The radiograph will thus show scratches and infill—when a man with a full head of hair was given a bald dome, for example. It will also show cracks, joins and additions, allowing the specialist to determine how a painting has aged, including the way it has warped or cracked. These ageing characteristics may not be consistent with the picture's reputed vintage: it is problematic if a painting alleged to be four hundred years shows few of the typical signs of ageing. The X-ray can show "garlands" (scalloped marks) from when a piece of canvas was first stretched—and if those are missing on two sides, it could reveal how an original painting was cut and altered.

After the film had sat in the developing bath for just fifteen seconds, Powell began to see an image. First a pair of dark eyes appeared, then the suggestion of hair. Next the curve of a mouth. Finally, a man's face, seen through the grey veil of an X-radiograph. When the developing sequence was complete, he lifted out the film and held it up against the illuminator right above the sink—a light box just like the one a doctor uses. The film held a ghost portrait, pale but clearly present on the film.

"Aha!" Powell almost said it out loud.

In outline and in detail, the radiograph image perfectly matched the painting through which the X-rays had passed.

There was no secret beneath the surface, no sign that it had been altered since it was first painted. There could be no better result for the portrait's second crucial scientific test. If the oak panel dated from 1603 and the paint on the panel was the paint originally applied, the odds were building that the Sanders portrait, whomever it portrayed, had been painted in 1603.

The portrait's story now took a frustrating turn. The scientists conveyed the happy news about the X-ray to Lloyd and told him what came next in the normal course of scientific analysis. But he took his picture home and put it back in the cupboard. He did not take it out again for almost four years. Through those years other family matters absorbed his attention, a great deal of his energy and a considerable amount of his money as well. "And I still didn't realize the potential of the painting," he says with a shake of his head, looking back at a four-year hiatus that seems, in hindsight, quite startling.

In the spring of 1999, he finally took his painting out of its hiding place and made the trek back to the Canadian Conservation Institute. When he got there, he discovered that a few crucial things had changed.

In the latter half of the 1990s the CCI (like many other Canadian cultural institutions) was under pressure created by deep cuts to the federal funding that provided its entire budget. Its directors faced the choice of eliminating some services and laying off staff or, for the first time, performing conservation and scientific work for foreign institutions and private clients. In 1997 the Institute had created a marketing department and a billing office and opened its doors for public business. And instead of the $50,000 estimated cost Lloyd says he was given back in 1993, he was now looking at more like $10,000. That was a price he might be able to afford. Moreover, the Institute would proceed with each phase in the analysis as he came up with money to pay for it.

He understood that each step carried with it the risk that evidence would emerge to cast doubt on the painting's authenticity—or even prove it was a forgery. But by 1999, after almost ten years of false starts and dead ends, Lloyd wanted the whole thing settled. He was not nervous, though he was aware of the possibility of a negative outcome—on his first visit to the CCI, John Taylor had told him a story about how the Institute had proved that an apparent Monet slated to be bought by a museum for huge sums of money was in fact a work by a student of the French impressionist. But the tests would tell him the truth. "I thought, I'm finally going to get an answer, and if it costs me money, I don't care." A decade into his project, Lloyd had moved from curiosity about the painting he inherited to an iron-clad conviction that it was authentic—and authentically Shakespeare.

Now the chemist Marie-Claude Corbeil took charge of the Sanders portrait project. When Corbeil was working toward her doctorate in inorganic chemistry at the Université de Montréal in the late 1980s, she never imagined applying the science to art. "Before I started this job, I had no idea that work like this existed," she says with a laugh. "I knew a little bit about art, I enjoyed going to galleries, but I would not say I knew much more than the average person in the street." But in 1988 the CCI needed a skilled chemist, and Corbeil learned that science could tell a great deal about art. "The main requirement for this job is to be a good scientist: we are doing chemical analysis, and you have to acquire the knowledge of materials, when they were used, their degradation."

Since she began to apply chemistry to art, Corbeil has seen her gallery-going from a new angle. "You find that you like art more, because you see it from a different perspective; you gain an appreciation for how art is made, with the materials—it's not just a beautiful image." Nevertheless, when she looked at the Sanders portrait, she saw specific technical questions. The identity of the sitter was interesting but irrelevant. In 1908 Spielmann suggested the portrait had been altered after it was created, that the doublet was changed and the collar added. He was also certain that the red paint of the date 1603 was added later. He concluded that the portrait was a "relatively modern" copy or fake. Corbeil and her colleagues had a question to answer: was the paint 150 years old, or 400?

The next step in the authentication process meant a return to Jeremy Powell's studio for two more non-destructive tests, types of photography that, like an X-radiograph, reveal different aspects of the painting without in any way harming it. These photographs would allow the scientists to see below the coat of varnish that had been thickly (and erratically) applied to the portrait surface at some point in its life. Varnish, an organic compound, darkens over time as it dries and eventually alters what we see of the colours beneath it.

Powell began with fluorescence, photographs taken using ultraviolet radiation instead of normal light, which may show if a painting has been extensively restored or altered. For this photograph, he used a technical camera; the light, in the otherwise darkened studio, came from four electronic flash-heads to which he had attached exciter filters that alter the wavelength emitted from normal or white light to long-wave ultraviolet radiation.

The molecules in varnish undergo a chemical change as it dries. Old varnish fluoresces—that is, the ultraviolet light is absorbed and a visible blue-green light is emitted. But newer varnish does not fluoresce, nor do unvarnished spots. So retouches, areas not under the older varnish, show up darker. The changes to a painting created in 1600 and modified in 1700 may not show up; those to a painting created in 1600 and modified in 1850 will.

When Powell developed his fluorescent photographs, he had images that looked almost exactly like the portrait itself. "There were no major disturbances or retouches," he says. Spielmann had been refuted on at least one point. The varnish of the Sanders portrait, however old, was of uniform application.

The next set of photographs might reveal any underdrawing or any pentimenti, what one might call a painting's undergarments. The underdrawing is a painter's sketch, often done in charcoal or graphite. Pentimenti are changes a painter makes in the course of creating the work. Pentimenti in carbon-based material would show up as well. To photograph this hidden evidence of the painting's evolution, the image specialist employed a film that can register infrared (electromagnetic radiation of a wavelength of 700 nanometres or more, compared with light visible to humans, which has a wavelength of about 400 to 700 nm). An infrared film registers where the infrared radiation is reflected or absorbed by different parts of an object. Infrared photographs are valuable for art historians because they may reveal the artist's technique. For a scientist looking for fraud, they can reveal how the final painting differs, if at all, from what was first sketched on the panel or canvas.

Carbon is highly absorptive of the infrared radiation; many

types of paint are not. Thus the clarity of an infrared photo will depend on the contrast between the absorptive qualities of the underdrawing and the absorptive qualities of the paint that covers it. A lead white pigment, for instance, absorbs relatively little infrared and would not disguise the underdrawing; an azurite blue absorbs more infrared and might mask what is underneath.

The developed infrared photos also closely matched the portrait. Beneath the paint surface there were neither underdrawing nor pentimenti—at least not in a carbon-based material. Perhaps the person who painted the Sanders portrait, like many painters of the period, did the underdrawing in paint rather than charcoal. (Rembrandt used a thin brown paint to sketch his compositions.) There was also the possibility that an underdrawing was present but obscured by the paint, a possibility further analysis of the paint could rule out. In sum, the infrared photographs proved only that the Sanders portrait did not start out as a charcoal sketch of someone else.

For the third and final non-destructive test, the painting moved from Powell's lair to Corbeil's laboratory, a space that resembles a spiffy high school chemistry classroom: big work tables, biohazard instructions on the walls, lots of microscopes. Her goal was to identify which chemical elements were present in the portrait's paint, and her means of identification was something called radioisotope-excited X-ray energy spectrometry, or REXES. "It's often enough to detect a fake or a modern copy," Corbeil says of the sophisticated but relatively straightforward technique. "On a painting like this, you're going to know there's a problem if you find titanium white, which has been used only since the twentieth century, or any of the cadmium pigments, which have been used since the nineteenth century."

It is complicated stuff, paint. When the painter of the Sanders portrait picked up his palette, the paint he used for the doublet was composed of a binding material (such as oil, glue, wax or egg); filler, to add body, usually a transparent mineral such as chalk, quartz (sand) or gypsum; and, of course, the pigment, which gave the paint its colour. Pigments could be inorganic (crushed lapis lazuli for a rich blue, or cinnabar—mercuric sulphide—for reds) or organic, extracted from plants, animals and insects. In the seventeenth century, a professional painter typically had an apprentice grinding and mixing the paints in only the small quantities that he or she was using at the time. Local materials were cheaper and easier to find than those obtained from trade, so painters preferred them; in a painting from Shakespeare's time, the composition of these materials can suggest its country of origin. English painters normally used abundant calcite, or chalk, for the preparation of their panels, while in Italy, the much more plentiful gypsum was used.

In preparation for spectrometry, Corbeil clipped a small radiation dosimeter on her lapel and slipped another on her finger, like a ring. (Her radiation dosage is checked every month.) From a case marked with the stern three-sided radiation symbol, she took out an X-ray source, a ring made of clear resin and brass and slightly smaller than a hockey puck. This source held a sample of the radioisotope americium-241. She attached this radioactive puck to the REXES X-ray detector, which is equipped with a container of liquid nitrogen to keep the detector cool. Now she was ready to discover exactly what chemical elements were present in the paint, one step in determining what pigments had been used to create the painting's still-vivid colours.

First the chemist used her microscope to select spots on the paint surface—each about fifteen millimetres (0.006 of an inch) in diameter—that together contained all the colours in the painting. Next she moved the source and X-ray detector over the first of the tiny areas of the painting she wished to test. Clicking an icon on the computer screen, she directed it to measure each spot for five minutes.

As the radiation from the americum-241 bombarded a minute area of paint, each chemical element in its pigments sent back a unique, characteristic pattern of X-rays, which were absorbed by the detector. It in turn generated pulses that could be counted by an X-ray spectrometer. Finally, each characteristic X-ray signal in the paint samples emerged in the form of a graph on the computer screen. Then the computer took over, searching a vast database of known chemical elements to match their X-ray patterns with those Corbeil had just recorded. After the five minutes were up, the computer spat out the answer.

Corbeil repeated this process for each of the areas she had chosen. The whole process took a couple of hours.

She found a variety of elements in the pigments on the Sanders portrait, such as lead and mercury, which indicated that lead white and cinnabar (both traditional pigments in use in 1603) were present. She found none that would indicate that the paint contained anachronistic pigments. All chemical elements found were indicative of pigments that were used in 1603.

Corbeil and her colleagues had now gone as far as they could without damaging the painting, however minuscule the damage might be. She knew Lloyd would be pleased that his portrait had passed yet another crucial test, but she now had a tough question to put to him: would he allow her to take a few microscopic samples of paint—to permanently remove them—for further analysis, in order to identify any chemical compounds present? "On a pristine, thinly painted painting, it will show," Corbeil explains. "But on most old paintings, there are cracks and losses. And we try to stick to the edges, or to the cracks. Obviously, we are concerned to limit our intervention." Once she had explained the process and its purpose, Lloyd gave permission to take samples as she needed them. He was increasingly anxious that the testing be as complete as possible.

To perform her delicate operation, Corbeil employed a surgeon's scalpel, a long tungsten needle and a thin set of tweezers. She focused the microscope, which magnifies the painting's surface forty times, on one of her chosen sample spots. With the scalpel she scratched the surface to loosen specks of paint that she could then pick up with the needle or tweezers and place on a welled microscope slide (for safekeeping until the samples were needed). On each of the four slides she made, the specks of paint were barely visible to the naked eye, tinier than grains of sand. In addition to samples scraped off the paint, she took two larger samples, made up of all layers, from the surface varnish down to the wood of the panel. Those samples would be used to look at how the painting was built up from the ground layer to the final layer of paint.

Now the science got trickier. Corbeil used several instrumental techniques to analyze these samples. She employed a method called X-ray diffraction to identify the compounds in the paint. While REXES had showed her the individual elements, the diffraction would allow her to identify specific chemical compounds, provided that their structures were crystalline.

Crystalline compounds are composed of atoms arranged in a repeating three-dimensional pattern, like bricks in a wall. These compounds can diffract X-rays—that is, the rays that hit a sample will bounce off the sample only in specific directions. The directions in which the X-ray beam is diffracted, or angled, and the intensity of the X-ray beam at each angle, are characteristic of a given chemical compound and serve as its fingerprint.

For this analysis Corbeil picked up a small cork, about the size of a pencil-top eraser, with a minute glass fibre embedded in one end. She dipped the exposed end of the fibre into silicon grease, then used the greased fibre to pick up a few particles of one of the samples from its slide. Suspended by this slender thread, the sample was ready for the diffractometer.

Corbeil fixed the fibre and its sample to a rotating stage and aligned the sample into the path of the X-ray beam using a microscope. Then she pushed the start button of the X-ray generator and began collecting data. The analysis of each sample took two hours. A curved detector collected the diffracted X-rays, produced as the sample rotated along three axes simultaneously, and the resulting signal was sent to a multi-channel analyzer. The final result, a diffraction pattern, was matched against the tens of thousands of patterns stored in a database of known crystals. A match identified each specific compound.

Corbeil also examined each paint sample by polarized light microscopy, a method of detecting pigments that might be present in trace amounts in the paint but undetectable by X-ray diffraction. For this test she placed each sample in a liquid mounting medium on a microscope slide and examined it in light transmitted from below and then in polarized light. Pigments have characteristic properties—such as size, shape, homogeneity, colour, transparency and refractive indices—and a single particle is often enough to identify the pigment.

Corbeil could now get a picture of what the artist had on his palette: lead white, charcoal black, red lake, cinnabar and orpiment (an orange-to-lemon-yellow arsenic trisulphide). Mixed in various combinations, those pigments produced the purple-blue of the doublet, the grey of the collar, the delicate white-grey lines that produce the effect of silver embroidery on the doublet and the orange-red of the date. Had she found a pigment not used in 1603, the portrait's claims would have been drastically undermined. For example, a shade called Prussian blue, made with ferric ferrocyanide, was first produced in 1704; a painting that contains this colour could not have been created before that date. All the pigments that Corbeil identified were in use in 1603.

Finally, she turned to the two larger samples, each of which comprised a complete cross-section of the paint from varnish on the top down to the oak board. She suspended these paint specks in a cube of epoxy resin, like ancient insects sealed in amber. Then she ground down one transverse side of the epoxy cube with silicon carbide papers, a delicate operation that involves holding the cube against what looks like a rough-surfaced potter's wheel. When she had ground almost to the middle of the cube where the paint speck lay, she switched to finer carbide paper. Once all layers of the paint speck were fully exposed, she polished the exposed cross-section with cushioned abrasive paper. The whole process took about five hours, producing two microscopic paint cross-sections fixed in cubes each about the size of a piece of Chiclet gum.

Corbeil then examined each of these under a microscope: first under normal light, then under ultraviolet light (a process known as fluorescence microscopy). Normal light would show her the order and colour of the different ground and paint layers that had been applied. (The ground is a layer of opaque paint applied to a panel to provide a suitable colour and texture to draw or paint on.) Fluorescence microscopy would reveal transparent varnish layers that were not visible under normal light. The layer of varnish fluoresced just as it had in Jeremy Powell's ultraviolet photographs. And Corbeil determined that the oak panel was prepared by its painter with a calcium carbonate and glue ground, a preparation typical of the Northern School (a geographic and stylistic grouping of painters from the Netherlands, France, Germany and England, who worked from the late Middle Ages through the Renaissance to the early modern period). The ground layer was covered with a thin layer of lead white and calcium carbonate in oil. The addition of the second thin layer was a practice that began in the sixteenth century. Such a professional preparation suggested a painter who knew what he or she was doing.

By looking at the layers in the sample taken from the date, Corbeil also sought to discover what did, or did not, lie between them. If she saw a layer of varnish between the red paint used for the "AN° 1603" of the date and the dark paint of the background below—if a thin fragment of varnish fluoresced beneath her microscope as the whole varnished surface of the painting had when Powell took his photos using ultraviolet light—she would know that the original painting was varnished before the date was added. Similarly, a tiny layer of dirt or dust between those two layers, visible only beneath her microscope, would indicate the date was added later. But there was no dust between the date and the layer below. The portrait was dated when it was painted. The picture had passed its final test.

Over several months of intermittent work, the scientists at the Canadian Conservation Institute had proved to their satisfaction that the Sanders portrait possessed no chemical or other anomalies that suggested forgery. They had satisfied their scientific curiosity about the Spielmann allegations, categorically refuting his published opinion that the painting was "relatively modern" when he examined it in 1908. In terms of scientific authentication, the Sanders portrait had survived more rigorous analysis than any of the other portrait contenders, including the Chandos, which has been examined only under X-ray and infrared spectrometry.

There was, in their estimation, little else that could be done to test the paint. And normally, the lab's analysis of a painting would end there. But the most controversial aspect of the Sanders portrait is not the paint on the front but the label on the back, which supposedly identifies the subject as Shakespeare. By the time the portrait got to the CCI, the paper was badly damaged—the scientists knew what it said only because it was reproduced in the 1909 Spielmann article. In the past ninety years, large fragments of the label had torn or flaked away. The writing on it, whatever it had once said, was no longer legible. "At first we were not so keen to look at the label," Corbeil says. There was no way of knowing when it was applied—only a minute amount of glue survived, not enough to date it using radiocarbon dating. "But the owner really insisted," she says—so the Institute agreed to do what it could.

First, Gregory Young, a biologist, put a small fragment of the label under his optical microscope to examine the structure of the paper. He was able to identify it as made from linen rag—a type of paper common in 1603—as opposed to tree pulp, which is the basis of most modern paper. The chemist Elizabeth Moffatt examined the glue, using a scalpel to scrape off tiny fragments at the edge of the label, then collected enough of the original adhesive to give her a useful sample. She put that under her microscope and analyzed it by infrared spectroscopy. When a substance absorbs infrared radiation, the bonds between its atoms vibrate with a characteristic frequency, and a characteristic spectrum is produced. The spectrum Moffatt observed indicated that the glue was made from a plant starch—rice or potatoes, perhaps—a finding consistent with the proposed date. (Polymer adhesives, like today's typical white glue, did not come into use until the beginning of the last century.)

Too little of the ink on the label remained to permit any kind of analysis, but there was one last possible test: radiocarbon dating of the linen rag. Having come so far with unbroken success, Lloyd was keen to proceed, accepting with resignation the news that dating just one sample would cost about $1,000. But was there enough of the label left to provide a sample without destroying it?

To answer this question, Marie-Claude Corbeil called Roelf Beukens, an applied nuclear physicist at the IsoTrace Radiocarbon Laboratory at the University of Toronto. Beukens told her that ideally he needed a sample of a hundred milligrams (15.4 grains or .0035 ounces) to get an accurate date reading but said he was willing to try with as little as twenty. Lloyd approved, so Corbeil took her scalpel and began to excise fragments of

The Picture Gallery

THE FOLLOWING PAGES represent the rooms of an imaginary art gallery, whose pictures explore the mystery of the Sanders portrait. They range from Martin Droeshout's engraving for the First Folio—the most familiar and reliable image—to a number of the contenders past and present. They include aspects of the forensic and art historical evidence and portraits of a number of Shakespeare's contemporaries. Together they present the visual case for and the case against the Sanders portrait.

This X-ray photograph of the Sanders portrait, one of the forensic tests performed by Ottawa's Canadian Conservation Institute, was the first solid evidence that the portrait had not been altered since it was first painted.

The four pictures on these two pages make up all the images—with the exception of the Sanders portrait—that have any claim to being Shakespeare. The 1623 engraving by Martin Droeshout (*left*), is the best known and is accepted as authentic. Was it the model for the Flower portrait (*below*)? Or was the Flower the model for the Droeshout? The memorial bust by Geraert Janssen (*inset opposite*), which has marked the playwright's tomb in Holy Trinity Church in Stratford-upon-Avon since it was erected in 1620, is accepted as authentic but condemned as characterless. The Chandos portrait (*opposite*) has many supporters, who attribute it to John Taylor, an artist with links to the Droeshout family. Its detractors point out that the Chandos is so different from the First Folio engraving that it could not portray the same man.

IVDICIO PYLIVM GENIO SOCRATEM, ARTE MARONEM,
TERRA TEGIT, POPVLVS MÆRET, OLYMPVS HABET
STAY PASSENGER, WHY GOEST THOV BY SO FAST,
READ IF THOV CANST, WHOM ENVIOVS DEATH HATH PLAST
WITH IN THIS MONVMENT SHAKSPEARE: WITH WHOME,
QVICK NATVRE DIDE WHOSE NAME, DOTH DECK Y TOMBE,
FAR MORE, THEN COST: SIEH ALL, Y HE HATH WRITT,
LEAVES LIVING ART, BVT PAGE, TO SERVE HIS WITT.

EACH OF THE five portraits on these two pages was at one time believed to depict Shakespeare. Every one of them has since been disqualified.

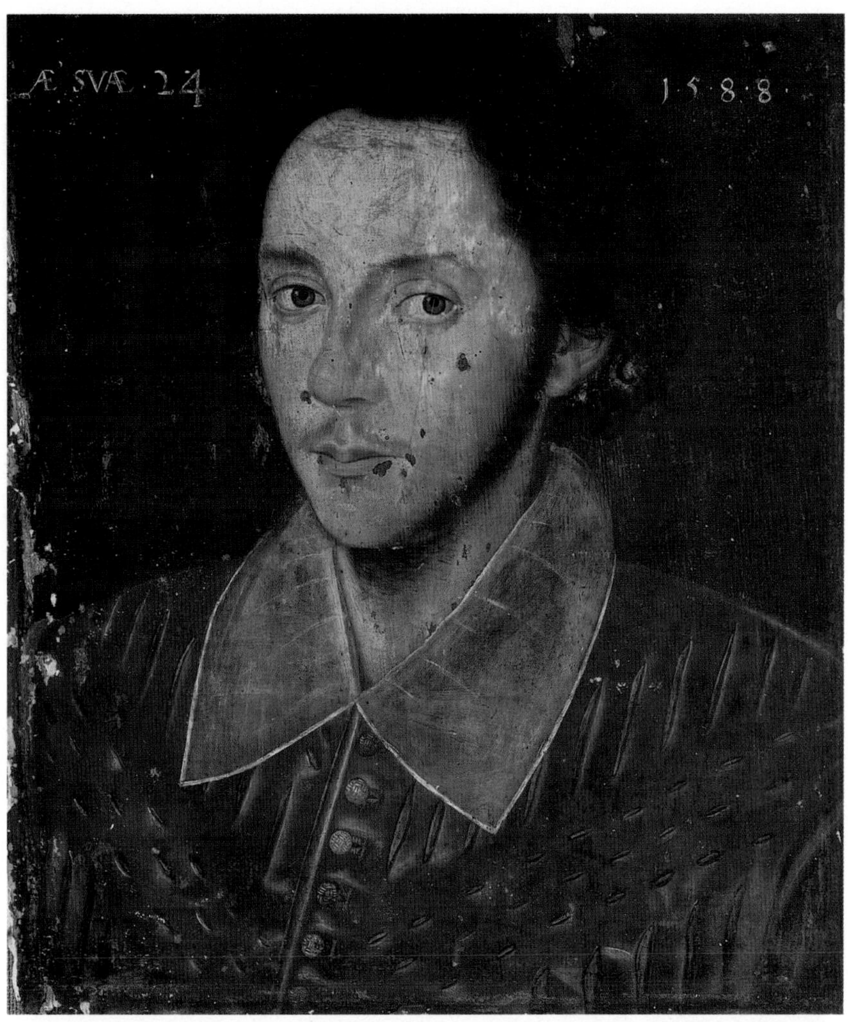

The Felton (*opposite top left*) is a classic example of a portrait altered, in this case by extensive overpainting, to look the way Shakespeare was thought to have looked. The Janssen (*opposite top right*) is another deliberate forgery. The date has been altered and the hairline moved back. (The original is believed to have been a portrait of the poet Sir Thomas Overbury.) The Zuccaro (*opposite middle right*) was believed to be the work of an Italian artist of that name until twentieth-century scholars discovered that Federigo Zuccaro had spent only six months in England in 1575, the year Shakespeare turned eleven. The Ashbourne (*opposite lower right*) fooled many until restoration in the 1970s and 1980s uncovered a coat of arms that identified the sitter as Sir Hugh Hamersley, Lord Mayor of London (*opposite lower left*). Before restoration, the sitter's ear was covered and the dome of the forehead altered to make it look more like the Droeshout engraving. The problem with the Grafton (*above*) is the date. In 1588 Shakespeare was a young man of twenty-four and a complete unknown who could not have afforded these rich clothes, even if he could have paid for the portrait.

VI The Picture Gallery

Each of the portraits on these two pages once laid claim to being Shakespeare. None is taken seriously today. Opposite page (*clockwise from top left*): the Burbage, the Lumley, the Shakespeare, and the Gunther (*in oval*). This page (*clockwise from top left*): the Staunton, the Vroom, and the Chesterfield.

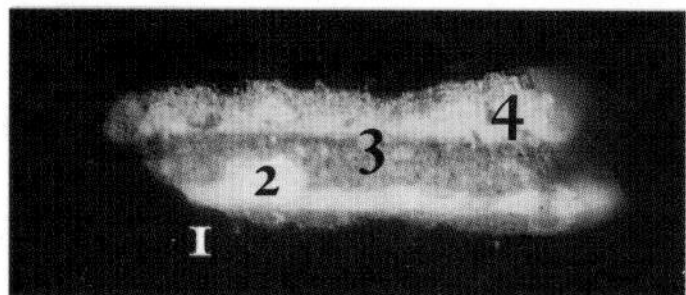

A photomicrograph cross-section of the paint that includes the red of the date (*4*) and the layers beneath (*1,2,3*) reveals neither dust nor varnish between the red and the lower paint layers, proving the date is genuine.

The letter and number forms in the date are correct for 1603 and bear a striking similarity to those in the *Portrait of an Unknown Boy* on p. xiv. (The lighter areas above and below the date were caused by the removal of adhesive tape.)

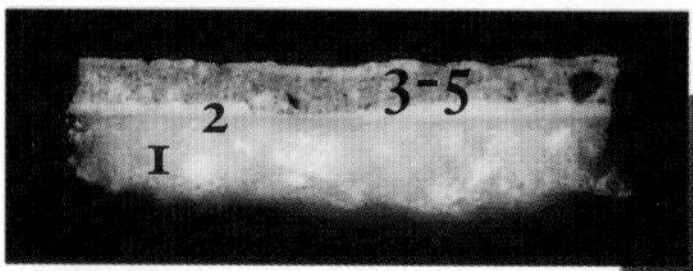

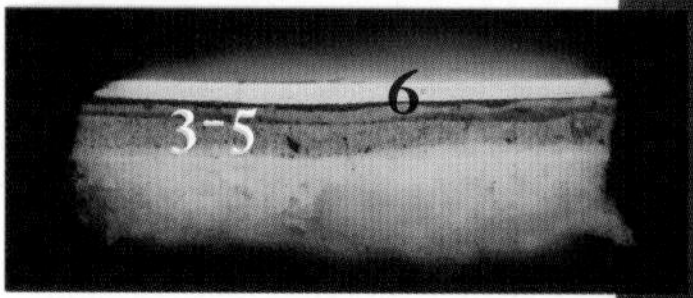

These two photomicrograph cross-sections of paint from the collar—one under reflected light (*top*), the other under ultraviolet light (*above*)—distinguish each separate paint layer: (1) glue ground; (2) white imprimatura; (3-5) grey paint; (6) varnish.

The ragged right edge of the painting has been badly damaged by woodworms. This is where a third wood panel, about 4.1 cm. wide, may have been attached.

Where the collar meets the flesh of the neck shows the differences in handling that suggest the costume and the face were painted by different hands.

The linen rag label is all but illegible to the naked eye, but photographed under ultraviolet-induced flourescence (*right*) some of the words can be made out.

Areas of adhesive tape residue, which correspond to the scratched areas on the painted side, can be seen near the top of the left edge of the back of the panel.

The seam where the two surviving oak boards were glued together.

A second, more modern label reads: "Panel might be enlarged this side about half an inch H.M." Beneath the ink there is a now-unreadable pencil inscription.

Grooves visible around the perimeter were caused by nails once used to hold a frame in place.

A detail of the side of the oak panel shows some of the growth rings Dr. Peter Klein used to date the wood.

X The Picture Gallery

The three portraits on these two pages depict men from Shakespeare's world. The playwright Ben Jonson *(above)*, painted around 1617 by Abraham van Blyenberch, was both friend and rival. The actor Richard Burbage (*right*), possibly painted by Burbage himself, was Shakespeare's friend and business partner. The younger playwright John Fletcher (*opposite*), painted by an unknown artist around 1620, was Shakespeare's protégé, with whom he collaborated on his three final plays.

Unlike courtly pictures, portrait miniatures of the time often communicate considerable personality. These two examples, by the English master of the genre, Isaac Oliver, portray an unknown man (1610) and the artist's wife, Elizabeth Harding (c. 1610).

(*Facing page*) This full-length portrait of Henry Wriothesley, 3rd Earl of Southampton and Shakespeare's patron, exhibits all the characteristics of the classic courtly portraits of the era, which were intended to project the subject's social status, rather than his personality.

Could this *Portrait of an Unknown Boy*, painted by an unknown artist or artists, come from the same source as the Sanders portrait? Only a comparison with the original, whose whereabouts are unknown, might settle the question.

These three pictures, all roughly contemporary with the Sanders portrait, demonstrate quite different motives for having a portrait painted. The 1604 portrait of the twenty-nine-year-old lawyer and antiquarian William Burton (*top left*) is meant to impress us with his ancestry (the coat of arms), his piety (the cartouche with its reminder of mortality), and his intellect (the moralizing motto in Latin). The severe 1588 portrait of the seventy-seven-year-old Lawrence Atwill of Exeter (*top right*) honours a civic benefactor for his service to the city and proclaims his standing as a leading citizen. His robes of office and his gloves denote freeman status within the community. The coat of arms and, possibly, the ring, identify him personally. By contrast, the portrait (*right*) of an unknown twenty-five-year-old *Gentleman of the Terrick Family* (c. 1600) bears an inscription that suggests its intimate purpose.

Ultraviolet-induced colour fluorescence photography allows us to see through the surface of the Sanders portrait to any underdrawing or a charcoal painter's sketch. None exists, and we can look beyond the face to the grained wood surface beneath.

paper from the label, concentrating on the edges and avoiding areas with words. After more than an hour, weighing each fragment as she added it to an aluminum foil container, she had what she needed: a tiny pile of material weighing only forty milligrams. But as Corbeil notes wryly, working as she does with microscopic samples, for her, "Five milligrams is huge." The precious pile of paper was dispatched to the IsoTrace lab.

Because every life form on the planet is carbon based, everything that was ever alive contains traces of carbon-14, one of the four isotopes of carbon. It decays at a half-life of six thousand years—that is, every six thousand years half the carbon-14 disappears. And because carbon-14 decays steadily over time, scientists can compare the amount of carbon-14 present in an object today with the amount of carbon-12 in the same object. (Carbon-12, as a stable isotope, does not decay, so the amount present remains constant.) The IsoTrace laboratory uses this comparison to calculate the age of material—that is, how many years have elapsed since it died. The calculation is easy. The hard part comes with measuring the infinitesimal amounts of the two isotopes present in a small fragment of organic matter—such as forty milligrams of ancient linen rag paper. To accomplish this, the IsoTrace laboratory employs an accelerator mass spectrometer, a machine that accelerates and separates isotopes of elements that differ only slightly in atomic mass. Theirs is the only one in the country and in such high demand that it works twenty-four hours a day, all year long; Lloyd's label got caught up in a backlog of months.

The process is tricky at the best of times, but Beukens is a master. A radiantly intelligent Dutch émigré, he was part of the Canadian and American team that invented this revolutionary carbon-dating technique back in 1977. Before then, radiocarbon dating meant counting the amount of radiation emitted by a quite large sample. The accelerator mass spectrometer, however, by measuring the amount of the isotope present rather than the amount of radiation it emits, made it possible to date small fragments—but usually samples from before about 1500, when the increased burning of fossil fuels began to measurably alter the amount of carbon-14 stored in organic matter. Still, Beukens was ready to have a go at the portrait label. It might just be old enough that he could say something conclusive about it.

Beukens always assumes a sample has been contaminated with carbon that is not part of the original material. Something as seemingly harmless as a human fingerprint can throw off his measurement, and much of his work is in the chemistry to clean the sample. Cleaning the label fragments took four days; he washed the sample with an acid bleach that oxidized potential contaminants but left the cellulose—the glucose units that make up the cell walls of plants—intact. (Alone among organic substances, cellulose does not oxidize.)

Beukens found the portrait's history intriguing, even given the exotic nature of his work. When he first went into nuclear physics, he spent his days with neutrons and ions and other subatomic particles. But these days he is called on to date whale skeletons, Viking dwellings and often art. "Physics was more interesting, but this is a lot more fun," he says with a chuckle. Frequently, there is a lineup of archaeologists in the lab waiting for a date to flash up on the spectrometer, placing bets on the age of artifacts they dug up.

When the acid bleaching was finished, the physicist was left with 250 micrograms of cellulose, a tiny percentage of the weight of the original pile of fragments Marie-Claude Corbeil had so patiently excised from the label. He now combusted the cellulose until the heat yielded a small graphite disc, and this he placed inside a tube in the accelerator. The isotopes were excited and counted—the carbon-14 to carbon-12 comparison was made in eight different spots on the disc, ten different times. Then Beukens, a man who puts a premium on precision, ran the eighty calculations a second time.

When his report finally arrived, it was stunning: the linen rag paper was dateable to between 1475 and 1640.

On August 15, 2000, a decade after Lloyd Sullivan had first set his mind to doing something with the picture his family called Willy Shake, the CCI delivered its formal report. "The materials and techniques of the panel painting known as the Sanders Portrait of William Shakespeare are consistent with the date of 1603 painted in the top right corner, as is the dating of the wood panel on which it is painted. . . . The dating of the paper label glued to the back of the panel, which identifies Shakespeare as the subject of the painting, indicates that the label was probably applied to the panel between the time it was painted and about forty years later, assuming the painting was executed in 1603."

Looking back, Marie-Claude Corbeil emphasizes the neutral nature of the Institute's work: "The materials in the paint are consistent with 1603, although that way of painting lasted a century, and you have no way of getting a precise date. The panel is the right period, the materials are consistent, the paper is from a broad range of dates, but old. If you take everything together, you have a painting that's old; that's all I'm saying." She says it with a wry smile. "For me, the attribution of the painting isn't CCI business, and even less determining who is the subject of a painting—for me that's so out of reach. I have no expertise in that." But working with Lloyd, who was so passionately interested in his painting, made it more than just a standard series of tests. "I was just very pleased that it turned out to be a legitimate painting. It was nice to work with somebody who is serious about the project and where the results will be helpful."

The report left Lloyd jubilant: as far as he was concerned, the picture was real. The science proved the date, and the label and his family story proved the subject. In truth, there were still questions with the label, because a fraud artist could have found a piece of seventeenth-century paper—torn out of an old book, perhaps—and affixed it to the back of the portrait. But that did not trouble him. If Beukens could have dated the original glue, that would have proved when it was attached to the painting, for such organic glues were used immediately after they were concocted. The date of the ink, too, would have helped. But neither of these substances survived in sufficient quantity to be tested with existing technology.

But there was something else, something far more important, that the scientists could not assess: the painting as a work of art. Despite everything he had done, Lloyd had not yet pursued the one avenue of authentication that most old paintings automatically undergo—an intensive examination by an art historian who is expert in paintings of the relevant period. In part, his reluctance to do so stemmed from the fact that the CCI tests had put a large hole in his retirement savings. To be fair, he was unaware of the value of such an examination. Lloyd's experiences of the high-art world had been discouraging, with the sole exception of Lord Crichton-Stuart's positive assessment all those years ago. He failed to see how some professor from an ivory tower could look at his painting and tell him anything conclusive. He was understandably wary of art "experts." Why, just look at Marion Henry Spielmann: when that noted art authority saw the portrait in 1908, he judged that parts of it were "no more than fifty years old." But the scientists at the Canadian Conservation Institute had proved Spielmann completely wrong: the Sanders portrait had been more than three hundred years old when Spielmann examined it.

Armed with the CCI findings, Lloyd began to seriously contemplate the sale of the Sanders portrait. Clearly, it could no longer remain tucked away in a cupboard. He had a report solid enough to satisfy the most skeptical buyer, he was sure. He and his lawyer friend, Ray, began to work evenings and weekends putting together a portfolio that would lay out the painting's history, detail its provenance, and compare it—with triumphant effect—to all the other Shakespeare portraits.

But those other claimants, it has become increasingly apparent, belong to a different world from the Sanders picture. Despite Lloyd's reservations about turning to scholars outside the precincts of science, only experts in history and art could finish what the forensic investigation had begun: first by evaluating the portrait in terms of the social realities of late-Elizabethan England; second by analyzing it closely with the trained eye of an art historian specializing in the English portraiture of Shakespeare's time. These two types of analysis would be the portrait's final tests.

An Actor's Face? The Sanders Portrait in Context

Robert Tittler

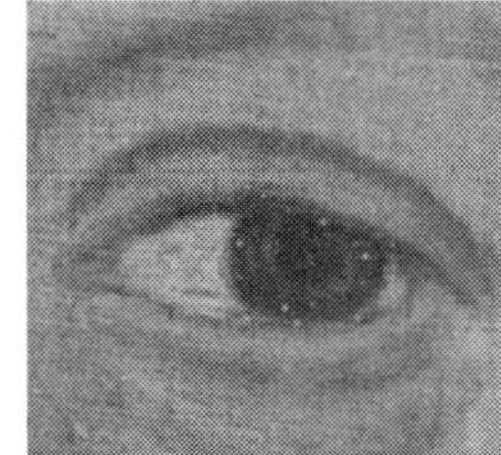

EVEN FOR THOSE who are more than casually acquainted with portraits of the English Renaissance, the Sanders portrait presents a puzzling picture. Observing few of the conventions that apply to most of the familiar portraits of its era, and unlike what we would find in major museum holdings of Renaissance painting, it raises a number of questions. What sort of painting is the Sanders portrait? Who might have commissioned it, and what sort of painter might have painted it? Where might it have been done, and for what reasons? How can we "read" a portrait that has so few of the standard elements of English Renaissance portraiture?

To understand what the Sanders portrait is, we must first determine what it is not and how it differs from most others of its time. The familiar portraits of the era depict royalty or members of the landed and gentle classes. Taken together, these form a corpus of paintings which, for the sake of convenience, and regardless of their stylistic attributes, we might call "courtly portraits." As statements of the sitter's identity, these portraits were almost invariably intended to serve as talismans of social and political status. As the eminent social and cultural historian

Lawrence Stone once reminded us, "Noblemen and gentlemen wanted above all formal family portraits, which take their place along with genealogical trees and sumptuous tombs as symptoms of the frenzied status-seeking and ancestor worship of the age. What sitters demanded was evidence of a sitter's position and wealth by opulence of dress, ornament and background."[1]

Courtly portraits commonly fulfil these functions by providing visual clues to the identity of the sitter, his or her status and even some information about the occasion or reason for the portrait. Inscriptions often convey personal mottoes, years of death and ages at death, and other critical bits of information. Coats of arms proclaim social status and reveal identity and lineage. Iconographic devices, worn by the subject or held in the hand, offer a wide range of clues. Such devices included scrolls that indicate the receipt of grants of land or title; skulls that suggest the transitory nature of life ("*in memento mori*") and perhaps the piety of the sitter; arms and armour that refer to knighthood or other chivalric associations; and items of jewellery or clothing that denote social—or in the case of chains of office, political—standing. Background scenes also prove enormously revealing. From the Armada ships in the famous, if anonymous, portrait of Elizabeth commemorating her forces' victory over the Spanish fleet in 1588 to the use of furnishings, classical columns or landscape in the more general run of courtly portraits, they allow us to know how the subject fits into his or her world.

Painters of courtly portraits conventionally used these devices often enough for them to become a familiar vocabulary. This vocabulary allows us—as it was meant to allow contemporaries—to "read" a portrait and thus learn the identity, status and accomplishments of the sitter. Courtly portraits were usually hung and displayed in such quasi-public venues as the long galleries and halls of country houses, precisely so that visitors could easily see and understand them.

The Welbeck Abbey portrait of Shakespeare's patron, Henry Wriothesley, the 3rd Earl of Southampton (see page xiii of "The Picture Gallery") illustrates this function quite well. The Earl poses in knightly attire, armour at the ready, sword in his scabbard and ornate helmet resting on a pedestal. While these objects suggest his military prowess, the elegantly turned out clothing, rich drapery and polished flooring speak to his social station and affluence.

There is another way we "read" courtly portraits: by identifying familiar elements of artistic style. The use of shading, perspective, brushstrokes, colour and even props and background scenes all provide clues to their genesis. Even when pictures remain unsigned and unattributed, these elements often allow us to feel we know who might have painted them, or at least in what tradition or school the painter may have worked. Faced with an unfamiliar painting, we instinctively turn to our mental checklist of these painterly characteristics and to the traditions of portraiture in which most of the known artists of this era (around 1603 still mostly Dutch, Flemish, French or Italian) had been trained, in an effort to assign attribution. When we undertake this exercise, we tend to assume that most portraits of any quality produced at this time probably came from one of a quite small number of known painters or their workshops. We may also assume that these men worked in and around London, though they accepted commissions from the courtly sorts of people in other parts of the realm. We know for certain that many of these professional artists were related to one another through marriage or kinship or training, or sometimes in several ways.

But when we try to read the Sanders portrait, we are stumped. Save for the date of 1603 in the upper-right-hand corner, we search in vain for a familiar visual vocabulary, the usual courtly attributes, the conventional painterly markers, that we count on to identify the subject or artist. The figure, or what we can see of it in this head-and-shoulders-only view, is stylishly dressed in a doublet, as was clearly appropriate for that time. But he has no distinctive symbolic or identifying features: no hands to hold symbolic items like gloves or swords, no jewellery or anything else of the sort. Nor does the background help us: the monochromatic deep umber pointedly (and perhaps even provocatively!) denies us any of the usual sort of clues or context for the sitter's identity or social context. We find no motto, no arms, no material to indicate status, occupation, genealogy or any other familiar signs or symbols that might allow us to interpret the scene. The linen label on the back of the panel purportedly identifying the sitter as Shakespeare speaks unambiguously enough and has been verified as deriving from this era. Yet it may have been added at any time after the completion of the painting. More to the point, it is not part of the work we are trying to interpret.

Not only is the Sanders painting unsigned, which was not unusual in itself, but none of its visual elements provide an obvious match with that mental checklist of stylistic traits of the known portrait painters of the era. This is all the more vexing because of the considerable degree of skill with which particular elements of the portrait have been rendered. Colours have been mixed patiently and expertly, the collar and embroidery have been worked with obvious care and attention to detail. The intriguingly emotional content of the face can hardly have been captured by a backroom dabbler whiling away a rainy afternoon.

The lack of courtly vocabulary or familiar stylistic markers pretty well rules out the conventional social motives that Stone described for the courtly portraits of this time. The painting thus sets its subject apart from any of the sort of people—royalty, the landed gentry, the court circle and so forth—whom we typically think of as subjects for portraits in Shakespeare's time. We are left to wonder what type of painting this is and how to find the key to its visual vocabulary. If it is not a courtly portrait, what kind of a portrait is it? How and by whom might it have come to be painted? Once we abandon our efforts to fit the Sanders painting into known but apparently inappropriate categories, we begin to see it for what it is: a vernacular work rather than an example of any particular formal or polite style, and the painting of a man who seems not to belong to the usual courtly elite. This perspective allows us to recognize it as a clearly competent work from a distinct and relatively unfamiliar tradition, thus one of a type far less familiar to us.

We seldom see these non-courtly portraits in our major art museums, although we might find a few in our folk or local history museums. Even fewer appear as reproductions in books or for sale in museum gift shops. We search almost entirely in vain for much discussion of such pictures in the standard textbooks of Art History 101, or in the canonical accounts of English portraiture itself. One might very easily assume that there were no non-courtly portraits, especially paintings of this quality, and that there was no particular urge to paint or possess paintings of the lesser or middling sorts of people in Shakespeare's era.

But these assumptions prove entirely erroneous, and most art historians specializing in this era know better than to insist on them. Though their aesthetic standards seldom come up to museum quality or attract the professional interest of the connoisseur or academic art historian, non-courtly portraits abounded in Shakespeare's England and had done so for at least a generation before the 1603 date of the Sanders painting. They were commissioned and collected by family members, friends and institutions. Their subjects included women as well as men and, very occasionally, even small groups. They were painted by people running the gamut from the famous to the anonymous.

Today such paintings tend to be hidden away in private collections. In London we find them still hanging in livery company halls and in the Inns of Court. We may find them displayed alongside more modern portraits in town halls or guildhalls throughout the realm. Their wide geographic distribution makes an interesting parallel to what the University of Toronto's Records of Early English Drama research project has taught us about the performance of plays and other dramatic activities in the same era. Much of the portraiture of the age, like much of its dramatic activity, lies outside the ranks of the formal, "polite," familiar and London based. Such works often remain, to put it another way, where we have not looked for them.

This vernacular, non-courtly tradition, displayed in places far removed from the conventional temples of art, provides us with an entirely more appropriate context for the Sanders portrait. While looking more closely at paintings like these will not tell us whether the Sanders sitter is William Shakespeare, it may at least suggest how and why its subject might have come to be painted, in what circumstances and by what sort of hand.

In contrast to many continental traditions, where non-courtly portraits appear on the scene at a much earlier time, non-courtly easel portraits begin to appear in England in the reign of Henry VIII (d. 1547). We find them among the early commissions that foreign-born artists, like Hans Holbein the Younger, were able to obtain in the 1520s and 1530s as they awaited steadier and more lucrative patronage from the "better sort" of people. We find them thereafter in the concentric circles of landed society that rippled outward, over a few decades' time, from the court itself and then from London as well.

And it seems not to have taken long at all for the idea of portrait painting to have spread to wider social as well as geographic circles. In what is conventionally considered the first known autobiography of an Englishman, Thomas Whythorne describes how, as a twenty- or twenty-one-year-old Oxford dropout working as a music tutor in London, he visited a portrait painter's workshop around the year 1549. Whythorne saw in that workshop numerous portraits in various stages of completion, and then he ordered one to be done of himself![2] Even if all the other paintings in the room were of courtly figures—Whythorne fails to identify either the painter or his other subjects—at least his own portrait, the first of four he would have done of himself by 1569, surely was not.

The scarcity of surviving examples would suggest that the production of non-courtly portraiture moved along slowly in the 1560s and 1570s but picked up steam steadily thereafter, both in London and elsewhere. Such pictures appear in several settings and with several sources of patronage. Towns and cities, many just then coming into their own as incorporated and politically autonomous entities, frequently commissioned portraits of notable citizens or benefactors as visual reminders of their own particular civic traditions. The resulting paintings, of mayors, aldermen, patrons and civic benefactors, were displayed and employed to enhance a sense of local pride and identity, and therefore also of deference to those who ruled in those communities.

We now know that at least fifteen provincial towns and cities, widely dispersed throughout the realm, had civic portraits painted or purchased before 1640 and hung in such places as town halls and endowed schools and hospitals. Nearly all these survive to the present day. Numbers range from one portrait each in, for example, Bury St. Edmunds, Leicester, Lichfield, Reading, Southampton and Winchester, to as many as twelve in Gloucester and no less than nineteen in Norwich.[3]

At roughly the same time as these civic portraits began to appear in provincial towns, some university colleges, public schools and London livery companies followed suit. At least forty livery company masters and benefactors are known to have been painted by the opening decades of the seventeenth century so that their portraits could be displayed in company halls.[4] Many of them remain there today. In addition, we have a variety of portraits of government officials, leading clerics and so forth, all of whom hovered on the edges of courtly society and whose portraits fit somewhere between civic and courtly traditions. Perhaps more to the point, there are even surviving portraits—though not necessarily easel portraits—of actors done in the same era: of Richard Tarlton (d. 1588), Edward Alleyn (d. 1626), Richard

Burbage (d. 1619; see page xi of "The Picture Gallery"); John Fletcher (d. 1625; see page x of "The Picture Gallery"); and John Lowin (d. 1659), though these men were well enough known in the London scene to have been part of the more formal portrait traditions of London painters.[5]

When portraits were intended for display in civic institutions, they would often have included identifying devices similar in function to those of their courtly counterparts—inscriptions, arms and the like—though the nature of those symbols may naturally have varied from one painting to another. These portraits served to honour the individual sitter, to be sure, but they were also consciously intended to honour the institution that would have commissioned or purchased them and also to have encouraged loyalty, deference or philanthropic instincts in those who viewed them.

As the civic observer John Earle put it in 1628, referring to the figure of a London alderman: "He is venerable in his gowne . . . wherein he setts not forth his owne so much as the face of a City. . . . His scarlet gowne is a monument, and lasts from generation to generation."[6] Therefore, we frequently find, in addition to personal arms or mottoes or inscriptions that identify the sitter directly, signs and symbols of that association. Mayors do indeed have gowns, as well as chains of office and sometimes references to maces or other implements symbolizing their authority. Philanthropists are often depicted holding a charter for the institution they may have founded. The subject's coat of arms, if any, frequently came to be coupled with those of the institution. In other cases, as with the very solemn portrait of the Exeter benefactor Lawrence Atwill (see page xv of "The Picture Gallery") painted in 1588, when he was seventy-seven, the coat of arms is matched with a distinctive robe indicating office or professional occupation and gloves to denote gentility and/or membership in the local freemanry, those who belonged to a guild and so had full economic rights in the community.

Not only can we be sure that civic institutions could commission and display portraits of their officials and benefactors during this era, but there can also be little doubt that individual people of at least middling ranks both served as the subjects of portraits and had come to own and collect paintings, including portraits, by the turn of the seventeenth century. The historian of Tudor portraiture Susan Foister established this last point some twenty years ago in her systematic examination of inventories post-mortem of private, largely non-courtly, individuals from this era.[7] An equally vivid—if less precise—attestation to this tendency may be noted in the play by Shakespeare's contemporary Thomas Heywood, *If You Know Not Me, You Know No Body*. In Part Two of the play, Heywood has the figure of Alexander Nowell, Dean of St. Paul's, show off the picture gallery in his London house to four of his friends. Nowell introduces the company to his collection ("A Gallery, wherin I keepe the pictures / Of many charitable citizens / That have fully satisfied your bodies / You may by them learn to refresh your soules"), and we learn that the subjects of the paintings were not courtly figures but Londoners: Sir John Filpot, Sir Richard Whittington, Sir John Allen, Agnes Foster and Anne Gibson, citizens and benefactors all.

Visual devices were similarly employed in paintings intended for family or domestic display, especially in great ancestral homes and the country houses of Professor Stone's socially competitive landed classes. Yet in a painting commissioned of oneself, or of a close friend or relative, such devices could well have seemed superfluous and would also have added to the cost of the work.

Young Thomas Whythorne's first commission of a painting of himself was meant as a companion piece to the portrait of a widow with whom he was then enamoured. Though neither portrait has survived, it is highly unlikely that Whythorne would have required an inscription or much in the way of props or furnishings in order to identify the subject. His social standing at the time would obviously have precluded a show of weapons, though (like Shakespeare) he would eventually acquire a coat of arms, and he included that device in the last of his four portraits. His own feelings about the value of having such portraits—which he sometimes referred to, in the usage of the day, as "counterfeits"—supports this idea. "Divers do cause their counterfeits to be made to see how time doth alter them from time to time," he tells us, "so thereby they may consider with themselves how they ought to alter their conditions." Whythorne proceeds to tell us that there was one more reason to have a portrait done, "the which is to leave with their friends, especially with their children. . . ."[8] Both of those sentiments inform us quite candidly of the personal motives for portraiture among at least some of the respectable, middling sorts of people of this era.

Such private portraits, done at the request of the sitter or of his family or friends and kept in homes, are much more difficult to track down than their courtly or institutional cousins. Access to them depends on the generosity of the owners as well as the time and resources of the would-be viewer. They are less likely to have survived than those done for the more stable environment of an enduring social or political institution. Paintings that pass from generation to generation of the same family, possibly as its members migrate from one area or continent to another, have a habit of getting lost or damaged or even discarded. Certainly they are less likely to be publicly displayed or reproduced commercially. Yet from Thomas Whythorne's time through William Shakespeare's and far beyond, family and personal portraits were indeed painted, and many of them have been preserved.

While some of these paintings, especially those of London figures, may have been the work of known painters, and painted in the formal and polite styles of the day, many others are vernacular and often more primitive in style and, being unsigned, remain anonymous. And if not all portraits of the age by any means were of courtly sitters, neither were their creators necessarily drawn from the ranks of professional painters known to have been working in London at that time. A considerable number seem to have been painted by less than full-time professionals—"picture painters," "picture-makers" or "limners," in the parlance of the day—but rather by craftsmen-painters, men and perhaps some women who might have painted fabrics, furniture, inn signs and other such objects as often as they did portraits.

Many, like Whythorne's painter of "old acquaintance," will remain anonymous. Some will have been London based, especially those of the second rank, who travelled widely, as did the English-born but foreign-trained Cornelius Johnson (also called Cornelis Janssen) from the late 1610s, for commissions wherever they could find them.[9] Foreign painters also came through England as itinerant artists, painting sitters wherever they received a commission to do so. Thus we read of "the Dutch painter" who painted two portraits of the Bristol merchant and official Nicholas Thorne around 1624,[10] and of similar references elsewhere. But there do indeed seem to be locally based portrait painters, and undoubtedly an even greater number of craftsmen-painters, working steadily in several of the provincial urban centres at this time, and we must assume that they also produced a considerable share of the non-courtly portraits outside London.

The twelve rather crude surviving portraits of Gloucester worthies, done sometime toward the very end of the sixteenth century and now to be found, with one exception, in the Gloucester City Folk Museum, fall into the general category of civic portraiture displaying civic iconography and do suggest a tradition of local painters. They seem clearly to have been painted by the same hand, though we will probably never know whose hand that was.[11] The nineteen much finer portraits done of Norwich officials and benefactors, prior to the year of Shakespeare's death in 1616, may or may not be by the same hand, but they surely do testify to a vigorous tradition of local portraiture in these years.[12] We know too that the Oxford/Abingdon area, including Oxford University, seems to have been served by the little-known Sampson Strong between about 1595 and 1605.[13] The Chichester area seems to have been the territory of three generations of painters of the Lambert family, though only one of Lambert's paintings have survived,[14] and a Christopher Carter seems to have been active in and around Leicester in the early seventeenth century.[15]

Nor should we assume that the subjects of portraits, including the subject of the Sanders painting, necessarily sat for their portraits. Queen Elizabeth herself is known to have sat for only a single portrait, a pencil sketch by the Italian Federigo Zuccaro in 1575, during her long and copiously illustrated reign. Many civic portraits were painted of civic worthies long deceased, for whom there could not possibly have been an accurate basis on which to establish a true likeness.

These observations about non-courtly portraiture in and around Shakespeare's lifetime provide a context for understanding the Sanders portraits in several respects. They establish that a widespread tradition of non-courtly portraiture flourished in England from the middle of the sixteenth century if not before, and that such a tradition included portraits of various occupational and social groups of what contemporaries would have known collectively as "the middling sorts of people." They establish that such traditions of non-courtly portraiture existed well beyond the boundaries of the London metropolitan area, even extending to certain urban areas being served regularly by some painters who may well have been resident in those towns. They indicate something of the range of artists—professionals and others, Londoners and others—who may have painted such works. They remind us too that we have many works that cannot be attributed to a specific painter, and that we also know of some painters to whom there are no surviving works that we may attribute. And they suggest that the subject did not necessarily sit for his or her portrait or indeed might not always have been aware of its existence.

So this foray into the little known but surprisingly robust world of non-courtly portraiture in Shakespeare's time provides a true context in which to consider the person who looks out at us from the Sanders painting. Now we can ask how this particular painting fits into these particular circumstances. For our answer, we must try to read the actual text implicit in the painting. In so doing, there are several things to consider.

For one, as I have noted, both courtly and many non-courtly portraits of this era tended to identify their subjects by the use of symbolic props and other devices. In the Sanders portrait, save for the date in the upper-right-hand corner, such devices seem to be absent. Yet non-courtly portraits, painted for the sitter or for close associates, or for the intimate gaze of close friends or families, often lack such devices. Indeed, in such close and familiar company, and especially if the portrait had been intended for display in restricted circumstances, such bona fides would hardly have been necessary.

And it is indeed likely that a painting of this modest size (42.3 x 33.0 cm, or 16½ x 13 inches) would not have been intended for the grand dimensions of a long gallery or grand parlour of the contemporary country house. A person close enough to the subject so as not to need symbolic devices to identify him or her would most likely have hung such a painting in a smaller and more private space: perhaps the parlour where the family would take its own meals, or the bedchamber. Susan Foister's study of inventories post-mortem does indeed suggest that many paintings were hung in smaller and more intimate rooms. It seems reasonable to assume that this would have been true of the Sanders portrait as well.

Facial expressions on contemporary portraits rarely convey the sort of emotional content that we find so strikingly here. Courtly portraits most often display the sort of exaggerated and—to our own eyes, strained—dignity that their sitters considered essential to proclaiming their social standing. Civic portraits almost always convey a weightiness and solemnity, what a contemporary observer termed "a sadd and wise manner," that was associated with the burdens of civic office. They usually come across to us as deeply solemn and even pained in appearance.

Only in portrait miniatures may we readily expect to find a more intimate, relaxed, emotionally candid visage: precisely the sort of face presented in the Sanders portrait. And these tiny paintings, frequently enclosed by a cover, worn around the neck or kept in the more private spaces of the household rather than hung for display, were meant, just as the Sanders seems to have been meant, for the private gaze of the close acquaintance. Rarely do they show, or have room to show, much in the way of symbols; almost never do they include arms or inscriptions. Only in the work of accomplished miniaturists like Isaac Oliver (d. 1617), or sometimes his teacher Nicholas Hilliard (d. 1619), do we find quite the candour and expressive quality of the portrait at hand. The lovely and very expressive miniature of Oliver's wife, Elizabeth, done sometime between 1610 and 1615, is an excellent example.

In the intriguing absence of any of the conventional props or objects that were a part of most portraits of the time, one looks carefully for any additional clues that might help us identify the subject of this painting. Though the first reading of the painting yields nothing of this sort, a long second look does turn up an intriguing possibility. Perhaps there is one prop, after all, that has simply not been perceived as such: it is the face itself.

The Sanders portrait stands out from the very large majority of contemporary works, courtly and non-courtly alike, precisely for its emotional expressiveness, a look that Stephanie Nolen in her first *Globe and Mail* article described as "mischievous, keen-eyed, almost flirtatious." In its sly smile and deviously captivating expression, it may well be, and may well have been intended to be read as, an actor's face.

A Painting with a Past— Locating the Artist and the Sitter

Tarnya Cooper

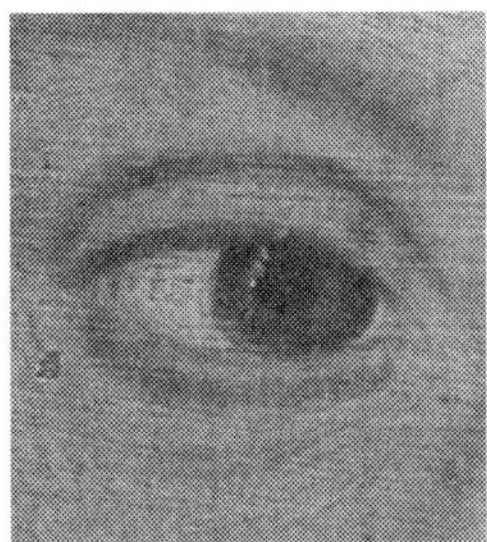

SCIENTISTS CAN ONLY go so far in helping us to understand the Sanders portrait. They can analyze the materials it is made of and prove that these correspond to the correct date and have not been altered since they were assembled. But scientists can tell us little, if anything, about the man in the picture or the person who painted him. They cannot consider the painting in terms of the values of the era when it was created or how it reflects and refracts its world. This kind of analysis is the province of the art historian, for whom a portrait can offer the potential of a window into past lives.

My first meeting with the Sanders portrait took place at the Art Gallery of Ontario only a few hours after my arrival in Toronto from England in early February 2002. After unfolding the tissue paper in which it was wrapped, I encountered a portrait of a young man with an unassuming yet enigmatic expression. My first response was of curiosity and surprise. The sitter's face was life-size and appeared to fill the frame in a way I hadn't quite expected from the colour photograph I had seen before my visit. Parts of the portrait were also beautifully painted and handled with a delicacy that could have been achieved only by a trained and practised painter, but the paint was obscured by a film of poorly applied, yellowed varnish that would require me to make educated guesses about the true colours. I was relieved to note that the quality of the brushwork and the manner in which the artist had portrayed the subject agreed with what we know about artistic practice in this period, and accorded with the date 1603 painted at the top right of the picture.[1]

Over the course of the next six hours, I considered the Sanders portrait not simply in terms of the artist's technique in relation to the artistic conventions of Shakespeare's time, but also the physical evidence provided by the condition of the paint and the state of the oak panel. All objects have a story to tell, but in the case of one so old and of unproved provenance, how can we discover it? Was the past life of the Sanders portrait, I wondered, written in a language of dents, abrasions, paint losses and missing pieces?

Close inspection of the two pieces of wood that make up the present panel, which now measures 42.3 by 33.0 cm (16 1/2 by 13 inches), suggests that a third piece is missing, a vertical plank that would have increased the total size of the painting by about 4.1 cm (1 2/3 inches) along the right-hand side. Part of the evidence for this consists of the fact that the bevelled edge visible on the back of the panel is narrower along the damaged side, suggesting that the damaged edge was bevelled at a different time from the other three. (Deep channels and holes visible all along the damaged edge are the vestiges of severe woodworm attack.) This loss is most evident when we consider the front of the painting (see page viii of "The Picture Gallery"), the composition of which now seems lopsided: the sitter's left shoulder and sleeve are missing. If this were the intended placement of the sitter, it would be highly unconventional. Portraits of this period consistently place the subject in the middle of the frame. Undoubtedly the woodworm damage caused the now-missing piece to loosen, become detached and ultimately misplaced.

The majority of sixteenth- and seventeenth-century portraits painted on wooden panels have since perished; many of those that survive are in worse condition than the Sanders panel. Despite the yellowed coat of varnish, the actual paint surface of the portrait has suffered no more than many surviving portraits of the period, if, unsurprisingly, it has been damaged over the years by rough handling. Examination of the paint surface under ultraviolet light revealed clear evidence of small areas of crude retouching applied in red paint to the brown background (probably executed sometime since the mid-nineteenth century). Dents, scratches and abrasions to the surface have caused such minor paint loss in many places, in some cases right down to the wood panel, in others down to the calcium carbonate ground. A poorly fitting frame has caused further abrasion and minor paint loss around all four sides of the painting, indicating that it has been framed at least once since the missing piece was lost. The three large holes on the panel just above the head of the sitter are likely the result of nails forced from behind to secure the panel to an old frame. Once the nails were removed, the weakened areas would have disintegrated, leaving the gaps we see today.

Among the most puzzling features of the painting's current physical condition are two areas of small scratches into the varnish at the top right edge of the panel. The scratches appear to be the result of determined scraping by someone intent on removing something from the painted surface. But what, exactly? On the back of the panel there are remnants of adhesive tape that correspond to these scratched areas on the front. It seems likely that these areas resulted from a determined attempt to remove the tape residue from the painted surface. Therefore the adhesive tape may have been used to secure the loose and now-missing piece of the panel in an attempt to hold it in place.[2]

I next turned my attention to the rest of the back of the panel. Here there were a number of other nail marks, or gouges, near the perimeter, evidence the painting has been reframed several times over the past four hundred years. (The nails would have been driven into the inside edge of the frame and bent back to secure the panel, causing severe stress on the wood.) The old label identifying the sitter as Shakespeare was now nearly illegible, even under magnification, but it was clear that the handwriting dated from a later period than the painting and partially obscured another, presumably earlier, hand.[3] (See "The Conundrum of the Label," page 274, for an analysis of the label by the Records of Early English Drama project.)

But what can we make of the work itself? Despite the yellowed varnish masking its true colours, the soft handling of the facial features and the delineation of the hair and beard suggest that the painter of the face was a practised professional. Across the face and parts of the hair, the paint appears to have been delicately applied, probably in a series of thin pigmented glazes that build up a depth of colour after repeated applications, providing an illusion of light, lustrous, gingery hair or palpably soft, flushed cheeks. It is possible that the hair in particular has suffered from overcleaning, although this point is controversial. (Conservators at the Canadian Conservation Institute and the Art Gallery of

Ontario question this analysis.) Yet it is curious that in some areas—for example, above the sitter's ear on the right side—this skilful artist has followed usual practice for the time and traced the hair with his brush, leaving clearly visible lines that emphasize the curls and strands. While what we see in other areas—particularly on the left side near the temple—are thinly painted patches of pigment and little evidence of brushstrokes, which may well indicate a partially abraded paint surface.

Typically for English painting of this period, the handling of the figure is also decidedly linear instead of tonal, the key features of the portrait, including the eyes and nose, being defined by line rather than by graduations of shading. The rather heavy brown lines that delineate the top of each eyelid and the top of each eye also appear in the work of the few well-known native painters of Shakespeare's day such as George Gower (d. 1596), who held the official post of Serjeant Painter to Queen Elizabeth I. The absence of underdrawing—as revealed by infrared analysis at the Canadian Conservation Institute—is not unusual. Numerous Netherlandish and English artists of the time worked directly on a primed panel, building up the figure in painted outlines. We have no way of knowing whether this artist worked from preliminary drawings of the subject taken from life; very few English drawings survive from this period. We do know that not all subjects sat for prolonged periods for their portraits—sometimes they left their clothes behind instead, to allow the artist to capture the elaborate details of their expensive attire. For important sitters, such as courtiers who might have their portrait painted many times, face patterns might be made and copied when needed. However, private individuals like the young man in the

Sanders portrait were almost certainly painted from life after at least one sitting.

When we move from the working of the face to the handling of the sitter's costume, we encounter a distinctly different style. Particularly with the doublet we find an alternative method of applying the paint to the panel, a method known as impasto (where paint is laid onto the panel far more thickly). This difference may be partly explained by the fact that the doublet's silver-grey material is embroidered, which caused the painter to embellish the illusion through the use of an embossed effect. But the collar has also been painted with some speed, and the paint has been more thickly and somewhat less skilfully applied. This is most evident when we compare the area where the collar and the neckline meet, showing the contrast between the more delicately painted flesh and the slightly heavier application of paint on the crest of the collar. The colour of the paint in this area now appears as a blue-green shade rather than the expected white or pale grey. This change is probably due to properties in the yellowed varnish that filter the mixture of lead white and charcoal black—a colour that frequently has a blueish hue—making it appear green to our eyes.[4] It must have been the contrast between the collar and the face that caused M. H. Spielmann to suggest in 1909 that the collar had been repainted or was a later addition. It appears far more likely that the portrait was finished by a second, less skilful, artist within a painters' workshop, perhaps someone who specialized in costume details. Such a division of artistic labour was reasonably common in busy workshops where numerous portraits were being undertaken simultaneously.

Most painters of this period were trained in England's major commercial centres, for example, in London, Norwich, Chester, Exeter and Newcastle. Customarily, an aspiring artist began as an apprentice to a master painter, probably eventually establishing himself in his own workshop. Many practising professional painters were men who had experienced a formal apprenticeship, although there were also those with some skill in other crafts who could turn their hand to painting when required. The few female artists we know of were almost certainly all members of the gentry who painted—or more likely produced drawings or miniatures—more for pleasure than for profit.[5] Within the City of London, the craft of painting was regulated by the guild called the Painter-Stainers Company, which attempted to restrict the practice of professional painting to its members. The records of this guild before 1623 have been lost, but they could have told us little conclusive about who painted the Sanders portrait. A significant number of artists in Shakespeare's time practised on the south bank of the River Thames, just outside the jurisdiction of the Painter-Stainers Company. By the 1630s, the author Henry Peacham tells his readers to acquaint themselves "with some of our excellent masters [painters] about London where there are many, passing judicious and skillfull."[6] We know that at least from the middle of the sixteenth century, if not before, many painters made livings from various types of work, including private portraits for London citizens and the gentry, as well as temporary painted decorations for theatrical events at court and elsewhere. Among these was the painter, or painters, of the Sanders portrait.

The authorship of an English painting from this period is extremely difficult to ascertain partly because two or more artists might work on the panel, and because few of these people thought to sign their work. Painting in Shakespeare's day was closer to the concept of craft than fine art. The artist or artists who painted the Sanders portrait would have worked with the sitter or patron in determining the format and composition. The placing of the subject close up to the picture plane against an unadorned background is distinctive, as in fact is the relatively small size of the panel. A *Portrait of an Unknown Boy*, dated 1605 (see page xiv of "The Picture Gallery") by an anonymous artist, is strikingly similar in size and composition. The shadowing of the jawline and the clear outlining of the eyes and nose at a slight angle and the rather stylized treatment of the lips are very marked in both portraits. The careful treatment of the young boy's hair, which appears to have been painted in thinly pigmented, single, flowing strokes of the brush, may hint at how the Sanders sitter looked before cleaning or abrasion. The lettering of the two inscriptions is also remarkably similar, and each exhibits a quite distinctive controlled flourish and a comma following the date. This evidence leads me to tentatively suggest that the *Portrait of an Unknown Boy* may come from the same workshop as the Sanders panel. The whereabouts of the painting depicting this unknown child of a gentry family—if it has survived—is unknown. (The photograph reproduced in "The Picture Gallery" was located in the costume files of the archives of the National Portrait Gallery, London, and dates from the 1930s, when the painting was held in a private collection in Germany).[7]

If the way the paint was applied can tell us something about the artist or artists, the composition and small size of the work suggest something about the motives of the person who commissioned the work, whether the sitter or his friend and patron. In terms of its overall composition, the Sanders portrait is quite typical of its period. Taking into account the missing piece along the right side, which would have placed the figure in the centre of the frame, the format is one utilized in many hundreds of portraits of early-seventeenth-century citizens and gentry. As Robert Tittler has noted, this work clearly falls outside the courtly tradition of portraiture with its grand poses, sumptuous costumes, informative emblems, coats of arms and inscriptions. Instead, the sitter is shown in a simple head-and-shoulders pose, his head turned slightly to the right, allowing a three-quarter view of the face so as to enhance the sense of lifelike presence.

The relatively small size of the panel tells us that the painting was probably meant to hang in a domestic setting, in an environment where the person in the portrait was well known. For such a painting, no inscription naming the sitter was needed. In fact, identifying inscriptions found on portraits of this period are quite frequently unreliable and many date from at least three generations later than the painting, presumably when the memory of its subject was beginning to fade. Perhaps, as the analysis by members of the University of Toronto's Records of Early English Drama project proposes, the label on the back of the panel was written for similar reasons.

Numerous contemporary inventories and surviving portraits of sitters from relatively modest backgrounds affirm that such images hung in domestic spaces. In this period private portraits were often commissioned by their sitters in order to commemorate a personal milestone, such as marriage, an honour or achievement, or were given as gifts to friends. The anonymous portrait of an *Unknown Gentleman of the Terrick Family* from around 1600 (see page xv of "The Picture Gallery") is similar in size to the Sanders panel and depicts a young man dressed in a wide cartwheel ruff. The painting includes at the top left a revealing inscription: "TO PLEASE MY FRENDE AND NOT MY SELFE." Assuming that these words do not postdate the painting, they can be read two ways: as a type of disclaimer to the charge of vanity inherent in presenting one's face to public view; as evidence that an English portrait of this period might be commissioned as a private memento for a friend.[8]

That the face in the Sanders portrait is painted life-size is also worth emphasizing. In the sixteenth and early seventeenth centuries, portraits were understood as records of an individual at a particular point in life. Only a life-size portrait could serve as a true likeness, or "counterfeit," to use the Elizabethan term for portrait, a visual record of the lost likeness of oneself, of a friend or of a loved one. Like a modern studio photograph, such personal images preserved a person's presence as if untouched by the ravages of time, thus reminding the viewer of the transience of life itself.

In an era when certain unwritten conventions governed the painting of portraits of male and female sitters, the pose of the Sanders sitter also indicates what the portrait is not. Double portraits of husbands and wives always placed the woman to the right and the man to the left, with each sitter frequently turned very slightly toward each other. Here, the sitter faces very slightly to his right, while his body is square to the picture plane. We therefore must conclude that the Sanders portrait is not one half of a double portrait but was commissioned as a single likeness painted on a single panel.

Although the Sanders portrait is in many ways quite typical of its period, it is also unusual—as Robert Tittler has rightly pointed out—in its lack of emblems, coats of arms or significant inscriptions. And this is another reason to link it with the same studio that produced the *Portrait of an Unknown Boy*. A more elaborate example of a picture of someone belonging roughly to Shakespeare's social class portrays the lawyer and antiquarian William Burton at the age of twenty-nine (see page xv of "The Picture Gallery") and painted the same year. As a landowner and member of the minor gentry, Burton was slightly higher up the social scale than a playwright with a merchant background. He was the brother of Robert Burton, the author of the *Anatomy of Melancholy*, a learned, university-educated and socially astute person. In this three-quarter-length view, William wears sober, yet expensive, attire and is surrounded by an elaborate shield of family arms, an inscription in Latin and a cartouche with a moralizing emblem about the vanity of life. Such a highly stylized image is designed to impress the viewer with the sitter's intellect, his piety and his family ancestry. Whoever commissioned the Sanders portrait, his motives did not include impressing the public with the sitter's worldly credentials.

The evidence uncovered so far perhaps raises more questions than it answers. Yet having examined the Sanders portrait as a physical object, as a work of art and as a social artifact, we may possibly draw some tentative conclusions. The work was almost certainly commissioned as a private record of an individual at a particular moment in his life. The sitter reveals himself as he wishes to be seen by his family and friends. I doubt we will ever know who commissioned the image, but it could easily have been the man in the portrait, who intended it as a keepsake or memento for someone who knew him well. We know that artists of this period would price their work by the size of the panel, and a head-and-shoulders portrait would undoubtedly cost significantly less than a three-quarter-length portrait such as the likeness of William Burton. For a successful businessman like Shakespeare in 1603, this modest format would have been well within his means. (No doubt the doublet the sitter wore cost considerably more than the painting.)

But what can the costume, pose and demeanour of this particular sitter tell us about who he might have been? His expensive and reasonably fashionable attire mark him out as a young man of promise, likely possessing some education and financial backing, perhaps a recent arrival in one of the urban centres of England from a country town. If only we knew his age, we might be able to come much closer to his identity. Here we are brought back to that tantalizing missing third piece of the panel that would have filled out its right side. What we have of the inscription painted in red lettering at the top right currently reads "AN°, 1603." As can be seen in the very similar *Portrait of an Unknown Boy* and the portrait of William Burton, in Shakespeare's day the date was invariably accompanied by the Latin formula "Ætatis Svae" or its shorter form, "Æt." (meaning "his or her age"), followed by the numerals of the sitter's age. On the Sanders portrait, the date ends just where the missing piece would have been attached.

We can only speculate about what, if anything, was painted

on the missing piece. But it is highly probable that it bore the sitter's age in the year he was portrayed. We may not know now how old the sitter is but we can tell that he is most probably from the middle ranks of society, an individual who could comfortably mix with minor gentry, prosperous clothiers, lawyers, physicians and city elite. The intensity of his gaze appears to reflect a powerful sense of self-awareness and a capacity for contemplation, both qualities we might expect Shakespeare to have in abundance. Yet exactly who he is will likely remain contentious. When this portrait was painted in 1603, it probably served as a memento for the eyes of the subject's family or his friend alone. It might, therefore, be fitting for the painting to retain the secret of the sitter's identity.

The Portrait Meets Its Pub

LLOYD SULLIVAN'S pursuit of proof that the Sanders portrait was genuine had lasted ten long years. If nothing else, he had proved that whoever painted it and whoever its subject, it was a work of art more than four centuries old. On the early evening of Thursday, May 10, 2001, as I sat down at the dining room table of my parents' house in Ottawa to pound out my first article about the picture, I had known of the rakish man in the portrait for only a couple of weeks. My part in the story was really just beginning.

At two minutes after 6:00 p.m., I plugged my laptop into a phone jack and attempted to send the fifteen hundred words I had written to *The Globe and Mail* in Toronto. But my parents' ancient pulse phone line refused to speak to my *Globe* laptop. And suddenly my parents' quaint refusal to join the touch-tone age, the subject of years of teasing, wasn't funny any more. After a few frantic minutes, I called Susan Allan, the *Globe*'s technical whiz. Sue has talked me through filing from satellite phones in the Nigerian wilderness and pay phones in Jerusalem, but this challenge stumped her. At six-ten, I gave up and dashed across the street, computer in hand, wires trailing, to knock on the door of a kindly neighbour, Elaine Gagné. As she led me to a telephone jack, Elaine politely asked what the story was, assuming from my wild-eyed look that I had a huge investigative scoop. But I was still in sworn-to-secrecy mode, so as I hooked up my laptop, I made extravagant changes of subject to avoid answering her questions. While I watched my words scroll across the screen as they travelled from a quiet Ottawa suburb to downtown Toronto, I instead quizzed her on her kids, her dogs and her renovations. Finally, my computer screen flashed relief: "Your Story Has Been Sent." I thanked Elaine profusely and headed back across the street.

But I had hardly collapsed on the living room sofa when the barrage of phone calls from the newsroom began. It seemed as if every editor at the paper was reading the story and that every single one of them wanted to double-check something: when did Shakespeare (and thus possibly John Sanders) join the Lord Chamberlain's Men? How precise was the radio carbon dating? If the label wasn't legible, how did I know what it said? *The Globe* was clearly going big on this story. One by one, the batteries in each of my parents' telephones died and I was left hollering into a tinny 1986 model left over from my all-pink teenage bedroom phase.

About nine o'clock in the evening, with the last of the phone calls dealt with and only seven hours before the Friday paper would start to arrive on doorsteps across Canada, I walked back over to Lloyd's house. He and his wife were settled in front of the television, watching a prayer gathering in Texas. He ushered me in and offered a beer, which I accepted gratefully.

Lloyd seemed a little startled that my story was already written, filed and edited. I tried to explain that I was fairly certain the piece would be featured prominently in the paper the next day and that it was likely to attract a lot of attention. And I asked him to please, please, get Shakespeare off the dining room table and find somewhere safer than a cupboard to put him. Lloyd had been at this project for a long time, in the course of which there were many conversations with friends and neighbours, just like the one with my father that had led to my article, and I could not even begin to guess how many people who read the newspaper would recognize him as the man with the painting. I didn't think the portrait should be in his house when they did. He promised he would take it somewhere safe, that very night. I suspected Lloyd had no idea just how big this story was going to be.

The next morning, Friday, May 11, I came down to the kitchen to find *The Globe* on the table where my dad had left it. Even though I had written the story myself and was by now intimately acquainted with the picture, the front page was a shock. The editors had thrown conventional newspaper layout to the wind. A portrait of a man in a doublet and a stiff linen collar occupied half the front page. Above the picture, in huge type, *The Globe* asked the mysterious question, "Is this the face of genius?" Below the portrait was the subhead: "Today we reveal what is believed to be William Shakespeare at 39—the only existing portrait painted while the playwright was alive."

Just after dawn, Lloyd went out and bought up every *Globe and Mail* in every shop in the neighbourhood. Then he cleaned out all the streetcorner newspaper boxes. He believed in his picture completely, but to see it like this, on the cover of Canada's newspaper of record, was a whole other thing. "We were in shock," he says. "I was amazed when I saw the paper." Finally, he understood the urgency of putting the portrait somewhere safe. After buying up forty *Globe*s, Lloyd took his painting back to the Canadian Conservation Institute, where it was safely stored in their vault.

For the first half of Friday, I was oblivious to the media storm that was brewing. I was back at my parents' dining room table, hard at work on a second article, a follow-up piece that would flesh out the portrait's history in the Saturday paper. Once again, I thought I was writing for a 6:00 p.m. deadline, and once again—this time around eleven in the morning—an editor called with a change of plan: the follow-up story would run in a section with a deadline of noon, twelve-thirty if I really had to push it. My mother shook her head: "They don't sound very organized," she said, in one of the great understated assessments of newsroom management.

In the afternoon, I got an additional assignment: the national editor, Bob Cox, said he wanted a story on the reaction to the portrait. From the dining room in Ottawa, I replied, "What reaction?" And that's when I got my first hint of just how extraordinary the reaction was. Cox told me the paper had received more than fifty calls from other news organizations, including CNN, ABC News, *Time* magazine, *The Washington Post* and a half-dozen British newspapers. Even a daily in Hanoi had called. They all wanted more details, and they wanted to reproduce the picture. The Canadian Conservation Institute was barraged with requests for Lloyd's name or details about him. *The Globe* had identified him only as a retired engineer in a mid-size city in Ontario. Former colleagues, friends from journalism school and people I barely knew left me messages begging for clues to his identity. Within hours of the story's publication, Shakespearean Internet sites were frenetic.

That night, all three of Canada's national television networks gave the story serious attention but played it skeptically. They had no shortage of critics to call on, such as a Chicago stock analyst cum Shakespeare scholar named David Kathman, who gave several interviews citing his comprehensive *Biographical Index of Elizabethan Theatre*, noting that it contains no record of any John Sanders in the theatrical companies of the time. I went to bed knowing Willy Shake had made a real splash, but with Kathman's doubts ringing in my ears, I wasn't sure the story would, as we say in the business, have legs.

When I got into the office on Monday, my voice mail was jammed, my e-mail inbox was groaning and faxes and letters had spilled off my desk and were heaped on the seat of my chair. The *Globe*'s editor-in-chief, Richard Addis, was clearly delighted. My colleagues were congratulatory in their usual arch sort of way. My deskmate, Margaret Philp, asked where I had got my mum, since clearly she needed a mother just like mine.

By Monday, most British newspapers had picked up the story. For the most part, they adopted the world-weary "another possible picture" tone I had first heard from the chief curator at the National Portrait Gallery. The Associated Press put the story of a new Shakespeare portrait—found in Canada, of all places—out on the wire. In the next few days it appeared in hundreds of U.S. and international newspapers, alongside a reproduction of *The Globe's* May 11 front page—the only image of the portrait that was available. Two weeks after the first *Globe* article, both *The New York Times* and *The L. A. Times* gave the story lengthy treatment. "A retired Canadian engineer, telling a tale of ancient family ties, mistaken judgments and surprise revelations, has roiled the world of Shakespeare scholarship by saying he possesses a striking portrait painted in 1603 showing Shakespeare as a coy man of 39, with a full head of hair and a Mona Lisa smile," wrote Anthony De Palma in *The New York Times.*

That Monday morning, my first day back at *The Globe* since the story broke, the phone calls came in a torrent. Richard Monette, director of the Stratford Festival in Ontario, called to tell me that Canada's centre for the production of Shakespearean drama wished to adopt the portrait as "Shakespeare in the New World." The Festival wanted to make the Sanders Shakespeare their Bard. I promised to pass the message along.

There was also an intriguing call from Matthew Teitelbaum, director of the Art Gallery of Ontario in Toronto, one of the country's top art museums. Teitelbaum wanted to know if I would relay a request to the mystery owner: Would he be willing to let the AGO put the Sanders portrait on public display? The idea was the brainchild of Christina Corsiglia, the AGO's curator of European art, who had been entranced by the front-page story that landed on her doorstep the previous Friday. By the time she got to work that day, she had prepared a pitch for Teitelbaum: if the gallery could exhibit the painting, it would give the public a rare opportunity to see first-hand how the art authentication process works. "This is what we do," she told me later, "but people never get to see this part of it. And I love that this picture has been investigated from the ground up." The AGO director immediately seized on the idea. In remarkably short order, he and Corsiglia had worked out the logistics of putting the portrait on display in time for the busy summer season. I wondered how Lloyd would react.

If *Globe* readers were any indication, Christina Corsiglia was right about the public wanting to see the portrait. On Saturday, the day after the first story appeared, the paper's letters page was already buzzing with commentary, pro and con. On May 16, the paper ran an extraordinary Letters to the Editor page of nothing but Shakespeare letters. "If this is the face of Shakespeare," wrote Barbara Pedrick from Victoria, "then I, for the first time in a long time, could really believe that he wrote all that delightful, insightful, sad, tragic and magical stuff. This fellow has an impish twinkle that suggests wit and wisdom, unlike the stodgy image that we all know from the Folio. That guy looks like a corn merchant. This guy looks like fun." Jon Preston of Victoria made a witty point: "The authenticity of the Sanders portrait of Shakespeare has been questioned, in that Shakespeare was too stingy or poor to pay for it. Perhaps that's why the Sanders family still owns it." And Anthony B. Dawson, professor of English at the University of British Columbia, raised serious questions about the story, but concluded, "The portrait could be Shakespeare; whoever it is, he's certainly a lot cuter than the guy with the great dome."

Others were not so taken with the face and for some reason were appalled that I had perpetuated the evil myth that the man from Stratford actually wrote the plays. Some simply scolded, some offered key bits of evidence and some heaped abuse into my voice mail. Supporters in the camp of Edward de Vere, the Earl of Oxford, seemed particularly outraged. "Academics and others in the Shakespeare industry are understandably reluctant to shake the boat in what has become a global multimillion-dollar business steeped in the mythology of a seemingly ordinary man reputed to create enduring words," wrote Alan S. Majauskas of Kitchener, Ontario. "The painting's authenticity is of technical interest. But its significance about authorship was sadly overlooked by *The Globe*, which owes its readers an objective look at this fascinating debate and nothing to the industry that strives to stifle the truth about Shakespeare's real identity." Many correspondents were far less polite than Majauskas, calling me a pathetic pawn of the Shakespeare Industrial Complex, which, they said, maintains the Stratford fiction in order to profit from the busloads of tourists who visit Anne Hathaway's Cottage and buy souvenir teaspoons.

The publication of the portrait served to uphold an age-old rule of journalism: the bigger the story, the taller the pile of letters from eccentrics. There were letters and phone calls from a vast array of people with, shall we say, unusual points of view. In a series of increasingly urgent phone messages, a very kind young man named Brad explained to me that Francis Bacon wrote the "Shakespeare" plays, and that many heretofore unseen manuscripts, products of the same great brain, were buried in a vault in Williamsburg, Virginia. He offered to fly me down to inspect possible sites for the Lost Vault myself. When I didn't seem keen to venture to Virginia, he made cheerfully insistent suggestions that he and his colleagues would come to me and do a little presentation right there in the comfort of my office. And then I heard from Dr. Rolph Z. Medgessy of Montreal, whose letterhead identified him as an art historian with a specialty in "Art Research—Discovery & Documentation." Medgessy had examined the image and had exciting news indeed—it contained several of the "microsignatures" he had made a career of unearthing, "representing unimitably [*sic*] conclusive 100 per cent evidence!" that Francisco de Goya had painted the Sanders portrait. Medgessy helpfully included a photocopy of the painting on which he had circled twenty-three of the barely visible scrawls he said were Goya's identifying marks.

The passionate response to the painting immediately set some people to thinking about how potentially valuable it was. A Sotheby's expert from New York called to ask me to tell Lloyd he would be glad to fly up and take a look at his most interesting work of art. The Heffel Fine Art Auction House in Vancouver started running ads in the papers reading, "Wanted: Shakespeare's Portrait. Desperately seeking eccentric Ontario resident with the only known portrait of William Shakespeare in history stashed under your bed. Isn't it better to collect bids from avid auction goers than dust bunnies? . . . We see millions in your future." I had calls from people pitching documentaries, books, canvas reproductions of the picture and any manner of merchandising ideas, all of which I dutifully passed on to Lloyd. He quickly realized that the reproduction of the image was going to be an important issue; he was also going to need help with the flood of proposals I was sending his way, and he hired a copyright lawyer.

For me, though, the most valuable responses—whether in the form of a letter to the editor or a direct message to me—were those that corrected my mistakes or added to my knowledge. A half-dozen *Globe* readers caught an error I made in my first story when I explained John Sanders's possible role in Shakespeare's theatre as a "set painter." Elizabethan theatres, such as the Globe and Rose, did not use sets. Reading through the letters, I wondered whether some new information might surface that would help or hurt the painting's claim—above all, some evidence linking John Sanders to William Shakespeare. The portion of the family legend that placed John Sanders in the London theatre at the time when Shakespeare was an actor and fledgling playwright—that was the weakest link in the case for the portrait. For scholars of Shakespeare, the Sanders portrait had meaning only if it portrayed the playwright. Proving a link, or at least placing Sanders on the London theatre scene in 1603, would make a huge difference.

It was a connection that *Globe* editors, having made so much of the story, rather hoped I would find. In the weeks following the first articles, many scholars wrote to tell me they had never heard of John Sanders, that he almost certainly did not exist. He soon became the centre of the ongoing story, and I was assigned to find out everything I could about John Sanders, mystery painter. (And always, in the back of my head, was Lloyd's point that he was fairly sure it was John, but there was a chance it *might* have been John's brother, Thomas, who painted the picture.)

The first big break, apparent evidence that a young man named Sanders knew William Shakespeare, came two weeks after the story broke, and from the first it seemed too good to be true. It arrived in the form of an overseas call from a warm-voiced Englishwoman named Veronica, who told me she lived in the village of Rowington, near Stratford-upon-Avon. Veronica had heard about the portrait on the local radio news—there were archly skeptical reports being aired in Stratford in those first few days—and had called to say that the skeptics were wrong. She knew this, she said, because she lived in a house once owned by the Sanders family. And they had owned the house across the road too, some four hundred years back, when the playwright William Shakespeare rented it for six shillings a year. It was widely known, she informed me, that the Sanders family and the Shakespeares had close ties. And she had wills and title documents that proved it all.

I made immediate arrangements to have Federal Express pick up copies of the papers from Veronica and speed them across the ocean to Toronto. But an hour later, I received a call from someone who said he was a friend of Veronica's. He was also a London public relations agent and was now representing her: we both know, he said smoothly, that Veronica possesses certain "papers of great interest to you." Papers that were probably quite valuable—to me . . . or to any other news organization to whom he happened to mention them.

The Globe does not pay for stories—ever. But the speed of this request for dollars had to set some sort of record. Polite but frosty, I told the London agent that *The Globe* was not interested—and then I did a little sleuthing on my own. It took only one phone call to Heather Wolfe, curator of manuscripts at the Folger Shakespeare Library in Washington, D.C., to dismiss Veronica's claim. If William Shakespeare—*the* William Shakespeare—had rented a house from the Sanders family, and if this transaction had been recorded on a lease that survives today, the scholarly world would know all about it. Veronica, she suggested, was likely a bit confused—for there was a William Shakespeare in Rowington—several, in fact. There were William

Shakespeares on juries, William Shakespeares on land grants, a plethora of William Shakespeares through the Tudor period in Rowington. But William Shakespeare of Rowington was not our Will, so his connection to the Sanders family was irrelevant.

But Veronica had set me thinking about historical documents. If our John Sanders could be found nowhere in the known records, just how good are those records? One of the first people I called, looking for an answer, was Andrew Gurr. As he has explained earlier, just because a John Sanders does not show up on surviving theatre records does not mean he wasn't in London or associated with the King's Men in 1603, since there was lots of work in the theatre besides acting. "The statistics about this sort of thing are pretty daunting," he told me. "We have records of two to three thousand named actors known to be active through this period." That compares poorly with the Spanish, the great bureaucrats of the age, who recorded everyone. A recently published index of Spanish actors published in 2000 lists ninety-three hundred names. "It's possible that there were [about] that number in England, so even if that evidence is only remotely parallel it is still likely that one-thirtieth of named actors are all that we've got record of," Gurr said. "So there is that likelihood of there being a John Sanders about at the time and our not having heard of him."

Others acknowledged the possibility that some record of John Sanders might yet be found. In recent years, Shakespeare studies have focused largely on reinterpretations of the playwright's life and work—feminist analysis, for instance, or Freudian. But very little current scholarship involves looking at original documents—court cases, manorial deeds—from the period. Such primary research is slow and tedious, and a scholar could easily spend her or his life squinting over bills of sale from the early 1600s and find nothing of relevance at all. There are thousands of Elizabethan documents that no one has examined since they were filed four hundred years ago. One day in the future some scholar may well turn up another reference as crucial as this one: "Edward sonne of Edward Shackspeere, Player: base-borne." These few words from a London baptismal record represent the sum total of the evidence that Edmund Shakespeare followed his older brother's path into the London theatre. (The names *Edmund* and *Edward* were often interchanged. "Base-born" means illegitimate.) Only the happenstance that Edmund fathered a child out of wedlock and had the child christened in a London parish tells us Edmund was a player.

Of all the specialists I consulted, the University of Toronto's Ian Lancashire held out the most hope of finding the actor John Sanders. The respected English professor agreed that there was no John Sanders on the extant rolls of the Lord Chamberlain's Men or the King's Men but proposed that he just might be the person called "Saunder" (a name then more or less interchangeable with Sanders) who shows up in Richard Burbage's company in 1591, around the time Shakespeare became an actor and playwright. We know of this Saunder because he is listed in the transcript of the "plot" of *The Second Part of the Seven Deadly Sins*,[1] written by the famed actor Richard Tarleton. (A plot was a pasteboard mounted backstage that offered actors a list of scenes and the characters in each, with stage directions.) Saunder played two women's parts, standard roles for young men whose voices had not yet changed. So it is plausible that the boy actors in Burbage's company included a young fellow from Worcester born in 1576. Other scholars had speculated that the Saunder in the *Seven Deadly Sins* was an abbreviation for the first name Alexander. "It's likely this 'Saunder' was not good enough to become an adult actor after his voice changed," Lancashire continued. "That's perhaps why we don't hear anything of him afterwards."

The Toronto professor also pointed the way to another possible clue. There is a John Sanders in the Worcestershire volume of the Records of Early Elizabethan Drama, an immense undertaking of Victoria University at the University of Toronto.[2] Begun in 1975, the REED project has brought together an international team of editors working to establish the broader context within which Shakespeare and his fellow dramatists lived and worked. These scholars transcribe every English historical record of dramatic, ceremonial and minstrel activity—including playbills, letters and pamphlets—that they can find, from the Middle Ages up to 1642, the year the Puritans closed the London playhouses. These documents are being collected and published in a series of annotated volumes. Twenty have so far been released and thirty more are anticipated.

With the help of Sally-Beth Maclean, executive editor of the Records, I found and deciphered the Sanders reference. It appears in a report from 1609, about a morris dance performed the year before. The dance was called "Old Meg of Herefordshire," and according to the report, it was put on by a group of nonagenarians and centenarians—this in an era when average life expectancy barely exceeded fifty. But the account of the ancient dancers is deadpan—and there was my Mr. Sanders. "The fourth was John Sanders of Walford, an Iron-worker; the hardness of which labour could not so wearie and wast his bodie, but that his courage hath overcome it, & carried him safely over the hie hill of old age, where she hath bestowed upon him one hundred and two yeares." John, at 102, was a whiffler—a bouncer, if you will, charged with controlling the crowd, lest they be whipped into an unruly frenzy by the sight of 120-year-old Meg Goodwin hopping away in the role of "Maide-marrian." This was too old to be our John, even allowing for a certain highly unprofessional exaggeration about his age on the part of the correspondent. And this John Sanders was from Walford, not Worcester. But Lancashire suggested it might be evidence that our John Sanders came from a performing family.

The overwhelming opinion of the scholars I interviewed can be summed up in the comments of Sir Roy Strong, former director of the National Portrait Gallery in London. Strong believes the portrait "looks perfectly authentic for 1603, and the costume addressed is absolutely correct," but unless the picture's provenance could be documented to early in the 1600s, its claim was tentative at best. There are "racks" of pictures from the 1650s onward claiming to be Shakespeare, he told me. In the end, of all the scholars with whom I spoke in my pursuit of the historical John Sanders, only Lancashire was willing to commit, to say he believed the painting to be genuine in every sense. Through me he sent Lloyd a kind letter that read, in part, "All Shakespeareans owe you and your family hearty thanks for your preservation of this wonderful portrait over almost four hundred years."

As the hunt for John Sanders progressed—or rather, didn't—I called Lloyd each day or two with an update. He had by now developed an optimistic myopia, discounting any hint of bad news, and enthusiastically embracing supporters. I also set out to try to fill some of the holes in Lloyd's efforts at authentication.

For one thing, the Sanders portrait offers up a whole set of clues to the identity of its sitter, if only you know how to read them. The clues lie in the smiling rogue's hair and clothing. As Robert Tittler has pointed out in his essay, a Tudor portrait typically conveys a great deal about the sitter's status. A painter in 1603 would have taken great care to depict a portrait subject in clothing, accessories and a hairstyle that told those who saw the picture, and who were highly literate in this language, a great deal about the subject. Doctors wore silk-lined gowns, soldiers wore leather jerkins, a lovelorn courtier wore his hair in flowing locks.

The man wears a doublet, the basic piece of apparel of all Elizabethan men. A doublet is made of at least two layers of material (hence, doublet) rising high on the neck with a tight collar. In addition, a man might wear a jerkin (a close-fitting sleeveless jacket) on top of a doublet and a waistcoat below it, but he always wore a sleeved linen shirt that opened in front and tied at the neck.

To learn what his costume conveys, I turned to Aileen Ribeiro, a warm and witty specialist at the Courtauld Institute of Art in London who is an acknowledged authority on what people wore in Elizabethan England. She was immediately intrigued by the portrait and believed that the costume and appearance of the sitter were perfectly correct for a date of 1603. In her opinion, however, the sitter could not be William Shakespeare.

The problem? For one thing, his hair.

"What makes me think it can't be Shakespeare is that his hair is very, very fashionable," she said. "It's cut short to stand up straight on top of his head. That is a fashion worn by young men, standing on end like a fire or a forest, curled over his ears and quite short. And the light frosting of beard also suggests a fashionable young man. Hair is always the more sensitive barometer of appearance." She cited *The Gull's Hornbook* written by Thomas Dekker in 1609, a satirical work of advice on behaviour for taverns and playhouses, wherein young gallants are told, "Let thy hair grow thick and bushy, like a forest or some wilderness."

The Sanders sitter is not a total slave to fashion, for he does not sport a lovelock (a lock of longer hair on one side) or a lock of his true love's tresses looped on an earring, but he has all the attributes of a young fop much concerned with fashion, as opposed to a thirty-nine-year-old gent with aspirations to respectability. A rich doublet like the one worn by the Sanders sitter, apparently decorated with silver thread, might have cost £20, a vast sum in 1603.

"This is a period when clothing, the outward person, really signifies what the inward person is," Aileen Ribeiro explained. Political allegiance and love affairs could be signified by clothing and hairstyles. And while there might be anomalies in clothing, she said, "People never mess with the hair and the face. That's your identity, your character, who you are."

There were other things that puzzled her about the Sanders portrait. The sleeves, for example. "It's fairly rare to see a portrait from this period without shoulder wings"—welted roles of material about an inch wide that project like epaulets and circle the whole armhole, where the sleeves join the body. Perhaps, Ribeiro speculated, the wings were just outside the portrait's boundary. Clothes were extremely expensive in this era and a shoulder wing allowed a man to make changes to the style of his sleeve without discarding the whole garment.

The collar also presents something of a mystery. Ribeiro had never seen anything quite like the construction of the Sanders collar: a long, rectangular piece of starched linen, pleated to fit around the neck. Normally a doublet neck was high, like that of a clergyman, and the collar folded out over it; the Sanders sitter wears his doublet open at the top one or two buttons and folded back. And the collar lacks tassels to hold it in place, something she would have expected, although the tassels were sometimes omitted from portraits. The collar (or "band," as the Jacobeans called them) is made of very fine linen, which is a young man's fabric: it is flimsy, it tears easily and it is a sign of conspicuous consumption, which, Ribeiro pointed out, "is all at one with the hairstyle."

Because the collar is so flat, we know it has been painted to emphasize the transparency of the linen and thus the wealth of the man who wears it—linen that fine was quite expensive. Yet we cannot see the pattern of the doublet through the linen. It might be that the painter was lazy, Ribeiro offered, "But these people aren't stupid. They were creating images for audiences who would understand the shorthand completely, who would know that underneath the collar the doublet could be seen." Perhaps the pattern has been left out to make the picture more interesting, maybe indicating "a higher degree of sophistication on the part of the painter."

There is also the question of colour. In this era, there was a revival of the medieval notion of colours being significant and symbolic. Elizabethans consulted *A Rare True and Proper Blazon of Colours and Ensigns*, published in 1583, which drew its information from mid-fifteenth-century writing on colours in tournaments. In the first reproduction of the portrait she saw, Ribeiro thought the doublet was black, faded to greeny grey as blacks in both old fabric dyes and paints tend to do. And that told her quite a bit—there are many portraits and miniatures of fine young men wearing black and white or black and silver, for those were the Queen's favourite colours. (We know this because Elizabeth confided as much to the Spanish ambassador in 1564, and he duly recorded the information, along with slightly more pressing political revelations, in a report home to Spain, collected in the Calendar of State Papers.) For a courtier, black indicates melancholy and constancy, while silver or white is about virginity and hope. A young man painted in black and white was showing that he was hoping against hope for the love of the Virgin Queen, or that he was constant in his devotion.

I told Ribeiro that the various art historians, curators and scientists who have examined the Sanders portrait assert that beneath the thick, discoloured layer of varnish, the doublet is not black but either "a greyed blue-green" (Art Gallery of Ontario) or purple-blue (Canadian Conservation Institute). Ribeiro doubted it was blue, a colour rarely seen in surviving portraits or clothing from Elizabethan times. Purple is even more unlikely: it is a royal colour, the colour of coronations and of royal mourning. Riberio thinks the doublet is something officially known as goose-turd green. "People were much more imaginative and enterprising about colours than we are," she said. "Goose-turd green was a greyish green—I think that's probably what he's wearing." Green was the colour of love.

Could this be an actor in foppish costume? I asked Ribeiro. This has been Lloyd's explanation for the rather rich doublet. Ribeiro quickly knocked the bottom out of that theory. There were no costumes in Elizabethan theatre: only a handful of roles such as Falstaff and Cardinal Wolsey were performed in specific attire. Most actors wore contemporary clothes on stage, even for historical dramas (with perhaps a plumed helmet added on), and the same outfits had to serve for comedies and tragedies. "There is nothing in the dress that says actor," Ribeiro said. "And there is no record of actors ever painted in something identifiable as a costume until much later."

On the other hand, costume historians agree that Henry VIII's sumptuary laws, regulating who could wear what fabrics and colours, while still in place in 1603, were rarely enforced and largely ignored. And actors had a sort of unofficial dispensation to wear clothes above their station because they often wore castoffs given to them by wealthy patrons. Thomas Platter, the young man from Basle who visited London in 1599, wrote in his account that "the players are most extravagantly and richly dressed" in their hand-me-downs.

And the late costume historian John Nevinson has pointed out that a portrait of an actor called Old Cartwright, one of the Lord Admiral's Men, shows him wearing a bright blue doublet slashed with red and a lace-edged collar, which Nevinson says "looks very much like the dress which an actor would have worn in the theatre and not in the streets."[3] Some of the other actors' portraits, such as the supposed self-portrait of Richard Burbage, show the men soberly dressed in the fashion of the sitter in the

Chandos portrait, while others depict men in fancier doublets with slashed sleeves or silk embroidery.

On balance, Ribeiro believes the Sanders portrait does not fit with what we know of Shakespeare in 1603. "The ultrafashionable hairstyle is totally inappropriate for someone of his status. He was a pretty wealthy [businessman] by then." A more plausible appearance for such a person would have been "a plain doublet, with more modest decoration and much plainer hairstyle." The costume expert also wonders at the lack of any evidence of Shakespeare's learning, of his status, "possibly a fur-lined gown, which quite wealthy middle-class men did wear—a modest interpretation of fashion for a man of status." And her conclusion was unequivocal: "I think it's a very interesting image. I just don't think it's Shakespeare." Ribeiro, it seems, can imagine no Shakespeare but a decorously dressed burgher of Stratford; if he had a mild fashion-victim phase at the beginning of his London celebrity, she cannot envision it.

When I told Lloyd of Ribeiro's assessment, he bristled and replied, "Experts can be wrong. Look at Spielmann." But a more positive assessment came from the art historian Tarnya Cooper. While she was troubled by the sitter's age, in her expert opinion it was definitely a portrait from the early seventeenth century. And it was of the size and style she would have expected for a man of Shakespeare's station.

The publication of my first articles about the Sanders portrait prompted a whole new line of inquiry. Many people who read the articles wrote to ask why the man with the painting or the *Globe* had not pursued paleography. Because neither he nor I knew it existed, I could have told them. I quickly learned that paleography is the study of old handwriting, and Lloyd readily agreed to submit the label to paleographic analysis.

Heather Wolfe at the Folger Library provided me with a list of some of the best paleographers in the world. I approached each of them with the request that they examine the label, or at least the set of ultraviolet photographs of the label that *The Globe* had purchased from the CCI, pictures that had been computer enhanced for maximum legibility (although the label still appeared indecipherable to me). The paleographers readily agreed to consider the label; their opinions were decidedly mixed.

The label, you may recall, read as follows, according to M. H. Spielmann's transcription of it in 1908:

Shakspere
Born April 23 = 1564
Died April 23 – 1616
Aged 52
This Likeness taken 1603
Age at that time 39 y^S

But Spielmann must have been reading an already faded script, so his interpretation cannot be considered indisputably accurate.

Wolfe was the first to question the information on the label, calling it anachronistic, since Elizabethan parishes recorded only baptismal dates, not birthdates. Shakespeare's official birthdate was not established till the 1740s. So a label written at the time the portrait was painted would be highly unlikely to refer to a birthdate and certain not to include a death date, since Shakespeare would live for another thirteen years. Other scholars would echo Wolfe's objection, adding the point that Shakespeare's birthdate has never been proved.

Peter Beal, the director of the department of books and manuscripts at Sotheby's auction house in London, wondered when William Shakespeare had come to be known only by his surname; certainly not in 1603, he was sure. And Beal was suspicious of the way the label was worded. "This does not strike me as the kind of inscription a contemporary would write. It's too crisp, efficient and comprehensive—in short, too modern. It's the kind of thing a later antiquary (or art dealer) would write.... From my experience, Elizabethan/Jacobean inscriptions recording the details of the sitter tend to be much briefer, or in Latin, and do not use phrases like 'Likeness taken.'"

Then there was the question of the style of handwriting itself. None of the experts I consulted thought the words could have been written as early as 1603. According to Elisabeth Leadham-Green, the long-serving, now-retired archivist of Cambridge University, "A contemporary of Shakespeare's would have used either a secretary hand (which has very distinctive letter forms, many of them quite different from modern hands) or an italic hand, or a 'mixed' hand combining features of the two. What we see here is a 'round hand' or . . . an attempt at such. Round hand does not appear until the eighteenth century and it continues into the nineteenth and indeed the twentieth. There is a further problem, which is harder to explain. [I] do not have the impression that whoever wrote the label was writing in his/her natural hand. The letters are carefully, too carefully, formed. It is the sort of writing that one finds in family Bibles: the very place one looks for examples of earlier handwriting [to copy for a spurious label]. If anything else, it resembles the writing of a studious child, or of someone not accustomed to writing, or not accustomed to writing script. It lacks fluency."

Beal did not think much of the style of writing either, declaring it definitely post-Jacobean. "It is in a rounded script nothing like early-seventeenth-century secretary script and with only minimal resemblance to Elizabethan/Jacobean italic. The words 'Born,' 'Died,' 'April,' for instance, would not have been written with those letter forms in the early seventeenth century. In my view, it is unlikely that this inscription was written earlier than the eighteenth century and more probably in the nineteenth century."

Laetitia Yeandle, the retired curator of manuscripts at the Folger Shakespeare Library and the doyenne of contemporary paleographers, also damned the script. "As far as I can tell from these photographs," she wrote, "the handwriting looks as though it dates at the earliest from the eighteenth century and possibly the nineteenth century."

However, some of these criticisms may be less grave than they first seem. Beal noted that "if the label is made of linen, it might partly account for why the writer is inscribing in a deliberate, rounded print-like hand, rather than a normal cursive style." Then a team of experts at the Records of Early English Drama project proposed a most intriguing hypothesis. (See "The Conundrum of the Label.")

Abigail Anne Young, Arleane Ralph and Alexandra Johnston of REED have studied the label first-hand—the only paleographers to have had the opportunity to do so—and they agree with Ian Lancashire that the label, which carbon dating had fixed as originating between 1475 and 1640, was most likely written and applied to the back of the panel one or two generations after the portrait was painted. "Labelling something when the people who know what it is are beginning to die off fits with human psychology," Johnston noted.

The REED team agreed with other experts that the writing on the label was certainly not early Jacobean. "Our suggestion is that somebody labelled the picture in the second half of the seventeenth century," says Johnston.

According to the REED hypothesis, after the label was first applied, the portrait was likely hung on a wall so that the paper became worn and faded to the point of illegibility. "In the late eighteenth century, somebody came along and overwrote it and traced the letters." The overwriting explains the sticky shape of the script, which does not flow normally. "It is like an overwritten passage in a fifteenth-century manuscript we have," Johnston noted. "It looks like somebody trying to preserve it. It is consistent with an overwriter."

REED's theory also helps to explain the anachronism of the birthdate. The notion that Shakespeare was born on April 23 hardened into orthodoxy with the publication of George Steevens's biography in 1773. "It got into the tradition at that point. If that's the case, the overwriter in the late eighteenth century supplied it," Johnston said. That explains the shades of eighteenth-century script that Leadham-Greene and Yeandle saw. The Toronto paleographers suggested the "born" may have been there in the late seventeenth century original, but not the death date, noting that "there is a mishmash of letter forms, word usage and abbreviations, which cannot be accounted for by any other hypothesis."

One reason REED's analysis differs from those of the other experts may lie in the kind of writing the project regularly examines: while museum curators typically see formal manuscripts written by educated people, REED looks at informal accounts of drama such as those found in letters or notes by church wardens. The manuscripts they examine were often written by less educated people, less comfortable with writing. In fact, Johnston says, the handwriting she and her colleagues deal with is typically "awful."

Johnston made one key point emphatically: "We are sure it is not a deliberate forgery. It would have been much better. The people of the nineteenth century were the world's great forgers. It was easy for them at the time to get seventeenth-century wood, seventeenth-century paper—they would get blank sixteenth-century paper and fake all kinds of things. Finding something about Shakespeare was really exciting in the nineteenth century, so lots of people were doing it. But if one were going to forge it, one would have forged the secretary hand, which is much spikier and much more elaborate. There were plenty of examples of it around."

The REED hypothesis will not suffice to totally satisfy the art historians, who want documentation that identifies the picture as Shakespeare from no later than 1650 and preferably from within a few years of the portrait's creation. The cult of celebrity around Shakespeare started some fifty years after his death. After that, all sorts of paintings from his time were falsely labelled as Shakespeare. "By the end of the seventeenth century, the mythology had built up so hugely. Even by 1650, people were creating Shakespeare myths," Andrew Gurr told me. "Anything after that is likely to have been sucked into the magnetic attraction for things tied to Shakespeare."

Lloyd, the pragmatic engineer, had no patience with those who suggested that the label was part of an attempt at fakery. "If you were going to conjure up a fake, you'd sell it. Why would you let it sit in the family for four hundred years?"

Only a few weeks after my initial *Globe* article appeared, the Art Gallery of Ontario was ready to put the portrait on display.

Once I had described the AGO's plan to Lloyd and told him about the gallery's sterling reputation, he agreed in principle to allow the Sanders portrait to go on show. After he received Matthew Teitelbaum's letter detailing the Gallery's careful plans for the exhibit and the insurance and security arrangements they would undertake, he gave his formal consent. Lloyd had always said the picture ought to be somewhere people could see it. And since he could not do anything with it for a few months anyway—not until he completed his portfolio of documentation—the portrait might as well hang in the Toronto art museum. Nor could it hurt his case to have the Sanders on display in a major Canadian art institution.

The curator Christina Corsiglia had inspected the painting and had an exhibit constructed that was scheduled to open on June 21. This would be the third time since the portrait's creation that members of the public would be able to view it but the first time it had been put on show in a reputable museum. In the exhibit and the publicity for it, the AGO would take no position on the picture's authenticity but would present it as an art historical mystery, under the suitably enigmatic title *Shakespeare?* The portrait would be displayed so that visitors could see both its front and back. Panels describing all the forensic testing—and the other contenders for the life-portrait title—would be displayed on the walls of the Gallery.

Late on the afternoon of June 20, I was on the phone in the *Globe* office checking some facts with Corsiglia when she mentioned that the AGO was admitting people to the Sanders exhibit a day early. Many visitors were asking about the painting—and the display was ready to go—so the Gallery had made the decision to open the doors that afternoon. I flagged down a cab and headed into the snarl of rush-hour traffic at the heart of the city. I planned to loiter in the hall outside the exhibit to observe the visitors. Would they react as I had, when I first met Willy Shake?

By the time I arrived, there was already a crowd in the octagonal exhibition room. The portrait stood by itself in the middle of the room, in a specially built case of reddish wood and thick, clear plastic. Visitors could walk around the picture and examine both the sitter's quixotic face and faded label on the back. Several of the people in the room were exclaiming over the enlarged photos of the CCI's analysis that adorned the walls, but Carole Brown was standing mesmerized before the picture. Brown is a lawyer from Ottawa and a lover of Shakespeare who happened to be in Toronto that day for meetings. In between her appointments she dashed over to the Gallery in the hope of catching a glimpse of a portrait. She circled the portrait a few times, then came back to stare at his face. "This is a gaze on humanity," she said quietly. "It's a critical but human gaze. And there's a steadfastness about the mouth. He wouldn't suffer fools lightly—we know where that phrase comes from." She stepped back, cocked her head. "This is right. It's a very intelligent face. There's a poet in that face."

Brown's reaction was typical. All summer long the Sanders portrait drew the passionate and the merely curious. Corsiglia later told me that anytime she stopped in to the exhibit, she would find thirty people reading the explanatory texts about the forensic tests the painting had passed, studying the reproductions of other portraits of Shakespeare, or, most often, standing and staring at the face. And most of them, it seemed, signed a comment book placed on a table in the exhibition room, which filled up rapidly with exclamations, written in a half-dozen languages but unified in opinion: visitors adored the portrait, they believed it was Shakespeare and they wanted it to stay in Canada.

And the portrait seemed to have galvanized the world of Shakespeare scholarship. Six months after I first reported on the picture, the Records of Early English Drama project at the University of Toronto and the AGO announced plans to host a symposium on the Sanders portrait in November 2002. Among items on the planned agenda is a report by William Ingram, professor emeritus of English literature at the University of Michigan at Ann Arbor. As this book went to press, Ingram was at work in London, searching for documentary evidence of John Sanders.

Which is not to say that the discovery of a John Sanders from Worcester, at work in the London theatre in 1603, would end the debate. Of course not. As Stanley Wells told me when I discussed the painting's prospects with him back in the summer of 2001, only a smoking gun will satisfy the greatest skeptics. "If the identity of the subject was on the picture itself in painterly handwriting of the period, that's the strongest you could get," he said.

Well, no chance of that. "Next would be a record in the painter's own catalogue of his own works, saying he painted William Shakespeare at this age of his life." This kind of record could yet be found. Next best would be solid evidence that not only put John Sanders in the theatrical world but also linked him specifically with Shakespeare. Perhaps William Ingram or another Shakespeare expert, intrigued by the portrait, will make this kind of discovery.

Proof positive that the Sanders portrait shows us William Shakespeare in his prime would add nothing to Shakespeare's literary legacy. *Hamlet* does not change if we know Will and John rehearsed lines together. But it would nevertheless matter immensely. "Given the choice between two discoveries—that of an unknown play by Shakespeare and that of one of Will's laundry lists—we would all plump for the dirty washing every time," Anthony Burgess wrote in *Shakespeare*. "That Shakespeare persists in presenting so shadowy a figure . . . is one of our reasons for pursuing him. . . . It is maddening that Shakespeare gives us nothing when Ben [Jonson] is only too ready to accost us with his mountain belly and his rocky face."[4] It seems almost deliberate and sly, that the man who gave us a wealth of immortal stories and characters, who forever reshaped the language—the man who *invented* us, in the words of the critic Harold Bloom—did not leave us a record of his face.

In the early autumn of 2001, Lloyd and Raymond paid a call on Christina Corsiglia, seeking the curator's advice on their portfolio documenting the case for the Sanders portrait. Corsiglia talked with them until after the AGO doors had closed and the day's visitors had gone. As she escorted her guests to the door, she asked if they wanted to stop to see the painting before it was taken down—the gallery had a pre-scheduled exhibit about to move into its space.

"I wasn't sure if I'd even see it again," Lloyd later told me, for he thought the family might sell it soon.

Corsiglia led the two men into the dimmed gallery. As they entered, a single light suddenly came on. Alarmed, Corsiglia left the men alone with the picture while she found a security guard.

"The light was right over Shakespeare," Lloyd confides with a smile, knowing he sounds sentimental. "And there he was looking at us. It was like he was saying goodbye."

The Conundrum of the Label

Alexandra F. Johnston,
Arleane Ralph and Abigail Anne Young

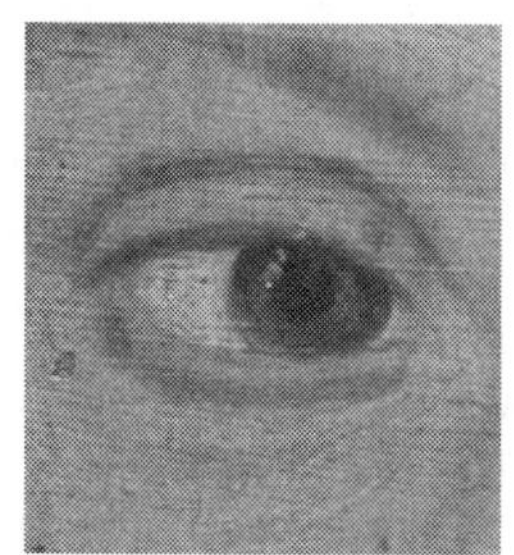

AFFIXED TO the back of the panel on which the portrait is painted is a small linen rag paper label, well worn and badly torn, that has been carbon dated to between 1475 and 1640. All that can be seen on this scrap of paper with the naked eye (and only in strong light with magnification) are traces of black ink. Attempting to read it under ultraviolet light has proved little better. However, the Canadian Conservation Institute has photographed the label under ultraviolet and has computer enhanced the photograph for maximum legibility. This photograph, which has been reproduced as faithfully as possible in colour in "The Picture Gallery" section of the book and in black and white on the opposite page, is all the direct evidence available to the contemporary paleographer. We emphasize at the outset that given the extent of the damage, all conclusions must be speculative.

Speculation is increased because of the anomalies that exist between the writing as it can be read today and the transcription made by M. H. Spielmann in 1909 (reproduced opposite).[1]

Between 1909 and 2002, a significant portion of the label

Shakspere

Born April 23=1564

Died April 23—1616

Aged 52

This Likeness taken 1603

Age at that time 39 ys

has been lost, but what remains indicates that Spielmann (or his typesetter) did not preserve the format of the lines. The name "Shakspere" that is centred in the Spielmann version is all but gone in the remaining label, although it is possible that it was there flush left and that the loop just visible in the top left of the surviving paper is from the bottom of the capital *S* and the other mark at the point of the tear is the descender of the *p*. The problem of reading the label is compounded by the holes that have been rubbed in the paper as the rough grain of the board has pressed on it either when hung on a wall or lying flat. What can actually be read today is:

B rn Ap 564
Died Apr l 23 1616
Aged 52
This Likene ta en 1603
Age at that time

The month and year of birth are correct for Shakespeare, as is the date of death. That is all that now connects this label with Shakespeare.

Should we then dismiss the label as a witness to the possible identity of the portrait? We think not. If the label is, as has been suggested, a forgery deliberately meant to deceive, it is a very bad attempt. The writing is not the familiar secretary hand of the early seventeenth century so ably recreated by such nineteenth-century forgers of Shakespeare as John Payne

Collier.[2] Any forger worth his craft would have produced a more credible script. We believe the hand could be from later in the seventeenth century. The letter forms are not unlike nonliterary hands from the mid-seventeenth century that we are familiar with through our work with manuscripts at Records of Early English Drama. The way "1616" is written is typical of that period. But as our colleague Elisabeth Leadham-Green of Cambridge has rightly noticed, "The letters are carefully, too carefully, formed. It is the sort of writing that one finds in family Bibles. . . . It lacks fluency." We suggest that this lack of fluency comes from the fact that the words were overwritten some years after they were first composed because the writing had faded and was becoming illegible. One of the documents we published in our first collection of dramatic records—the records of York—was overwritten in a much later hand in an attempt to make the original clearer.[3]

We believe that a plausible hypothesis can be proposed that fits the tradition behind the provenance of this portrait. The University of Toronto's Ian Lancashire has made the point that people begin labelling possessions (and the most common thing today is old photographs) when the memory of what the object is or where it came from begins to fade. We suggest that the writing on the label was first composed sometime after 1650 in the later years of a family member who knew the tradition of the portrait. As the original lettering began to fade—sometime in the late eighteenth century—this later family member traced over the original inscription in order to keep the family tradition alive.

Such a hypothesis would account for the fact that the paper of the label dates from the rough period of the painting but that some of the odd letter forms in the inscription (such as the rounded *a*'s and the capital *B* in "Born") as they can now be deciphered do not. It would also meet several objections that have been raised about the content of the label. First, the birthdate of April 23 would be an anomaly if the label were dated soon after 1616. As several commentators have observed, the Elizabethans were not concerned with birthdates. We know from the baptismal register of the parish church of Stratford that William Shakespeare was baptized April 26, 1564. The tradition that he was born April 23 grew up much later, partly to create symmetry with his death date but also to fulfil the romantic desire to have the nation's greatest playwright born on the feast day of England's patron saint, St. George. The tradition became part of "common knowledge" about Shakespeare after the publication of George Steevens's edition of the plays in 1773.[4] If the "23" was indeed there in 1909 and not provided by Spielmann himself, who would, of course, have known the tradition, it could have been provided by the late-eighteenth-century overwriter.

Second, literary scholars have objected that the phrase "likeness taken" does not appear in the *Oxford English Dictionary* until 1647. Although we do not consider this a valid objection since the *OED* is based on literary sources, and both "likeness" and "to take" appear separately much earlier with the meanings of "picture" and "to draw or depict," our suggestion that the original writing is post 1650 meets that concern.

If we dismiss the idea of a deliberate forgery and consider the family tradition that maintains the portrait has been passed from generation to generation in a single family since it was first painted, we believe our hypothesis embraces all the objections that have been raised. While our hypothesis does not prove that the Sanders portrait is of Shakespeare, we believe there is nothing in the label that disproves the ascription.

The Man Who Will Not Meet Your Eyes

Alexander Leggatt

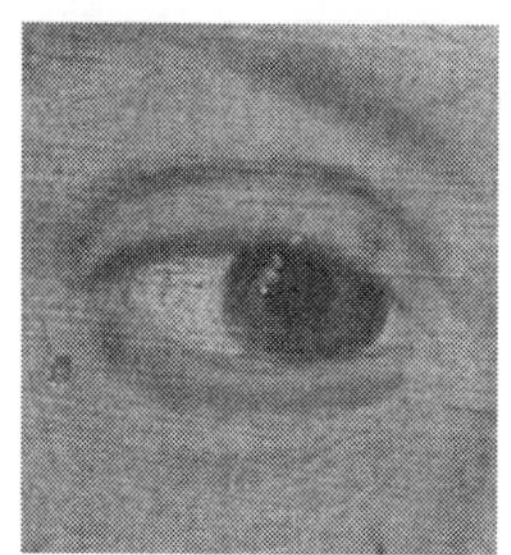

IT IS A JUNE DAY in 2001; I am standing in an octagonal room in the Art Gallery of Ontario, where the Sanders portrait is about to go on public display for the first time. The walls are hung with an exhibit showing other versions of Shakespeare's face and describing the technical tests that have established the age of the materials in the portrait, opening the possibility that it may indeed be what the label on the back claims it to be—a likeness of William Shakespeare in 1603. In the centre of the room, in a double-sided glass case raised on a pedestal, is the painting itself. I am getting a preview arranged by a local television station, which wants my views on the portrait based on a first-hand look, supplemented by footage of me walking around it, closing in on it, preparing to make a pronouncement. Shakespeare's four hundred years of fame have become my fifteen minutes of fame, mine being more evanescent than his: on the news broadcast I watch that night, none of the footage is used. No matter. By getting up close and personal, I have learned something.

Like everyone else who has seen the portrait reproduced in *The Globe and Mail* I have been struck by the engaging personality of the face, so unlike the flat inexpressiveness of the familiar

Droeshout likeness in the Folio. This man is young, he has hair and he is smiling. But given the opportunity to walk all around him, to see him from various angles, I find I can't make contact with him. There is a painter's trick that allows you to think, as you walk around a portrait, that the sitter is following you with his eyes. These eyes, as I look at them from different angles, seem to be looking sideways, downward and above all inward. They are the eyes of someone absorbed in his own thoughts; I cannot get him to look at me.

Pictures can help us organize our ideas, and a picture of a writer can help us organize our ideas about the writer. The tight-drawn line of T. S. Eliot's mouth, the broad bare chest of Ernest Hemingway, the Druid-in-tweeds look of Robertson Davies—all these are with you in your imagination as you read. Is this a face we can take into our reading of Shakespeare? In particular, how does it relate to what we know of the man and his work in 1603? I stress 1603 because while the Droeshout portrait in the Folio is Shakespeare in black and white, dead and collected, setting his stamp on a posthumous anthology of his work, the Sanders portrait is Shakespeare alive, in colour, in mid-career. The Droeshout face is for book buyers; the Sanders face is the one you might have encountered if you were hanging around the Globe Theatre.

I begin with the smile. The man in the Sanders portrait has an amiable face, and early accounts of Shakespeare suggest an amiable man. Near the start of his career he was attacked by a senior playwright, Robert Greene, who on his deathbed denounced him as an "upstart crow," a mere actor who presumed to set himself up as a playwright.[1] Another playwright, Henry Chettle, who had been involved in the publication of Greene's attack, took the trouble to apologize: "I am as sorry as if the original fault had been my fault, because myself have seen his demeanour no less civil than he excellent in the quality he professes [i.e., acting]. Besides, divers of worship [many of good social standing] have reported his uprightness of dealing, which argues his honesty, and his facetious grace in writing, that approves [demonstrates] his art."[2] "Facetious" to us is a word that suggests superficial flippancy; it was more of a compliment in Shakespeare's time, and combined with "grace" suggests a polished, stylish wit. Chettle links the virtues of the man with the virtues of his art and evokes a Shakespeare who is talented, charming, polite, well-connected and trustworthy. Is it any wonder that Greene, who had messed up his own life and was dying in poverty, resented him?

This is no tortured, temperamental artist but a smooth-mannered fellow who knows how to make himself agreeable. In contemporary tributes to his work, the recurring note is sweetness. In 1598 Francis Meres declares, "the sweet witty soul of Ovid lives in mellifluous and honey-tongued Shakespeare, witness his *Venus and Adonis*, his *Lucrece*, his sugared sonnets [among his private friends]."[3] A verse tribute by John Weever (1599) addresses "Honey-tongued Shakespeare" and pays tribute to his characters' "sugared tongues."[4] The foolish Gullio, in the Cambridge play *The Return from Parnassus, Part One* (c. 1599), gushes about "sweet Mr. Shakespeare," whose picture he wants in his study.[5] Here the sweetness seems to be not just that of the work, but of the man.

Back to the Sanders portrait: the smile is certainly sweet, even gentle; and when we look at Shakespeare's early work we can see the smoothness that seems to have made people like the man. He knows how to make potentially controversial material easier to take, filing down the rough edges. We see this when we compare his villain-heroes with those of his most important predecessor, Christopher Marlowe. When Marlowe had died in a tavern brawl in 1593, respectable moralists rejoiced that the blasphemer had got what was coming to him. Marlowe's rebellious heroes defy conventional morality and religious belief. The title character of his two-part epic *Tamburlaine the Great* (c. 1587–88) conquers country after country, burning cities and massacring their inhabitants. When one of his sons shows pacifist tendencies, Tamburlaine kills him. No power on earth can stop him; as though bored by the lack of competition, he challenges Heaven. He burns the Koran, and defies "Mahomet" to do anything about it. Shortly after, he feels the first twinge of the sickness that will kill him; but it never occurs to him that he is being punished, or that he has anything to repent. While looking to a triumph beyond the grave, he is still fixated on his earthly career (Part Two, 5.3.121–25):

> In vain I strive and rail against those powers
> That mean t'invest me in a higher throne,
> As much too high for this disdainful earth.
> Give me a map; then let me see how much
> Is left for me to conquer all the world.[6]

Once a conqueror, always a conqueror. Barabas, the villain-hero of *The Jew of Malta* (c. 1588), goes from moneymaking to large-scale murder and treason. In the end he makes a fatal mistake: he trusts a Christian, who catches him in his own booby trap, a boiling cauldron. Barabas dies not repenting but cursing: "Die, life! fly, soul! tongue, curse thy fill, and die!" (5.5.94).

Shakespeare's Richard of Gloucester, who in the *Henry VI* plays (c. 1589–92) and *Richard III* (c. 1593) murders his way through the royal family to make himself King, shares the ruthless ambition of Tamburlaine and the intriguer's cunning and daring wit of Barabas. At the opening of *Richard III* he declares, "I am determinèd to prove a villain" (1.1.30). He starts by having his brother George imprisoned and murdered and goes on from there. You know where you are with Richard. But toward the end of the play, in a dream before his final battle, the ghosts of all the people Richard has killed appear and denounce him. It is a long procession. He wakes in panic, and the shameless self-confidence in villainy he has shown up to now suddenly breaks apart (5.5.145–55):

> I am a villain. Yet I lie: I am not.
> Fool, of thyself speak well.—Fool, do not flatter.
> My conscience hath a thousand several tongues.
> And every tongue brings in a several tale,
> And every tale condemns me for a villain.
>
> I shall despair. There is no creature loves me,
> And if I die no soul will pity me.

He recovers; but Shakespeare has allowed him something Marlowe never gives his defiant villain-heroes: a moment to feel the pain of being excluded from the human community, to wish he had the pity and love he has denied himself. Marlowe was a tough customer and shaped his heroes accordingly; Shakespeare was more humane.

Marlowe's Barabas has one apparent soft spot: he loves his daughter Abigail. But when she turns against him, converts to Christianity and enters a convent, he dispatches the entire convent with a bowl of poisoned porridge in order to kill her. Aaron the Moor, the principal villain of Shakespeare's *Titus Andronicus* (c. 1590), is a close counterpart to Barabas, with the same tendency to gloat over his own evil. His hobbies include murder, rape, arson and digging up dead bodies. But Aaron too has a child, the product of his affair with the Empress Tamora. When Tamora's sons, offended at the sight of a black baby, prepare to kill it, Aaron intervenes to save it, declaring, "Sweet blowze, you are a beauteous blossom, sure" (4.2.72). In that line we hear a note of unguarded affection virtually nowhere else in this violent play—and we hear (coincidentally?) the word so often applied to Shakespeare: sweet. While Marlowe gives his villain a touch of humanity, then withdraws it, Shakespeare can surprise us with gentleness from the most unlikely character, in the midst of the bloodiest revenge tragedy he ever wrote.

You do not get a reputation for being civil and honest (Chettle's words) if you put people's backs up too much, and there are times when we can see the younger Shakespeare deciding to play it safe. Once again a comparison with one of his predecessors is revealing. John Lyly, who wrote courtly comedies for all-boy companies in the 1580s, set an important precedent for Shakespeare in his use of fantasy and stylization. In Lyly's *Gallathea* (c. 1584) two girls, Gallathea and Phyllida, both disguised as boys, fall in love with each other. Even when the truth comes out, they still want to get married, despite the obvious practical and social difficulties. The gods, who have taken an active part in the story, debate the problem. Neptune takes the view that same-sex love is a contradiction in terms: "An idle choice, strange and foolish, for one virgin to dote on another, and to imagine a constant faith where there can be no cause of affection." But when he appeals to the specialist in love—"How like you this, Venus?"—Venus replies, "I like it well and allow it . . . never shall it be said that Nature or Fortune shall overthrow love and faith" (5.3.131–36).[7] She says, in effect, it's love, don't worry about the details. In a final concession to heterosexual assumptions, she promises that just before the girls are married one will be transformed into a boy. She does not say which one—we never know—and the girls are perfectly content. What the audience sees at the end of the play is two girls, both dressed as boys, both played by boy actors, going off to get married. Even allowing for the play's air of fantasy, there must have been a few raised eyebrows in the auditorium.

Shakespeare also puts his heroines (played by boy actors) into male dress. In some comedies, such as *The Merchant of Venice* (c. 1597) and *As You Like It* (c. 1599), they reappear as women at the end of the play. But Julia in *The Two Gentlemen of Verona* (c. 1592) and Viola in *Twelfth Night* (c. 1601) are dressed as boys right up to the end. Their lovers are men—Shakespeare does not go so far as Lyly—but in *Twelfth Night* he teases us with the possibility that he might. Viola has spent most of the play disguised as the boy Cesario, serving Count Orsino and falling in love with him. Orsino has shown a growing, more than friendly interest in Cesario, but the male disguise stops him from admitting even to himself the full depth of his affection. When Viola's name and sex are revealed, he turns to her with relief and starts the conversation he has always wished he could have: "Boy, thou hast said to me a thousand times / Thou never shouldst love woman like to me" (5.1.260–61). He asks to see her in women's clothing, but here and right to the end of the play he continues to call her "boy" and "Cesario." Audience members who think conventionally could simply take this as a joke, but the joke may have a point: Orsino fell in love with a boy, and the boy, looking no different, is standing in front of him. There is a sense in which the Count is going to marry Cesario. In *Twelfth Night* Shakespeare plays Lyly's game—more tactfully, but it is the same game. When we look at the Sanders portrait, we see a smile that is accommodating, with just a hint of private amusement.

That hint takes us away from the sweet and gentle Shakespeare who knows how to be agreeable, and toward the man who will not meet our eyes. This young man likes to tease us, and some of the teasing is erotic. In *Romeo and Juliet* (c. 1595) we expect bawdy puns in the comic scenes dominated by Romeo's witty friend Mercutio, and we get them: "the bawdy hand of the dial is now upon the prick of noon" (2.3.99–100). What we do not expect is that the scenes of stormy lamentation the lovers have after Romeo's banishment will be touched by similar jokes. Finding Romeo prostrate with grief, the Nurse remarks that Juliet is just the same: "O, he is even in my mistress' case, / Just in her case" (3.3.84–85). The repetition of the key word is a nudge to the audience to remember that "case" can mean "vagina." When the Nurse goes on to urge Romeo, "For Juliet's sake, for her sake, rise and stand" (3.3.89), we do not need footnotes. But the jokes come so fast we might miss them, or catch them just a moment too late, asking ourselves, "What did she just say?" The smile is teasing.

The full collection of Shakespeare's sonnets did not appear until 1609, but two of them were in print by 1599, in a collection called *The Passionate Pilgrim,* and in both there is a playful wit that lightens what could be a painful account of deception in love. The 1599 version of Sonnet 138 reads:

> When my love swears that she is made of truth
> I do believe her though I know she lies,
> That she might think me some untutored youth
> Unskilful in the world's false forgeries.
> Thus vainly thinking that she thinks me young,
> Although I know my years be past the best,
> I, smiling, credit her false-speaking tongue,
> Outfacing faults in love with love's ill rest.
> But wherefore says my love that she is young,
> And wherefore say not I that I am old?
> O, love's best habit's in a soothing tongue,
> And age in love loves not to have years told.
> Therefore I'll lie with love, and love with me,
> Since that our faults in love thus smothered be.

From the first two lines, we see a relationship that depends on game playing, on agreeing to believe a lie. Shakespeare—it is a critical convention to call the first-person voice in a poem "the speaker," avoiding the whole question of whether he is meant to be the author, but in an essay on the Sanders portrait such caution seems misplaced—Shakespeare, then, dwells on the mutual pretence he and his lover make that he is still young. She lies about it, and he pretends to believe the lie: "I, smiling, credit her false-speaking tongue." The smile is unique to this version of the sonnet. In the 1609 version the line reads "Simply I credit her false-speaking tongue." Back to the Sanders portrait: is that smile a little rueful? It is a common observation that the portrait looks young for a man of thirty-nine. Was it—just a thought—part of the game of pretending to be young? But he is not meeting our eyes; the game involves concealment. And it may involve pretending not to notice that on a closer look those eyes have faint bags beneath them.

In two of the changes it makes, the 1609 version of this sonnet is more straightforward, less enigmatic. The incomprehensible 1599 line "Outfacing faults in love with love's ill rest" becomes the crystal clear "On both sides thus is simple truth suppressed." The new version also makes it clear through wordplay that part of what keeps this relationship going is sex: "Therefore I lie with her, and she with me, / And in our faults by lies we flattered be." The 1599 version, "Therefore I'll lie with love, and love with me, / Since that our faults in love thus smothered be," is lighter and more intricate. Instead of the straightforward pun on "lie," which brings out the sex in blunt language, there is a play of suggestions in "lie with love" that includes lying about love as well as lying with one's lover. Their faults are not "flattered," with the harsh edge that word brings, but "smothered," hidden and suppressed as if under the bedclothes. This was the version available in 1603, and it is lighter and more enigmatic than its successor.

In the other sonnet published in 1599, the sonnet now known as 144, Shakespeare imagines that his two principal lovers, whom he does not name but whom critics have called the young man and the dark lady, are betraying him by having an affair with each other. He calls them his good and evil angels and visualizes them in the sexual act: "I guess one angel in another's hell." It is all suspicion, a jealous fantasy: but he expects to find the truth when the dark lady infects the young man with venereal disease: "my bad angel fire my good one out." This time the changes between 1599 and 1609 are less extensive, but one of them shows the early version, again, as a little lighter. Shakespeare imagines the lady seducing the young man, "Wooing his purity with her fair pride." In 1609 this rueful compliment to her beauty has turned into a straight attack, with "fair pride" becoming "foul pride." In neither version, however, does the poem seem particularly "sweet": the joke is bitter. Yet it is still a joke. Marlowe's *Doctor Faustus* (c. 1592), drawing on the traditions of earlier religous drama, had shown Faustus accompanied by a Good Angel and an Evil Angel, the first trying to save him by drawing him away from the forbidden arts of magic, the second trying to tempt him into damnation. The Evil Angel wins. For once, Shakespeare is more impudent than Marlowe; he imagines an evil angel tempting not a human subject but a good angel—and succeeding. Abandoning Shakespeare, the angels go off to bed with each other.[8] It may be painful fun, but it is still fun.

And it is all speculation; in both versions of Sonnet 144 Shakespeare admits he knows nothing. Did anything like this really happen? The only thing we know for certain is that Shakespeare never knows for certain. Or rather, the speaker of the poem (to be cautious again) claims he does not know for certain. What that has to do with the reality of Shakespeare's own love life remains as elusive as the identities of the young man and the dark lady, if indeed there ever were such people. Rivers of ink have flowed, forests have been felled, and we are none the wiser. The man in the picture will not meet our eyes. The more we notice his avoidance, the less his smile looks sweet and amiable, the more it looks enigmatic, sphinxlike.

As was the public Shakespeare—or what we know of him up to 1603. Henry Chettle's tribute, defending Shakespeare from Greene's attack, suggests an agreeable man; but whatever Shakespeare himself may have said to, or about, either Greene or Chettle, remains unrecorded. There is a graceful tribute to Marlowe in *As You Like It*: "Dead shepherd, now I find thy saw of might: / 'Who ever loved that loved not at first sight?' " (3.5.82–83). (Marlowe was the author of "The Passionate Shepherd to His Love," and the line is quoted from Marlowe's *Hero and Leander*). That one line apart, Shakespeare does not comment on the work of other writers. He does not attack them as his younger, more satiric contemporary Ben Jonson does.[9] When around the beginning of the seventeenth century playwrights began to write commendatory verses complimenting each other in the preliminaries to printed editions of their plays, Shakespeare did not join in. He did not solicit compliments either; there are no commendatory verses from other writers to the editions of his plays published in his lifetime. Was there, beneath the agreeableness, a certain aloofness and a sense of privacy others learned to respect?

How did he feel about his own reputation for sweetness and gentleness, this man who will not look us in the face? We have no direct knowledge of his attitude, and it would be surprising if we did. But there are teasing hints in his work. The 1599 version of Sonnet 138 includes among the equipment of lying lovers "a soothing tongue." (This becomes "seeming trust" in 1609.) Do you trust someone who is too agreeable? As to that stock compliment, "sweet," there is a little outburst of irritation in *Love's Labour's Lost* (c. 1594), when Biron asks the Princess, "White-handed mistress, one sweet word with thee," and she snaps back, "Honey and milk and sugar—there is three" (5.2.230–31). One line leaps out of the text of *King John* (c. 1596): "Sweet, sweet, sweet poison for the age's tooth" (1.1.213). As for the smile: that inveterate phrasemaker Hamlet (c. 1600) is so arrested by the thought "That one may smile and smile and be a villain" (1.5.109) that he pauses to write it down. The eyes look away; are they a bit tired of the compliments? What is that smile concealing?

That Shakespeare's work can be enigmatic, entertaining a wide variety of interpretations but refusing to let any one lock into place as unquestionably right, is one of the chief sources of its fascination. In *The Taming of the Shrew* (c. 1592) Katherine, a high-spirited young woman who terrifies anyone who comes near her, is wooed by Petruccio, who is determined to marry her for her money and to tame her. At the end of their first interview, she absolutely refuses to marry him. We next see her on her wedding day, waiting at the church, fuming because Petruccio is late. What happened between those two scenes? In the subsequent action, when Petruccio tames Katherine through a combination of brainwashing techniques—depriving her of food and sleep, scrambling her sense of time—is she really tamed, is she acquiescing as a survival strategy, or is she joining in, actively enjoying the game? (*Is* it a game?) There is another play of the time, the anonymous *The Taming of a Shrew* (c. 1592), which is so close in character and action to Shakespeare's that one play has to be seen as a version of the other, though how exactly the relationship works is much debated. The shrew of this other play, even as she defies her Petruccio, lets us in on her strategy in an aside (5.40–2):

> But yet I will consent and marry him,
> For I methinks have lived too long a maid,
> And match him too, or else his manhood's good.[10]

This character's motives and intentions are clear. Looking back to Shakespeare, we realize that his Katherine has (like her successor Cleopatra) no asides or soliloquies. We never know what is going on in her mind; we have only her reactions to events, which bear different possible interpretations. If we try to look into her eyes, we cannot get her to look back.

However Shakespeare may have tamed the ending of Lyly's *Gallathea* when he wrote *Twelfth Night*, elsewhere he picked up and expanded one of the earlier playwright's devices to tease the audience. Lyly never tells us which girl will be changed into a boy. We have to decide—or decide if it is even worth deciding. In *Love's Labour's Lost*, four lords woo four ladies, and since this is a comedy we know what will happen: after the requisite conflicts and misunderstandings they will get married in the end. Except they don't; we forgot about the title. (That smile again.) The decision is deferred for a year, one of the men notes, "That's too long for a play" (5.2.855), and there the matter rests, unresolved, leaving an uncertain future where another writer would put an ending.

Paradoxically, Shakespeare can also construct enigmas by giving us not less information but more. In his *Henry IV* plays

(c. 1596–97), he inherits the popular tradition of the wild Prince Hal leading a playboy life in the taverns of London only to repent and reform when on the death of his father he becomes King Henry V. In the anonymous *Famous Victories of Henry V* (c. 1586), the legend is played straight: the Prince rampages through the taverns and brothels with the same thuggish energy he brings to the conquest of France after he becomes King. Shakespeare transforms the character. At the end of the first tavern scene in *Henry IV, Part One* the Prince is left alone to do something Katherine never does: he speaks his thoughts to the audience. What he tells us is that the playboy image is a calculated performance, an exercise in what a modern spin artist would call the raising of negative expectations: he is making himself look bad now so that his later reform, which he has already planned, will look even more stunning: "I'll so offend to make offence a skill, / Redeeming time when men think least I will" (1.2.194–5).

The explanation raises more questions than it answers. Hal's tavern cronies, led by Falstaff, think of Hal as a friend. Can anyone really calculate his human relationships so coldly, over such a long range, and if so what do we think of such a person? What kind of virtue is it that uses other people in this way? Hal enters into the tavern life, matching wits with Falstaff, with what looks like real panache and enjoyment. Is none of the pleasure real? Does he manage to enjoy himself even while keeping his spin game going? Is the explanation he offers in soliloquy the truth about his plans or a rationalization? What about other, more reasonable-sounding motives, such as a desire to learn about the people he is going to govern? We could sympathize with such a motive, and some critics offer it as a theory about him; but if this is his purpose, why does he not say so himself? Amid the fun and bustle of the tavern scenes there is one character who may or may not be enjoying himself, who has a hidden agenda he may or may not have revealed to us, who will not meet our eyes—even when he seems to be looking right at us.

When Shakespeare puts Prince Hal on the throne in *Henry V* (1599) as the hero King who won legendary victories in France, the enigma deepens. Much of the play seems a genuinely stirring celebration of the war. That is what the Chorus's opening speech leads us to expect. But the first scene of the play proper takes us to the ecclesiastical equivalent of a smoke-filled back room in which two worldly bishops fret over an impending bill in Parliament that would strip the Church of a substantial amount of its property; they plan to win the King's favour by giving a large cash grant to his war effort—in effect, a bribe. Then we are off to the throne room, and to the justice of Henry's cause, the excitement of his battle poetry—but for a moment we have glimpsed something shabby behind the glory and the glamour. Later in the play, even the great victory at Agincourt raises questions: if Shakespeare had wanted us to see Henry as a straightforward national hero, why did he include one of the historical Henry's most controversial acts, the killing of French prisoners? The play marches on, its characters seemingly untroubled by the awkward questions their actions are provoking. Some judicious cuts would have eliminated those questions; some more explicit pointing would have called decisive attention to them. The play does neither. Its intention, like its author, remains enigmatic.

That was where Shakespeare was in 1603: provoking questions he did not answer. Why does Hamlet delay his revenge? Hamlet's own answer (in one of the play's three surviving versions; that's another problem) is "I do not know" (4.4.33). If Shakespeare is the sitter in the Sanders portrait, it is possible that between sittings he was working on *Measure for Measure* (c. 1603), one of his most problematic and hotly debated plays, which concludes with the Duke proposing marriage to Isabella, a proposal to which she does not reply. Will she accept him or not? Critics debate, productions decide one way or another; the text is silent.

Shakespeare's work to this point has been engaging and entertaining, popular then as now. His tragedies *Romeo and Juliet* and *Hamlet* are more fun than many other authors' comedies. John Weever's 1599 verse tribute ends with a hope that Shakespeare will continue in his present honey-tongued vein.[11] The Shakespeare of 1603 must have heard that one a lot. But the man in the picture is looking away; he has his own agenda. In *Troilus and Cressida* (c. 1601) and *Measure for Measure* there is a new harshness, even in the laughter. In *Othello* (c. 1604), *King Lear* (c. 1606) and *Macbeth* (c. 1607), which lie just ahead, "Sweet Mr. Shakespeare" will be giving his audience nightmares.

The Sanders portrait, amiable and engaging but somewhat withdrawn, may or may not be Shakespeare as he looked in 1603. Others who have looked into this face have reported on the kind of man who looks back them from the picture; I have reported that I could not find that man. We seem likely to go on debating this face, as we debate the plays and poems. We debate Shakespeare's work because we do not know his characters fully, and this is a key to our sense of their humanity. With conventional characters, drawn to a formula, we know everything there is to know—as we never do with real people, even our closest friends.

If Shakespeare fools us into thinking of his characters as real people (and he does, over and over) it is because, as with real people, we never fully know them. The Droeshout Shakespeare gives us a flat stare; the Sanders Shakespeare looks away; the Sanders Shakespeare is more human. That face keeps its secrets—including the secret of its identity. The fact that it does so may be, paradoxically, one of the best arguments for seeing it as the face of Shakespeare.

Is This the Face of Genius?

SINCE LLOYD SULLIVAN first pulled a peculiar old picture from beneath his grandmother's bed, the Sanders portrait has been part of his life. After his retirement, it grew from a diverting hobby into a consuming passion, ultimately leading me to his door on a May morning in 2001, then to my first articles about the portrait, and finally to *Shakespeare's Face*.

To help us know that face, this book has called upon a cast of scholars whose wide knowledge and differing perspectives have helped complete the picture. Now these experts take the stage once more, this time to weigh the evidence and offer their parting opinions. Do they think the portrait is authentic to 1603? If so, is it a portrait of William Shakespeare? Does it really matter either way? If it matters, what will it mean for Shakespeare studies, for a world so far removed from the time and place in which the face was born?

Stanley Wells

Wherever it is shown or reproduced the Sanders portrait—as it will continue to be known, whether or not it was painted by someone named John Sanders—will be the subject of intense interpretative activity as spectators puzzle over what it may tell us about its subject: who he was, how old he was and what sort of a person he was. Inevitably it will be compared with the only two images of Shakespeare that have any real claim to authenticity, the Droeshout engraving and the Janssen portrait bust in Holy Trinity Church, Stratford-upon-Avon. Neither of these can be precisely dated but they were produced after Shakespeare's death, and it is impossible to say whether their artists ever even saw their subject. The engraving seems likely to derive from a drawing, or even possibly an earlier engraving—like the one of Ben Jonson I mentioned—done from a lost drawing. It is virtually certain, in other words, that Shakespeare did not sit for Droeshout and quite possible he never laid eyes on him. The fact—I think it is a fact—that it seems to depict a younger man than the subject of the Stratford bust may encourage the speculation that Droeshout was working from a relatively early image. The bust was clearly carved specifically for the monument, which was in place by 1623, within a few months of the first appearance in print of the engraving. Though the bust's subject resembles that of the engraving closely enough for us to believe that it is a portrait of the same man, it does not appear to derive either from the engraving or from whatever may have served as the source of the engraving. It must therefore derive either from a separate image, perhaps a drawing supplied by Shakespeare's family, or from the sculptor's personal knowledge, or from his imagination, perhaps aided by the memories of other persons. And it probably depicts the sitter toward the time of his death.

None of this can give us great confidence in either the engraving or the bust as a true and faithful likeness of the man they claim to represent, and this in turn makes it all the more difficult to assess the authenticity of the Sanders painting by comparison with other images. One reason why the Sanders portrait is being taken so seriously is, I think, because the sitter looks so much more interesting than the subject of the engraving and the bust. And of course we feel that Shakespeare should have looked interesting. The engraving is mask-like, the bust provincial-looking. By comparison, the Sanders sitter is more characterful. As in the other images, he has elegantly arched, slender eyebrows, a faint line of moustache, more beard but a wispier one than is visible in the engraving, and he wears his hair long over his ears. He is less bald, which helps to make him look considerably younger even than the sitter for the engraving, but his hair is starting to recede. The nose is less prominent, the lips are less full, the eyes are set farther apart. The angle of the head is similar to that in the engraving, which encourages the notion of resemblance, and the ruff is not dissimilar, though in the painting it is turned down, revealing a long and possibly hairy neck. The expression—and this is what gives a sense of character—is less bland; there is just a faint hint of a smile, of a twinkle in the eye, even of disdain. The costume does not look aristocratic; the man looks self-confident, a bit raffish, a good listener—as I feel sure Shakespeare was.

It is—just—possible to see him as a younger version of the man in the engraving. But here the matter of the date enters into the picture. To me—and this is inevitably a subjective impression—the Shakespeare of the engraving looks like a man in his late thirties, whereas the man in the portrait looks some ten years younger. But we have every reason to believe that the portrait was painted in 1603, when Shakespeare was thirty-nine, around the age that he appears to be in the engraving. It would be far-fetched to suggest that the painting deliberately flatters its sitter by representing him as younger than his actual age. This is not a formal, "official" painting, but one that seems designed to represent its sitter as he appeared to his friends and relatives.

Attractive as the Sanders portrait is, I find it hard to match William Shakespeare at the age of thirty-nine with the man in the picture.

Andrew Gurr

What Shakespeare looked like is not really very important. He has been dead for nearly four hundred years, so his face is not going to launch any new ships and we are hardly likely to meet him in the street. Getting a fresh idea of what his face looked like cannot alter much of what he has left us. It might shift a few perspectives about his life a little, but it can add nothing to the corpus of his writings, on which his reputation and our valuation stand. The Sanders portrait, if it really shows us the man as he wanted to be seen in 1603, might satisfy a kind of curiosity, but it is a pretty idle one. I can't see it adding much to the value of the written texts that we have lived off for more than four centuries.

Given the subject of this book, it's tempting to quarry those written texts to see what Shakespeare made his characters say about the art of painting portraits. Most of their comments are fairly cynical, like Dumain's when watching Don Armado try to act Worthy Hector in *Love's Labour's Lost* 5.2, "He's a God or a Painter, for he makes faces." Armado is neither a God nor a good artist, and actors make only false faces. So why bother with a painted portrait of an actor? The plays have nearly as many references to face-painting as a form of female trickery as to faces that can show their owners' truth. The tempter Antonio can say to Sebastian, "methinks I see it in thy face, / What thou shouldst be" (*The Tempest*, 2.1), that is, in truth a murderous king of Naples, but *Macbeth* and *The Taming of the Shrew* offer more substantially what Duncan says of the first Thane of Cawdor, "There's no art / To find the mind's construction in the face" (*Macbeth*, 1.4).

So why all the bother about a possible portrait of a man who at the time it was painted was an actor-poet well known only in his own small world? Interest in finding a more acceptable face than the one in Droeshout's engraving really began in the nineteenth century because readers of Shakespeare's work could not believe that a man from such a small country town could have written such great works. In its way that interest counters the multitude of theories claiming an alternative author, fostered as they were by the delights of subverting established ideas and by the underdog's pleasure in conspiracy theory. A better face than the Droeshout, one showing more obvious glints of genius, would help to counter the anti-Stratfordians. But any search for an authentic and properly authenticated portrait of Shakespeare made in his lifetime will get muddied by fights between hagiographers and alternative-author theorists with their murky rivers of speculation and misinformation.

By far the most convincing evidence for the authenticity of the Sanders portrait is the dendrochronology establishing the age of the wood, which corroborates the specific date on the painting itself. But the subject's name was not painted on that handsome piece of Baltic oak along with the date and the subject's age, as was usual at the time. That is one anomaly. More suggestive is the fabric the sitter wears, which seems to have a silver weave indicative of the sort of claim for gentle status that literally thousands of men could assert. The portrait has the right kind of date, and it is the kind of picture Shakespeare might have wanted done, either for a friend or for his absent family. But it does lack the name.

Except, we are told, on a scrap of old paper stuck to the back of the panel. Apart from that, nothing would ever have suggested that it is of Shakespeare beyond the Sanders family tradition (when and how did that start?). The apparently overwritten inscription on the paper is undoubtedly late, and its extra detail acquired in later centuries infects it with the suspicion that it was created by some nineteenth-century Bardic hagiographer. Whatever lay under it may be the crucial clinching evidence, and it would be nice to think that modern techniques of microanalysis of the chemical traces left by the original ink may make it possible to identify the scripted words of the original writer. Without that, the Sanders portrait must stick in the mud with all those other unprovable theories that claim some hidden truth about Shakespeare's life.

The two Fleming émigré Southwarkers who produced the best-attested representations of the playwright, Martin Droeshout and his older associate the Dutchman Geraert Janssen who carved the bust for his tomb in Trinity Church, Stratford, have generally been criticized for incompetent workmanship. People look for better representations of the great national poet. The balding middle-class burgher had to be replaced by someone more slim and anguished, more like Joseph Fiennes in *Shakespeare in Love*. Given this raw need to dismiss the engraving and the bust as not impressive enough, the Sanders portrait really is attractive. It looks quite good alongside the familiar candidates such as the so-called Chandos portrait, an anonymous oil painting that at least seems to make the great author appear suitably dignified and intelligent. But that very comfort should serve as a warning that we may in some degree be joining up with the cranks and conspiracy theorists who find it hard to believe that a young man from Warwickshire without aristocratic rank or a university education could have written such immortal works.

For all the wishful thinking that needs something impressive to fix the imagination on, the two Southwark productions—each made by a man who lived near the Globe and who could have seen the poet himself—remain the only substantial depictions with a good claim to present a recognizable likeness. It is true that the one engraved for the First Folio in 1623 was done by an artist who was barely a teenager when Shakespeare died in Stratford. It has, however, the unique credential of being verified as a good likeness by Shakespeare's friend Ben Jonson. If only the Sanders portrait could acquire a credential with comparable authority.

I have to confess to being almost seduced into *wanting* the Sanders portrait to be of Shakespeare, if only because the thought that he might have agreed to have his portrait painted in 1603 prompts so many colourful ideas about his state of mind in that remarkable year. We know that Ben Jonson mocked him in 1599 for his social climbing, and we know that Francis Beaumont followed Jonson more sourly and derisively in 1605. Could Shakespeare's insecurity over his status, born not a gentleman, dyed by the less-than-gentle trade that kept him from the noble young patron he loved, have made him overcompensate when he acquired his courtier status in 1603? The promotion to Groom of the Chamber must have been a surprise, and his exultation at achieving what had been denied him for so long may well for a while have been more than he could encompass with a more rational view. We might even speculate that his own sensitivity to his long-running social insecurity was what made him don gentle but not courtier attire for his portrait—the silver-threaded fabric. But not too far along that way lies the madness of self-deception and conspiracy theory, and scholarly assessors should be committed to the honest face of truth, however burgherish it looks. Thus far, the Sanders portrait question must remain a question, though one that makes a rich addition to the mythology of ideas about Shakespeare that Sam Schoenbaum captured so wonderfully in his (cautionary plural) *Shakespeare's Lives.*

Jonathan Bate

There are three *prima facie* possibilities: that it is an authentic portrait of Shakespeare, that it is an authentic portrait from the period but not of Shakespeare, and that it is some kind of forgery or fake from a later era.

The classic instance of the third possibility is the so-called Flower portrait of Shakespeare. When this painting was discovered in the mid-nineteenth century, it was proclaimed to be the original upon which Martin Droeshout based his engraving in the First Folio. In fact, it turned out to be a painting copied from the Droeshout engraving. The first thing that strikes the viewer of the Sanders portrait is that it is not at all like the Droeshout or the bust by Geraert Janssen on the memorial to Shakespeare in Holy Trinity church in Stratford-upon-Avon. This immediately suggests that the painting is not an eighteenth- or nineteenth-century forgery intended to represent Shakespeare. The forger's starting point would have been one or other of the two authentic images from the years immediately after the poet's death. The fact that the painting does not conform to our prior expectation of Shakespeare's face is, paradoxically, the first thing to be said in its favour.

Partly for this reason, my immediate instinct on seeing the painting was that it was an authentic—rather good—portrait from the period, not a later forgery. The forensic examination of the picture itself decisively supports this view. But just as there has been a long tradition of forged or faked Shakespeare paintings, so there has been an equally long tradition of claims that this or that unidentified portrait from the period is an authentic image of Shakespeare. M. H. Spielmann's 1909 article in *The Connoisseur*, which first brought the Sanders portrait to the attention of the scholarly world, dwelt at greater length on the so-called Grafton portrait, a classic example of this phenomenon. The Grafton is a fine portrait, authentic to the period, but no evidence can be found to support the claim that it is Shakespeare. Were it not for the label on the back of the Sanders portrait, we would say exactly the same about it.

It was, however, the inscription on the label that made me suspicious from the start. "This Likeness taken" does not sound to me like an Elizabethan formulation. The birth and death dates are even more problematic. A painter or owner in 1603 could not have known that Shakespeare would die in 1616. At the very least, the inscription must have been added after the sitter's death. What is more, no one in the period knew that Shakespeare was born on April 23, 1564. His date of birth is not a fact, but an inference—first drawn in the eighteenth century—from the date of his baptism. Behind the inference was a piece of wishful thinking: Bardolaters liked the idea that the national poet should have been born on the feast day of St. George, England's patron saint. It follows that the April 23 date is a myth contingent on Shakespeare's elevation to the status of England's national poet. That elevation took place in the course of the eighteenth century. The only conclusion can be that any document which proposes April 23 as Shakespeare's date of birth belongs to the eighteenth century or later.

The handwriting on the label confirms this conclusion: it is in neither the secretary nor the italic hand of the early seventeenth century but a rounded script that did not appear until the eighteenth century. Even if the linen rag label and its glue belong to the seventeenth century, the inscription does not. It is especially noteworthy that when Spielmann examined the portrait in 1908, when the writing was in much better condition than it is now, he concluded that whatever the age of the portrait, the label was "apparently some fifty or sixty years old."

I believe, then, that the label tells us no more than that someone in the eighteenth or nineteenth century believed—or wished others to believe—that the portrait is of Shakespeare. It does not support the inference that the portrait is *really* of Shakespeare. My initial inclination was therefore to place the Sanders in the large category of authentic Elizabethan and Jacobean portraits of unidentified sitters.

The other reason for discounting the label is that it is the kind of "evidence" that is somehow too good to be true. Authenticity does not often reveal itself in this convenient way. More often, it has to be teased out through such tortuous routes as provenance. Consider the case of the Chandos portrait, which still has the best claim to be the only surviving authentic likeness of Shakespeare painted in his lifetime. It resembles the authentic posthumous images—the Droeshout engraving and the Janssen bust—sufficiently for it to be plausible that it is the same man (that domed forehead). But it does not resemble them so closely as to raise the suspicion that it was based on those images, as the Flower was. And it has the strongest provenance of any of the so-called Shakespeare portraits. It was owned by the late-seventeenth-century actor Thomas Betterton, the leading Shakespearean player of his age. Its authenticity was taken for granted by this time, to the extent that copies were painted by several artists, including the distinguished Sir Godfrey Kneller. There is fairly firm evidence that before Betterton, the portrait was owned by William Davenant, who was Shakespeare's godson and his foremost fan. Recent research on the Davenant family has confirmed their close links with Shakespeare. Furthermore, the Chandos was ascribed at an early date to a named artist, and independent evidence has confirmed the existence of that artist. All this puts the Chandos in a league of its own.

The case for the Chandos draws on oral tradition but is strengthened by circumstantial documentary evidence. The strong likelihood of its authenticity shows us that oral tradition often has some kind of truth behind it. Once we have discounted the label, the case for the Sanders falls back on oral tradition. The only hope of its being authentically Shakespeare is the fact that the family has for a long time believed that it is Shakespeare. Maybe we simply have a case of a long history of wishful thinking, rather as it sometimes seems as if almost every large old house in England has a bed in which, according to family tradition, Queen Elizabeth once spent a night. But then again, although she couldn't have slept in all those beds, she, or at the very least someone associated with her court, probably did sleep in some of them. By the same account, there *may* be some grain of truth in the Sanders family tradition. It often happens in oral tradition that a connection of some kind is magnified into a connection of a stronger kind (thus Davenant was Shakespeare's godson, but oral tradition had it that he was also his illegitimate son!).

Could it then be that the portrait had *some* connection with the world of the early-seventeenth-century theatre and that oral tradition exaggerated that into an identification with Shakespeare? The more I looked at the portrait, the more it started reminding me of someone. A figure engraved on the frontispiece of an influential First Folio of plays. Not, however, the Shakespeare First Folio of 1623, but the Beaumont and Fletcher First Folio of 1647. The long face, the thick curly hair receding at the temples, the cut of the beard and moustache, the rounded eyebrows: everything about this face seems to me more like John Fletcher than William Shakespeare. I find it hard to believe that the Sanders portrait shows a man of thirty-nine, Shakespeare's age in 1603. It looks to me more like a man of twenty-four: Fletcher's age in 1603. Furthermore, the surviving images of Shakespeare suggest that such hair as he had was very dark, whereas the portraits of John Fletcher that now hang at Knole House in Kent and at Montacute House in Somerset reveal him to be red-haired, as is the man in the Sanders portrait. In 1603 Fletcher was a young man seeking to establish himself on the literary and theatrical scene: such a figure accords well with Aileen Ribeiro's brilliant analysis of the significance of the fashionable hairstyle and dress of the Sanders sitter.

I do not want to go so far as to propose decisively that this *is* an authentic image of John Fletcher. I wish only to suggest that a possible explanation for the oral tradition associating the image with Shakespeare is an indirect connection of this sort: by a "Chinese whisper" effect, a close associate of Shakespeare may have been metamorphosed into Shakespeare himself.

Suppose, though, that it is a portrait of Fletcher. That would be something to celebrate. John Fletcher, one of the finest and most versatile dramatists of the age. Co-author of Shakespeare's last three plays, *Henry VIII*, *The Two Noble Kinsmen* and the lost *Cardenio*. Shakespeare's own chosen successor as "in-house" dramatist for the King's Men. Co-author, first with Francis Beaumont and then with Philip Massinger, of some of the best non-Shakespearean plays of the period. If Fletcherian authenticity were to be proved, the picture would deserve to hang in the National Portrait Gallery, just below the Chandos Shakespeare.

But there would be one problem: it wouldn't be worth quite so much money as the Chandos. I am reminded of one of the very first great debates about Shakespearean authenticity. In the early eighteenth century, the scholar Lewis Theobald discovered the manuscript of a somewhat adapted version of a lost

Shakespeare play that he called *Double Falsehood*. For a time, he appeared to have made the greatest literary discovery of the age. He went so far as to obtain a special royal warrant giving him the exclusive right to publish the play for a period of fourteen years. But then a rival scholar demonstrated that the play was stylistically much closer to Fletcher than Shakespeare. Theobald backed off from his high claims for his discovery, though he always vigorously denied that his manuscript was a forgery. In my book *The Genius of Shakespeare* I argued that this was one of the first moments when Shakespeare was valued above Fletcher: the *Double Falsehood* affair occurred in the 1720s, a key decade in Shakespeare's rise in status from *primus inter pares* to unique genius.

What Theobald and his contemporaries did not know was that the play—originally called *Cardenio*—was in fact one of Shakespeare and Fletcher's collaborative works. Paradoxically, the marks of Fletcher were signs of the manuscript's authenticity, though at the time they were considered to be indications that Theobald was engaged in forgery. Should our portrait prove to be Fletcher, people (and especially potential purchasers) will lose interest in it, as they lost interest in the manuscript of *Double Falsehood/Cardenio* all those years ago. As then, so now, this would be a matter for considerable regret. Why should we not be content with the face of the genius chosen by Shakespeare himself as his theatrical successor?

Marjorie Garber

The reproduction of the Sanders portrait in *Vanity Fair* magazine (December 2001) bears a kind of inscription, in the form of a caption printed in the dark field to the left of "Shakespeare's" face. "Wherefore art thou?" it demands. What does *VF* think it is asking with this rhetorical question? It's a common modern mistake to understand "wherefore" as a version of "where," but in fact the word means "why"—for what purpose, reason, or end. Juliet's "Wherefore art thou Romeo?" means not, "where are you, Romeo?" but rather, "why are you called Romeo? Why is your name Montague, the name of my family's enemy clan?" The "wherefore" line is in fact the entry into Juliet's famous speech beginning "What's in a name?"

I'm guessing that the *VF* caption writer meant to underscore the long quest for an accurate visual image of Shakespeare by evoking this famous phrase. "Shakespeare, where are you?" seems to be the general sense intended here, at least that's what I suppose. But what if we were to view the apparent misuse of "wherefore" as a happy accident and to take the caption's question straight? "Wherefore art thou Shakespeare?" would then mean not "where are you, [the true image of] Shakespeare?" but rather "Why are you [the Sanders portrait] Shakespeare?" *VF*'s caption goes on to amplify or flesh out its message: "Believed to have been painted in 1603, during Shakespeare's lifetime, this long-lost study of a red-haired Elizabethan may or may not be the Bard."

What are the "whys and wherefores," the causes and reasons, for wanting to believe that the Sanders portrait is Shakespeare?

M. H. Spielmann's 1909 essay on "The 'Grafton' and 'Sanders' Portraits of Shakespeare" concludes with his acknowledgment that although he "never for a moment believed the latter picture to have been intended as Shakespeare's portrait," he "was at once attracted to it." Almost one hundred years later, amateur enthusiasts, and some professionals, have registered the same attraction, together with what might be described as a kind of cultural erotics—the excitement not only of finally seeing "Shakespeare" face to face but of recognizing him as someone they would like to know.

For Spielmann both the Grafton and the Sanders portraits had a salient characteristic, one that explained their appeal—they *looked right*. They looked *English*. "Both pictures," he wrote, "belong to the same period and both present the same type of Englishman—fair, refined, and mildly determined, and about as different from the swarthy Italianate breed represented in the Chandos picture as could well be imagined."

Not too much stress, perhaps, should be put upon the word "breed" here, which in context simply means something like "type" or "kind." But in the (dim) light of late-nineteenth-century genetics, "breed," when conjoined with "swarthy" and "Italianate," suggests a heritage and a physiognomy that was distinctly *not* an Englishman's fantasy of the national poet. In my essay in this book I have noted that "Italianate" seems to have alternated with "Jewish" as a way of characterizing the foreignness of the Chandos portrait in the later nineteenth and early twentieth centuries. It is of some interest that Spielmann, in his account of the doubts surrounding Grafton and Sanders, mentions a number of other comparison images (the Droeshout engraving, the Ely Palace and Flower portraits, the supposed Death Mask, the Welcombe portrait, and the Stratford bust) but not, until the final sentence, the swarthy Italianate Chandos. So the punchline of the Spielmann essay has to do with his own attraction and ambivalence, despite what he characterizes in his close study of the Sanders portrait as "the stupidity of the faker," the "obvious . . . addition" of the collar, dress and date, and the "irreconcilable elements" of the face, which "even were all other details satisfactory, would prevent us from accepting the attribution." Spielmann ridicules the notion that the "downy" young man pictured in the Sanders portrait could possibly be, as the supposed label declares, thirty-nine years old. He regards the collar ("apparently of steel plate") and the tunic as patently spurious. Yet he likes the look of the man. He would rather that Shakespeare look like an Englishman—a certain "type" of Englishman—than an exotic foreigner.

It seems that for many twenty-first-century viewers, Spielmann's "very fair, gentle youth" is likewise attractive. The antitype for them is not the swarthy Chandos Shakespeare, with his sexy earring—an appealing artistic type to many modern eyes—but the balding guy in the Folio engraving, who looks (perhaps) wise but distant, not One of Us. We don't mind if our Shakespeare looks like an Italian, or a Jew, or a Bohemian—but we'd rather that he not look like an egghead. The Sanders Shakespeare looks cool—there's hardly a better word to describe his insouciant glance and crinkly Woody Allen hair. If the Sanders was "downy" to Spielmann, it is Robert Downey Jr. ("the most talented actor of his generation"—Charles Taylor, *Salon*) to us. If we think of recent film portrayals, not only of Shakespeare (Joseph Fiennes) but also of his reputed alter ego, Hamlet (Kenneth Branagh, and especially Ethan Hawke) we can far more easily fit the man in the Sanders portrait in among those other modern actors. And Shakespeare for us is an actor as well as an author.

Spielmann makes another important point in his essay: period portraits tend to look alike. One young Elizabethan man is very like another. The same would be true if we were to look at clusters of portraits of Victorian industrialists, or Gatsby types and flappers from the 1920s, or photographic portraits of contemporary Hollywood pretty boys (and girls) in soft focus. Hair, clothing style, makeup, the fashion in portraiture, all conspire to make the faces of a generation more like one another than like those of their ancestors. As Marcel Proust somewhere remarks, all the portraits of the same era have a family resemblance.

Spielmann's article speaks without rancour about several different kinds of "Shakespeare" portraits: the "sham Shakespeares" that were produced to meet the booming market for Shakespeare stuff after the bicentenary of 1764 and Garrick's Shakespeare Jubilee in 1769; the considerable category of "genuine portraits which are authentic likenesses of somebody else" or where the resemblance is an "accident of type"; and the rarest category of all, a true "likeness of Shakespeare." To which of these categories the Sanders belongs is not yet clear. But the reasons, the "whys and wherefores," for the new celebrity of this image are not far to seek:

- It is attractive; it looks like someone we would find interesting, good company, appealing and even sexy.
- It is timely; a Shakespeare public just getting over its crush on *Shakespeare in Love* is ready for a new Bardic heartthrob.
- It is romantic; the story of its discovery and rediscovery makes good telling.
- It is a relic, a fetish, a numinous whiff of the past; a high-

class souvenir or remembrance, a sign of "the real thing," whatever we think that is.

- It is new; we are ready (as every other era has been, from the seventeenth century to the present) for a Shakespeare in our own image, and for our own time.

Like the two recently rediscovered poems supposedly written by Shakespeare, each unearthed and analyzed by a reputable Shakespeare scholar, the Sanders portrait will ultimately be judged as much by how much the public likes it (is it "Shakespearean"?) as by whether the wood, paint and label are authentic, and the provenance unimpeachable. Every age gets the Shakespeare it wants, and perhaps even the Shakespeare it deserves.

Robert Tittler

Having had a long and careful look at the Sanders portrait "in the flesh," I would raise two final thoughts.

The first concerns the painting itself. I had begun to think seriously about the picture on the basis of the photograph reprinted in Stephanie Nolen's initial articles in *The Globe and Mail* in May of 2001. But as is perhaps always the case, that reproduction failed fully to convey the visual impact of the work. Since that time, a long and leisurely examination of the original, undertaken in the company of Christina Corsiglia, in whose curatorial care at the Art Gallery of Ontario the painting rested, greatly enhanced my appreciation of it. It is a much finer and more subtly worked portrait than reproductions had led me to believe.

As I have indicated in my essay, it *could* conceivably have been done by any number of painters—full-time portrait painters or part-time painters-of-all-work—and almost anywhere in England at the opening of the seventeenth century. But a close inspection of the original compels me to think it more likely to have been done by an experienced and expert hand than by a part-timer, and by one more likely to have been based in London or one of the larger provincial cities. Its vernacular character seems to make it somewhat less likely to have been painted by anyone trained abroad, where formal styles had taken a much firmer hold by this time. Its sheer competence leads me to doubt that its artist would have been based in any smaller centre.

The Sanders family has attributed the work to their ancestor, John Sanders, and this leads me to my second point. It is indeed possible that someone named John Sanders had the expertise and experience to paint this portrait, and that we have heard nothing else of him as a painter because none of his works have been signed or are known to have survived. But though there are a few people from that era who might fit such a description, I think it highly unlikely that a John Sanders is one of them. The experience and assurance indicated by this work tell us that its painter had almost certainly painted a great many portraits, and must have been commissioned to do so by a wide range of patrons, possibly over a wide geographic area and over a substantial period of time. If Sanders is indeed the painter, that considerable activity would almost surely have brought him and his work to our attention by now: in some signed paintings, in the accounts of those who might have commissioned or purchased his work, in earlier descriptions of portrait collections, or in references to paintings in wills or memorials. So far as I am aware, and despite the rather intense search for more clues to Sanders's life and activity, no such evidence has surfaced.

To carry this skeptical note a bit further, it also seems reasonable to wonder whether John Sanders was indeed even the patron of the work, or whether the work has been in the family since 1603 as is alleged. I must confess to being troubled by the assumption that John Sanders knew Shakespeare well enough to paint him.

When Thomas Hales-Sanders brought this painting to the attention of the art historian M. H. Spielmann in 1908, he indicated that the work had been in his family for "nearly a hundred years past," which dates its presence in the Sanders family only to the beginning of the nineteenth, rather than the seventeenth, century.[1] At least as of this writing, no one has successfully traced the ownership of the painting earlier than the early 1800s.

In addition, if this is a painting painted or even commissioned by a Sanders, and based on his own intimate familiarity with Shakespeare, it seems odd that we have such scant record of his connection with any of the touring companies to which Shakespeare is known to have belonged. It would indeed be fascinating to know for sure who painted the picture, and how it came to the Sanders family, and what role Shakespeare's contemporary John Sanders may have played in those events, but these facts continue to elude our grasp.

These, then, are the caveats I feel obliged to express as part of the discussion about the Sanders portrait, of which this book marks only the beginning. I think it is entirely plausible that this portrait was painted at the request of, and perhaps by the hand of, someone who knew the subject very well. We may never know for certain whether or not this is a portrait of William Shakespeare. Yet a close look at the little-known traditions of non-courtly portraits of this time and place at least allows us to see it and its world more clearly. When added to the appearance of the work itself, that context suggests that the Sanders' family identification of the sitter as Shakespeare might just possibly be correct.

Tarnya Cooper

In all likelihood the Sanders portrait owes its survival to the fact that since sometime in the third quarter of the seventeenth century it has been assumed by its owners to represent a literary giant of English literature. Portraits on wooden panels from this period have proved exceptionally vulnerable to decay, and those showing sitters from the middling sort—usually those without a secure family estate to provide their images with centuries of refuge—were even more likely to fall into disrepair or be painted over. At least from the date that someone applied the identifying label to the back of the panel, the Sanders portrait has been saved by the celebrity of the supposed sitter. Who the sitter was believed to be before that date will be exceptionally difficult to discover.

The first decade of the seventeenth century saw a significant rise in the production of portraits for the middle ranks of society, where William Shakespeare found himself. Yet unlike many of the era's surviving portraits of such sitters, where the subjects appear alongside trappings of their office or worldly status, the sitter here is depicted as a private person, a life-size head and shoulders on a small panel that provides us with an intense and touching illusion of personal presence. The gentle, intelligent face that we encounter in the Sanders portrait seems to match our desire to meet the private Shakespeare, a Shakespeare with a face whose sensitivity and insight matches his talent for creating dramatic personae.

People from this period tended to have their portraits painted at particular times of life, soon after having met with some level of worldly success. Certainly, as Andrew Gurr has noted, what we know about Shakespeare's life in 1603 would make this a very probable year for the playwright to commission a portrait. In the autobiography of the Elizabethan scholar and astronomer Simon Forman, we find a short but revealing commentary on the commissioning of his own image. Forman notes that in 1599, at the age of twenty-seven, he "had" his "own picture drawen" and this was not long after his marriage, the purchase of leases on houses, a gelding and numerous elaborate suits of clothes.[2] It is interesting that Forman chooses to do this at a time when he is consolidating his assets and fashioning his status as a gentleman, part of the social act of learning to both play and look the part. He notes that in the same year he had allowed his hair and beard to grow, as if this point in his life marks his coming of age as a gentleman of some means.

Forman's comment about the shaping of his outward appearance to fit his status brings me to one of the central problems I have with accepting the Sanders portrait as depicting William Shakespeare. We know that Shakespeare was around thirty-nine years of age in 1603, having established himself as a man of impressive wit and personal means, so it seems likely that he would want to appear reasonably distinguished and would want his likeness to mirror the way he looked at that time in his life. To my eyes, the man we encounter appears considerably younger than thirty-nine, with his soft, downy facial hair, smooth skin, flushed, soft cheeks and full head of hair.

Without further evidence we simply will not know who this beguiling image represents or even who painted it. Only future investigation will reveal whether other surviving images of this modest size and format can be grouped around a particular painter's workshop. As I have pointed out, the true authorship of an unsigned portrait claiming to be Shakespeare is almost impossible to discover: the best known claimant, the Chandos portrait (see page iii of "The Picture Gallery"), is attributed by tradition to a painter called John Taylor, and while Taylor's name appears in the minute books of the Painter-Stainers Company in the 1620s, very little else is known about him. Whether John Sanders was in fact a painter, and if so whether he was capable of producing a painting of this type and quality, must await further exploration.

Alexander Leggatt

It seems churlish to complain about the label on the back of the Sanders portrait; after all, there would be no story without it. Yet a consensus has emerged that the label, like those tight-fitting shorts worn by cyclists, tells us more than we care to know. Giving us Shakespeare's years of birth and death, even his birthday, it seems too eager to inform, too anxious to prove its case. Therein lies the paradox: the one piece of evidence for the Shakespeare identification is also the strongest evidence against it. If the label is on a mission to prove this is Shakespeare, it is a suicide mission. It needs to be rescued from itself, a rescue the REED hypothesis elsewhere in this volume performs admirably. We need that hypothesis, or something like it, to keep open the possibility that the label, though it protests too much, is still telling the truth, reporting it from an earlier source we would find easy enough to believe if only we had it.

At the moment all we have is the possibility. What we need in order to have certainty is, let's say, an entry from Shakepeare's diary: "Mr. Sanders finished his portrait of me today. Can't say I like it. He may keep it for his family; it may be of some value to them if they ever emigrate to Canada." I'm not holding my breath. Yet the need for certainty is a natural human trait. In the days after the story broke in *The Globe and Mail*, I was corralled—once at a concert, once at the local market—by acquaintances who know what my day job is and who had the same question: "So, is it really him?" And I would be as delighted as anyone if we could simply say yes.

Behind the need for certainty about this one portrait is an appetite for information about Shakespeare that other contributers to this volume have addressed in various ways. If only we knew more. Yet how would we like it if we did? As the complaints about the label suggest, there may be such a thing as knowing too much. When we had simply the poetry of Philip Larkin, we could enjoy its bracing cynicism. We now have more information about the man, including his letters and a number of poems he chose not to publish. In the light of this new information, the bracing cynicism begins to look like mere unpleasantness. The poetry remains; but we have to cut away the new information to enjoy it again—and perhaps to remind ourselves that the real Philip Larkin may have been in the poetry, after all. The appearance of previously unpublished work by T. S. Eliot has a similarly damaging effect: *Prufrock*, *The Waste Land* and *Four Quartets* have now been joined by racist, scatological verses that seem to belong not in the literary canon but on the walls of a lavatory. We can remind ourselves that Eliot chose not to publish this stuff, but we may still wonder why he wrote it in the first place, and why he did not destroy it. (I should add that publication of work a writer did not publish himself is not always a bad thing; without it, most of Shakespeare's output would be lost.)

By the same token, it can be fatal to meet a writer whose work you admire. Keats loved Wordsworth's poetry, but when he met the man he found him pompous and egotistical. The list goes on: Wagner, Brecht, Picasso—while loving the art, you want to send the artist to his room until he has learned to behave himself. But if he did, would he be the same artist? And what does that tell us about art? Contemporary artists are frequently unhelpful, even hostile, to interviewers, as though they need to protect the artistic process by not letting anyone get too close. We may think this is because the creative life is a frail plant that will not stand a strong light; but there may be other reasons why it needs to be kept in the dark.

During my preview of the Sanders portrait before it first was put on show, I leaned close to get a better look, incautiously putting my foot on the pedestal that supported the display case. In short order, a Gallery official relayed a message from the security staff, who were watching on closed-circuit television from another room. The message was polite but slightly pained: please *don't* do that. I had got too close. When I visited the portrait again during the public exhibition, the design of the pedestal had been modified, and there was a rail around it.

Proof that this portrait is Shakespeare would do no harm at all to his reputation; indeed, it would add an attractive visual image to it. But would it damage, if only slightly, an important part of our response to him, making us a little too certain, too familiar, like the person who shows how well he knows you by using your nickname and gets it wrong? Is it better not to get too close? In a famous letter to his brothers George and Thomas (December 1817), John Keats pays tribute to what he calls Shakespeare's "Negative Capability," and goes on to explain the term: "that is, when a man is capable of being in uncertainties, mysteries, doubts, without any irritable reaching after fact and reason." This has long been accepted as a shrewd account of the spirit in which Shakespeare wrote, and as good advice about the spirit in which we should read him. It may be a good way, certainly a Shakespearean way, to read the Sanders portrait.

Stephanie Nolen

Each of us sees something different when we look at the Sanders portrait. Many of those who admire Shakespeare's works see a face that looks. . . *right*, somehow. The scientists and scholars tend to see something much more specific, a picture placed in a narrower frame: growth rings on a tree, chemical compounds in a pigment, silver threads in a doublet, wormholes and scratches on an old oak panel. To Lloyd Sullivan, the man who grew up with the painting as an heirloom with a family story attached, it is simply Shakespeare.

The modern story of the portrait always comes back to Lloyd Sullivan. Some people will inevitably question his version of events and suggest that he has doctored the facts to make the painting more plausible. I think those people are wrong. I do not believe Lloyd has in any way falsified the evidence or misrepresented what he knows of the painting's story. He is a sincere and honest man. But the evidence he has gathered in support of the portrait is coloured by the very personal process of authentication he has undertaken.

Some of his evidence is crisp and comfortingly conclusive—particularly the results of the various scientific tests the painting has undergone. Other parts are problematic. The Sanders family genealogy is neither solidly established nor complete all the way back to the key date of 1603. Even if the genealogy were rock solid, we must still take the painting's provenance—the story that it has passed through generations of this family and only this family—on faith, as Lloyd has done. We have no documentation to show who owned the portrait before the mid-1800s.

Putting questions of genealogy and provenance aside, we find serious problems with the claim that the portrait shows us Shakespeare. As Stanley Wells has pointed out, the Sanders does not bear much resemblance to the First Folio engraving or the bust that marks Shakespeare's grave in Stratford-upon-Avon, the only two unquestioned images. Some of the Shakespeareans and art historians believe the Sanders sitter looks too young to be thirty-nine, an age when the poet was burdened with many worldly cares. The costume historian Aileen Ribeiro sees a sitter dressed and coiffed like a fashionable young fop, not a serious social climber on the cusp of forty, and this in an era when such public presentation was of the utmost importance. The art historian Tarnya Cooper believes the portrait was painted by two hands of discernibly different skill, which undermines the family tradition that a lone jobbing actor named John Sanders is its only creator. As yet we have no known work by a young Sanders from Worcester, nor any record of his running an artists' studio staffed with apprentice-assistants in later Elizabethan London. Tarnya Cooper also notes that the sitter's age, which one typically finds on portraits of the period, is missing. And what of that faded label? The experts believe it was written well after the portrait was painted, by which time a cult had grown up around the memory of the Stratford playwright. As Jonathan Bate and others have observed, the label bears information (Shakespeare's birth and death dates) that the artist could not have known in 1603. All in all, the case against the portrait as Shakespeare seems to be quite a strong one.

And yet. The label is made of a linen rag paper that radiocarbon dating has shown to be from Shakespeare's time. It is inscribed with handwriting that may have been written as little as fifty years after the portrait was painted. It identifies the sitter as Shakespeare. What motive could there have been in the 1650s to fake the attribution, unless the owner intended to sell the portrait? But the Sanders panel did not then come to light, as so many others did. It remained unknown and in private hands until 1908, when Thomas Hales-Sanders Jr., Lloyd Sullivan's great-grandfather, took it for evaluation to Marion Henry Spielmann. And experts in Elizabethan handwriting are convinced that the label shows no sign of being a forgery. The writer did not deliberately falsify the sitter's identity. Nor, it would appear, did any of its owners over four hundred years attempt to alter the paint surface to make the sitter resemble someone different. While the picture has probably lost a narrow slice along its right side and been amateurishly touched up in a number of tiny spots, there is no sign of deliberate falsification. This claim is backed up by what the REED paleographers see in the writing on the label and in its wording: a textbook example of what less-educated people would write to identify a family heirloom, not an artful forgery. In fact, the more one examines the label, the more it tends to support the Sanders family tradition.

The label would be useless, though, if the wooden panel and the paint applied to it came from a later date. Instead, dendrochronology confirms that the Sanders portrait was painted within a few years either side of 1603. All the elements and compounds in the paint are correct for the time. Andrew Gurr tells us that 1603 is a logical year for the increasingly successful, yet introspective, William Shakespeare to choose to have his portrait painted. Tarnya Cooper argues convincingly that the Sanders portrait is every inch a late-Elizabethan work and is very much the type of picture that someone of Shakespeare's social standing would have wanted painted.

And what of the manner in which the sitter is portrayed? This question elicits some of the most interesting scholarly analysis. The social historian Robert Tittler wonders if the very absence of the usual identifying devices of Elizabethan portraiture—and the unusual degree of personality the artist has conveyed—subtly suggest this is an actor's face. Alexander Leggatt sees a witty, humorous and provocative face, just what we would expect, given what we know of Shakespeare's life and plays up to 1603. It is perhaps the very unconventionality of the Sanders portrait, the fact it does not fit easily into known categories, that makes its claim most persuasive. The sitter wears a fancy doublet with a fine lace collar—a sign of wealth and status—and yet he hides (perhaps disguises?) his identity. It's a suitably ambiguous, in fact a very Shakespearean, puzzle.

Short of the invention of a time machine that will take us back to the room in England in 1603 where the portrait was being painted, we will never know for certain who created it and why.

We can, however, imagine. We can imagine a crisp afternoon in London in early spring, during the last days of the reign of Elizabeth I. Our playwright, having written his quota of lines for the day and settled his accounts, decides on a whim to have his hair cut by that new and fashionable barber on the South Bank, only a short walk from the Globe Theatre. Sporting his stylish new coif and feeling younger than his years, he borrows a rather flashy new doublet from the costume cupboard. It looks so fine that he decides to wear it to an assignation with a young woman he is to meet at a local tavern. She has put a gleam in his eye these past few weeks. While he awaits her, a young friend from the theatre, a recent arrival from the provinces, asks to sketch his face. Shakespeare consents.

But when, a few weeks later, he is presented with a modest portrait made from the sketch, our hero scowls. His fresh romance has soured and his light-hearted mood has passed. The Queen has died, the playhouses are closed, and there are hints the plague is returning. This foolish little picture makes him look like a gallant, almost fey, he tells the painter. He reneges on a casual offer to pay, and he and the painter quarrel—so badly that the young man from Worcester vows then and there to quit this business of painting, to go home and join his father in the family cloth business.

This is, I know, a fanciful scenario. It is just one of many we might construct to fit the facts we have, using as fodder a life as extraordinary and ill-documented as Shakespeare's. Jonathan Bate tells us that the label on the back of the oak panel is the kind of evidence that is "too good to be true." But every so often the evidence is this good, and it is also true. Sometimes, portraits of Shakespeare really are kept under Granny's bed.

As our assembled cast of experts make their exit and I too move once more toward the wings, the portrait is left alone at centre stage. Alone with its audience—who can decide for themselves, one way or another. For as Antonio says to Sebastian in *The Tempest* (2.1), Shakespeare's last play,

> And yet methinks I see it in thy face,
> What thou shouldst be.

Choosing Your Shakespeare

Alexander Leggatt

The endless fascination Shakespeare exerts is reflected in the wide variety of Shakespeare editions on the market; there is room here to mention only a few. Each edition represents a set of decisions about how to treat the Quarto and Folio texts that provide our only source for the plays.

I'll begin with collected editions of the complete works. *The Riverside Shakespeare*, ed. G. Blakemore Evans (2d ed. Boston and New York: Houghton Mifflin, 1997) has good introductions by a variety of scholars and helpful background material. It is illustrated from sources contemporary with Shakespeare and includes photographs from modern productions. In common with other widely available editions, it modernizes the original spelling, but more conservatively than most, preserving some archaic forms to give a flavour of the original. *The Complete Works of Shakespeare*, ed. David Bevington (4th ed. New York: HarperCollins, 1992), is the work of one of the most experienced Shakespeare scholars of our time and is notable for its solid, straightforward treatment of the text. Like Riverside, it contains useful introductions and background material. It is not quite so lavishly illustrated. Both editions provide a full commentary.

Among collected editions the most provocative and controversial is *The Oxford Shakespeare, The Complete Works*, ed. Stanley Wells and Gary Taylor (Oxford: Clarendon Press, 1986). This edition challenges tradition in many areas—for example, changing the forms of some familiar character names. In modernizing the text it goes to the opposite extreme from Riverside, sometimes replacing Elizabethan words with their modern equivalents. This was the first edition to face head-on the challenge posed by the growing belief among Shakespeare critics that when the original texts, Quarto and Folio, disagree, particularly in the matter of cuts, the solution is not to combine all the available material in a single conflated text—thereby producing, in effect, a new text—but to respect the individuality of each original edition. Thus the Oxford edition provides two different versions of *King Lear*, one based on the Quarto and one on the Folio, and follows the Folio text of *Hamlet* with passages the Folio cuts relegated to an appendix.

The Oxford edition signalled a revolution in editorial thinking, but its usefulness to general readers is limited by its lack of commentary and its very brief introductions. *The Norton Shakespeare*, gen. ed. Stephen Greenblatt (New York: Norton, 1997), presents a modified version of the Oxford text, preserving many of its innovations; it adds introductions by a variety of scholars representing current critical approaches, a commentary, background information and illustrations drawn from Shakespeare's time.

There are also several different Shakespeare series that present each play in a separate volume with its own editor, allowing fuller introductions and commentary than a collected edition makes possible. The *Arden* editions, published originally by Methuen, then by Routledge, and now by Thomas Nelson, were unchallenged in this area for most of the twentieth century. The series began in 1899 and was completely revised from the middle of the twentieth century onward; a second revision, sometimes known as *Arden 3*, is now well under way. The Oxford University Press is producing a comparable series under the *World's Classics* imprint. This, like the Oxford *Complete Works*, is marketed as *The Oxford Shakespeare*, and its general editor is Stanley Wells. However, in the *World's Classics* series, each play has its own individual editor, and the degree to which these editors follow the practices of the collected edition varies. The *World's Classics* editions, like the more recent *Arden* editions, give much greater attention to Shakespeare in production than editions used to do. The Cambridge University Press has a similar series, *The New Cambridge Shakespeare*, slightly slimmer than the *Arden* and *World's Classics* editions, but containing, like them, full introductions and commentary, with illustrations of the plays in performance.

Notes

Prime Suspects

1. David Piper. *O Sweet Mr. Shakespeare I'll Have His Picture: The Changing Image of Shakespeare's Person, 1600–1800* (London: National Portrait Gallery, 1964), 3.

2. J. Hain Friswell, *Life Portraits of William Shakespeare: A History of the Various Representations of the Poet, with an Examination into Their Authenticity* (London: Sampson Low, Son & Marston, 1864), 40.

3. Mary Edmond, "It Was for Gentle Shakespeare Cut," *Shakespeare Quarterly* 42 no. 3 (fall 1991): 343. See also Christiaan Schuckman, "The Engraver of the First Folio Portrait of William Shakespeare," *Print Quarterly* 8, no. 1 (1991): 40–43, for another argument on the life of Martin Droeshout.

4. Cited in Katherine Duncan-Jones, *Ungentle Shakespeare: Scenes from His Life* (London: Arden Shakespeare, Thomson Learning, 2001), 280.

5. Samuel Schoenbaum, *William Shakespeare: A Compact Documentary Life* (Oxford: Oxford University Press, 1987), 315.

6. Friswell, *Life Portraits of William Shakespeare*, 44.

7. Cited in Duncan-Jones, *Ungentle Shakespeare*, 197. "Self-satisfied pork butcher" is the assessment of J. Dover Wilson, English academic and critic (1881–1969); Duncan-Jones quotes him before adding her own assessment of the "dull eyes and fat jowls."

8. Piper, *O Sweet Mr. Shakespeare*, 4.

9. Friswell, *Life Portraits of William Shakepeare*, 74.

10. Ibid., 109.

11. Spielmann, "The 'Grafton' and 'Sanders' Portraits of Shakespeare", 100.

12. Friswell, *Life Portraits of William Shakepeare*, 107.

13. William L. Pressly, *"As Imagination Bodies Forth": A Catalogue of*

Paintings in the Folger Shakespeare Library (New Haven: Yale University Press, 1993), 264.

14. Paul Bertram and Frank Cossa, "Willm Shakespeare 1609: The Flower Portrait Revisited," *Shakespeare Quarterly* 37, no. 1 (1986): 95.

15. See Roy Strong, *Tudor and Jacobean Portraits* (London: National Portrait Gallery, 1969), 279–86.

16. Edmond, "It Was for Gentle Shakespeare Cut": 344.

17. J. L. Nevinson,. "Shakespeare's Dress in His Portraits," *Shakespeare Quarterly* 18, no. 2 (spring 1967): 102.

Picturing Shakespeare in 1603

1. Two versions of a picture of this event in 1604, *The Conference of English and Spanish Plenipotentiaries,* painted in what the art historian Ellis Waterhouse calls the "Flemish style," exist, in the National Portrait Gallery, London, and the National Maritime Museum, Greenwich.

2. Edward Alleyn worked as a "servant" of Charles Howard, the Lord Admiral. At first he was simply a player in the company that Howard gave his name to. From 1591, however, when Alleyn switched from the Admiral's Men to Lord Strange's, he retained his allegiance to Howard and was so distinguished in court records and on the title pages of the plays he acted in. His was a unique case, which probably reflects the value that Howard found in him not only as the most famous actor of the time but as a potential manager of new enterprises. In 1594, when Howard and his father-in-law, the Lord Chamberlain, set up a duopoly to replace the monopoly of the Queen's Men, he started his recruitment with Alleyn, who by then had the added status of being partnered with his father-in-law, the owner of the Rose playhouse, to which the new Lord Admiral's Men were assigned as their London base. There is no other sign that great lords were ever prepared to become patrons of individual players.

3. The quotation is taken from the edition by George Walton Williams in *Beaumont and Fletcher, Dramatic Works,* Fredson Bowers, gen. ed., 9 vols, (Cambridge: Cambridge University Press, 1966–96), I.164 (1.3.13–21).

4. Printed in E. K. Chambers, *William Shakespeare,* 2 vols (Oxford: Clarendon Press, 1930), II, 213.

5. One of the reasons why Shakespeare never went to university was that he got married at eighteen. Students had to be bachelors.

6. Chambers, *William Shakespeare,* II, 153.

7. J. Overbury, *New Characters,* 1615, M6v.

8. See Duncan-Jones, *Ungentle Shakespeare,* 99–103.

9. Quotations from the sonnets are taken from the edition of Stephen

Booth, *Shakespeare's Sonnets* (New Haven: Yale University Press, 1977). The sonnets quoted are 111 and 110.

10. The bequest underwent a lengthy process of law before the College could get its hands on the pictures, and many of them were lost to theft or sale by Cartwright's two servants, who claimed them on the grounds that the deed of gift to the College was invalidated by a subsequent will that left everything to them.

11. Sometime before his death, Cartwright made his own inventory, listing and describing all his original 239. The inventory survives, except for numbers 186–209, where pages are missing. Of particular interest for our purposes are number 103, described as "a womans head on a bord, dun by mr burbige *ye* Actor," and number 105, "mr burbig his head." The portrait of Burbage, which has no artist's name on it, has been assumed to be a self-portrait, but is now thought to most closely resemble the work of the Southwark painter Marcus Gheeraerts the Younger. Besides Burbage and Field, other portraits of actors are of Richard Perkins (166), also a King's player for a while, and Thomas Bond (148). These were probably among Cartwright's acquisitions, since all three actors were in the same companies in the 1620s and 1630s. The portraits of Perkins and Bond were most probably painted in the 1640s. Another, the head of a burly figure, is marked in the Inventory as "mr Slys pictur *ye* Actour," but cannot be of the Shakespeare company's Will Sly. Nicola Kalinsky and Giles Waterfield, *Mr Cartwright's Pictures: A Seventeenth Century Collection*. Catalogue of an exhibition, 25 November 1987–28 February 1988 (London: Dulwich Picture Gallery 1987), 44–45.

12. "Theise are to Certifie you. That Edward Knight, William Pattrick, William Chambers, Ambrose Byland, Henry Wilson, Jeffery Collins, William Sanders, Nicholas Underhill Henry Clay, George Vernon, Roberte Pallant, Thomas Tuckfeild, Robert Clarke, John Rhodes, William Mago Anthony Knight [and other names added in margin] are all imployed by the Kinges Majesties servantes in their quallity of Playinge as Musitions and other necessary attendantes." *The Control and Censorship of Caroline Drama*, N. W. Bawcutt, ed. (Oxford: Clarendon Press, 1996), 158. Edward Knight was the company scribe. Robert Pallant rose to become a sharer in the company. Byland, Rhodes and Wilson were musicians, the last becoming a King's violinist. Vernon, Tuckfield, Underhill and Mago were players, Underhill starting as a boy player in 1613 and continuing with the company until at least 1636, Pattrick staying until 1637.

13. Mark Eccles, *Shakespeare in Warwickshire* (Madison: University of Wisconsin Press, 1961), 94.

In Search of Master Shakespeare

1. Friswell, *Life Portraits of William Shakespeare*, 1.
2. Schoenbaum, *William Shakespeare*, 4.
3. Anthony Burgess, *Shakespeare*, (Chicago: Ivan R. Dee, 1994), 166.
4. Schoenbaum, *William Shakespeare*, 209.

Family Traces

1. Cited in Charles Allen, *Notes on the Bacon-Shakespeare Question* (New York: AMS Press, 1970; first published Boston: Houghton, Mifflin and Company, 1900), 274.
2. Cited in Bertram and Cossa, "Willm Shakespeare 1609."
3. Spielmann, "The 'Grafton' and 'Sanders' Portraits of Shakespeare."

Looking the Part

1. Henry James, *The Aspern Papers and The Turn of the Screw* (London and New York: Penguin, 1984), 108–109.
2. E. T. Craig, *Shakespeare's Portraits Phrenologically Considered.* (Philadelphia: Printed for private circulation by J. Parker Norris), 1875.
3. John Corbin, *A New Portrait of Shakespeare: The Case of the Ely Palace Painting as against that of the so-called Droeshout Original* (London and New York: John Lane, The Bodley Head, 1903).
4. Leslie Hotson, *Shakespeare by Hilliard: A Portrait Deciphered* (Berkeley and Los Angeles: University of California Press, 1977), 9.
5. Marjorie Weeden Champlin, *Changing the Face of Shakespeare* (privately printed, 1996).
6. William Stone Booth, *The Droeshout Portrait of William Shakespeare, An Experiment in Identification* (Boston: W. A. Butterfield, 1911), 2.
7. Olive Wagner Driver, *The Shakespearean Portraits and Other Addenda* (Northampton, MA: Metcalf Printing and Publishing, 1966), 13.
8. Corbin, *A New Portrait of Shakespeare*, 95.
9. Charles Dickens, *Letters*, G. Howarth and M. Dickens, eds. (London and New York, 1893), 173. Cited in Samuel Schoenbaum, *Shakespeare's Lives* (Oxford: Clarendon Press; New York: Oxford University Press, 1970), 470.
10. Craig, *Shakespeare's Portraits Phrenologically Considered*, 1.
11. Ibid., 2–3.
12. Ibid., 6.
13. J. Parker Norris, "Shaksperian Gossip," in *American Bibliopolist* 8 (1876): 40.

14. J. O. Halliwell-Philipps, *Folio Edition of Shakespeare* (London, 1853), 1: 230. J. Parker Norris, "The Portraits of Shakespeare," *Shakespeariana* (Philadelphia: Leonard Scott, 1883–1884), 4–5.

15. C. M. Ingleby, "The Portraiture of Shakespeare," in *Shakespeare, the Man and the Book* (London, 1877).

16. J. S. Hart, "The Shakespeare Death Mask," *Scribner's Monthly* 8, no. 3 (July 1874): 313.

17. Abraham Wivell, *An Inquiry into the History, Authenticity, and Characteristics of the Shakespeare Portraits* (London, 1827), 140.

18. Schoenbaum, *Shakespeare's Lives*, 6–7.

19. Ibid., 281.

20. J. Parker Norris, *Shakesperiana* 1, no. 3 (January 1884): 65.

21. George Steevens, quoted in Schoenbaum, *Shakespeare's Lives*, 282.

22. Friswell, *Life Portraits of William Shakespeare*, 31.

23. "Many other scholars are skeptical, in part because [the Chandos portrait] shows a swarthy Italianate Shakespeare who does not much resemble the bust or the Droeshout." Stephanie Nolen, "Is This the Face of Genius?" *The Globe and Mail* (Toronto), 11 May 2001.

24. John Dover Wilson, *The Essential Shakespeare* (Cambridge: Cambridge University Press, 1932; reprinted 1960), 5–8.

25. "The Merry Bard Himself," *Courier Mail* (Queensland, Australia), 14 May 2001, 3.

26. Verlyn Klinkenborg, Editorial Notebook: "A Knowing Smile on an Unknown Face," *The New York Times*, 27 May 2001, Section 4, 8.

27. Tim Rutten, "The New Face of Shakespeare," *The Los Angeles Times*, 1 June 2001, Part 5, 1.

28. Josephine Tey, *The Daughter of Time* (New York: Scribner, 1995), 29–30.

29. Emmanuel Levinas, *Ethics and Infinity*, conversations with Philippe Nemo, Richard A. Cohen, trans. (Pittsburgh: Duquesne University Press, 1985), 85–86.

30. Alexander Leggatt, quoted in Nolen, "Is This the Face of Genius?"

31. Oscar Wilde, "The Portrait of Mr. W. H.," in *The Complete Works of Oscar Wilde* (New York: Harper and Row, 1966), 1150–1201. The narrator of "The Portrait," who is a stand-in for Wilde, offers the opinion that "so-called forgeries were merely the result of an artistic desire for perfect representation," and that "all Art being to a certain degree a mode of acting, an attempt to realize one's own personality on some imaginative plane out of reach of the trammeling accidents and limitations of real life, to censure an artist for a forgery was to confuse an ethical with an aesthetical problem" (p. 1156). His companion asks him what he would think of "a young man who had a strange theory about a certain work of art, believed in his theory, and committed a forgery

in order to prove it." The test case is the portrait of Mr. W. H. (Willie Hughes), which is now in the possession of the host: a "full-length portrait of a young man in late sixteenth-century costume, standing by a table, with his right hand resting on a book. He seemed about seventeen years of age, and was of quite extraordinary beauty." The portrait, it turns out, is itself a forgery, created by the young man with the "strange theory" to demonstrate that "W. H." was not an aristocratic patron of Shakespeare's but the boy-actor who inspired him. When the forger was confronted with his act, he explained that he had done it to make a point. "You would not be convinced any other way. It does not affect the truth of the theory." Told that the fact of the forgery invalidated his argument, he committed suicide, leaving behind a letter enjoining his friend to present the theory to the world and "unlock the secret of Shakespeare's heart" (p. 1156).

An Actor's Face?

1. Lawrence Stone, *The Crisis of the Aristocracy, 1558–1641* (Oxford: Oxford University Press, 1965), 712.

2. James M. Osborne, ed., *The Autobiography of Thomas Whythorne* (Oxford: Oxford University Press, 1961), 134. I am grateful to David Dean and Norman Jones for bringing this reference to my attention.

3. Robert Tittler, "Civic Portraiture and Political Culture in English Provincial Towns, ca. 1560–1640," *Journal of British Studies* 37 (July 1998): 306–29 and especially Appendix I, 326–29.

4. I draw this figure from the database of my current research-in-progress on the subject of civic portraiture in London and elsewhere.

5. I am grateful to Dr. Sally-Beth Maclean, Executive Editor of Records of Early English Drama, who has made this information available to me from REED's databases.

6. John Earle, *Microcosmography, or a Piece of the World Discovered in Essays and Characters (1628)*, Edward Arber, ed. (1895), 26–27.

7. Susan Foister, "Paintings and Other Works of Art in Sixteenth-Century English Inventories," *Burlington Magazine* 123, no. 938 (May 1981): 273–82.

8. *Whythorne Autobiography*, 134. I have modernized the spelling.

9. Johnson, also known as Janssen and Johnson van Calen, painted hundreds of portraits in his time, the vast proportion of them courtly portraits of people outside London.

10. Richard Quick, ed., *Catalogue of the Second Loan Collection of Pictures Held in the Bristol Art Gallery, 1905* (Bristol: Bristol Art Gallery, 1905), no. 202.

11. Brian Frith, *Twelve Portraits of Gloucester Benefactors* (Gloucester:

Gloucester Folk Museum, 1972).

12. Andrew Moore and Charlotte Crawley, *Family and Friends, A Regional Survey of British Portraiture* (London: HMSO, 1992), 196–99.

13. Mrs. R. L. Poole, ed., *Catalogue of Portraits in the University, Colleges, City and County of Oxford* (Oxford: Oxford Historical Society, vol. 57, 1912; vols. 81 and 82, 1926), vol. 57, 244; vol. 81, xii; Berkshire County Record Office MS. D/EP 7/55; Mary Edmund, "Sampson Strong," in *Dictionary of Art*, Jane Turner, ed. (New York: Grove Dictionaries, 1996) xxix, 781.

14. The family included Lambert Bernard (d. 1567/8), his son Anthony (d. 1619) and his grandson Barnard (d. 1655), though none of their portrait work is known to have survived. Ellis Waterhouse, *Dictionary of 16th and 17th* [sic] *British Painters* (Woodbridge, Suffolk: The Antique Collectors' Club, 1988) 20.

15. Leicester Museum, *Catalogue of Local Portraits*, (1956), 12–13; Waterhouse, *Dictionary*, 43.

A Painting with a Past

1. I am exceptionally grateful to Christina Corsiglia, curator of European Art at the Art Gallery of Ontario, who supervised my examination of this painting and whose helpful and patient advice prompted several of the observations made in this essay.

2. This observation I owe to Christina Corsiglia, who noted the connection between these scratches and application of adhesive tape on the verso.

3. The second, later label, which is also written over, may have been applied by M. H. Spielmann when he examined the picture in 1908. However, it carries the set of initials "H.M.," which have so far defied identification.

4. I am grateful to Libby Sheldon from the Painting Analysis Unit of the History of Art Department, University College London, for her advice on the effects of varnish on painted colour values.

5. An exception is the artist Levenia Teerlinc, c. 1510/20–1576, daughter of a Flemish illustrator, Simon Bennick. Teerlinc worked for the court of Elizabeth I, principally as a miniaturist.

6. Henry Peacham, *The Compleat Gentleman* (London: Francis Marriott, 1634), 137.

7. All the observations here have been based on an examination of this black-and-white photograph.

8. Private Collection. Dimensions approximately 44 x 35 cm (17 x 14 inches). The man may be a member of the Terrick Family. The sentiment here records an unease with the nature of portrayal that we know was a serious concern among those of the middling sort, and a similar senti-

ment is found in a painting within a private collection by Hans Eworth (active 1540–1574) of an English merchant's wife known as Joan Wakeman, dated 1566. See Elizabeth Honig, "In Memory: Lady Dacre and Pairing by Hans Eworth" in *Renaissance Bodies: The Human Figure in English Culture* c. 1540–1660, Lucy Gent and Nigel Llewellyn, eds. (London: Reaktion Books, 1990), 60–85.

The Portrait Meets its Public

1. See Sir Edmund Chambers, *An Index to "The Elizabethan State" and "William Shakespeare"*, Beatrice White, comp. (New York: Benjamin Bloom, Inc., 1968).

2. David N. Klausner, ed. *Herefordshire and Worcestershire: Records of Early English Drama* (Toronto: University of Toronto Press, 1990), 130.

3. Nevinson, "Shakespeare's Dress in His Portraits": 101.

4. Burgess, *Shakespeare,* 10.

The Conundrum of the Label

1. Spielmann, "The 'Grafton' and 'Sanders' portraits of Shakespeare": 101.

2. For an example of Collier's "secretary hand," see Anthony G. Petti, *English Literary Hands from Chaucer to Dryden* (Cambridge, Mass., Harvard University Press, 1977), 88.

3. Alexandra F. Johnston and Margaret Rogerson, eds. *York, Records of Early English Drama,* 2 vols. (Toronto: University of Toronto Press, 1979), 61, 871.

4. Schoenbaum, *William Shakespeare,* 21.

The Man Who Will Not Meet Your Eyes

1. Greene's attack is reproduced in *The Norton Shakespeare,* Stephen Greenblatt, gen. ed. (New York and London: Norton, 1997), 3321–22. All references to Shakespeare's plays are to this edition (which is based on the Oxford edition) and are identified by act, scene and line number. Unless otherwise specified, other texts from Shakespeare's time are quoted from this edition and identified by page number. Spelling and punctuation have been modernized.

2. Ibid., 3322. To explain the square brackets: in the appendix in which they quote the passage, the Norton editors cut it short just when it is getting interesting; I have restored the missing words.

3. Ibid., 3324.

4. Ibid., 3328.

5. Ibid., 3326.

6. All Marlowe references are to Christopher Marlowe, *The Complete Plays*, J. B. Steane, ed. (Harmondsworth: Penguin, 1969).

7. John Lyly, *Gallathea* and *Midas*, Anne Begor Lancashire, ed. (Lincoln: University of Nebraska Press, 1969).

8. See Helen Vendler's reading of this sonnet in *The Art of Shakespeare's Sonnets* (Cambridge, Massachusetts, and London, England: The Belknap Press of Harvard University Press, 1997), 605–606.

9. The second part of *The Return from Parnassus* (c. 1601) contains what sounds like a reference to a literary feud between Shakespeare and Jonson (3327), but the reference is cryptic and no other evidence of such a feud survives.

10. The text is from *Narrative and Dramatic Sources of Shakespeare*, vol. 1, Geoffrey Bullough, ed. (London: Routledge and Kegan Paul; New York, Columbia University Press, 1966). The reference is to scene and line; there are no act divisions.

11. *The Norton Shakespeare*, 3328.

Is This the Face of Genius?

1. Spielmann. "The 'Grafton' and 'Sanders' Portraits of Shakespeare": 100.

2. Simon Foreman, *The Autobiography and Personal Diary of Dr. Simon Forman, The celebrated astrologer From AD. 1552 to AD. 1602 from unpublished Manuscripts in the Ashmolean Museum Oxford*, James Orchard Halliwell, ed., (1849), 31.

Useful Sources

Stephanie Nolen

I began this project with only a very basic knowledge of Shakespeare's life and work, but I fast discovered that hundreds of years of scholarship have generated whole libraries full of studies of his writings and, to a lesser extent, the man himself. There is also a smaller but intriguing body of work dealing specifically with images of Shakespeare. I drew on many such sources, the best and most useful of which are listed alphabetically by author below.

Bloom, Harold. *Shakespeare, The Invention of the Human.* New York: Riverhead Books, 1998.

Burgess, Anthony. *Shakespeare.* London: Jonathan Cape, 1970; reprint, Chicago: Ivan R. Dee, 1994. An enchanting biography by a famous English novelist that attempts to impute human motivations where we have only a slim documentary record.

Dobson, Michael, and Stanley Wells, eds. *The Oxford Companion to Shakespeare.* Oxford: Oxford University Press, 2001. The definitive encyclopedia on all things to do with both the playwright and his work, this reference work is as engaging as it is useful.

Duncan-Jones, Katherine. *Ungentle Shakespeare: Scenes from His Life.* London: Arden Shakespeare, Thomson Learning, 2001. A recent biography that paints a vivid picture of the man, strongly supporting it with the existing evidence.

Friswell, J. Hain. *Life Portraits of William Shakspeare: A History of the Various Representations of the Poet, with an Examination into Their Authenticity.*

London: Sampson Low, Son, & Marston. 1864. One of the most thorough studies of Shakespeare iconography in its era, it remains interesting today, in part as a barometer of how modern scholarship has changed the evaluations of some of the life-portrait contenders.

Halliday. F. E. *Shakespeare.* London: Thames and Hudson, 1956; reprint, London: Thames and Hudson, 1998.

Honan, Park. *Shakespeare, A Life.* Oxford: Oxford University Press, 1999. A solidly researched, evidence-based biography.

Piper, David. *O Sweet Mr. Shakespeare I'll Have His Picture: The Changing Image of Shakespeare's Person, 1600-1800.* London: National Portrait Gallery, 1964. A comprehensive survey of the iconography.

Pressly, William L. *A Catalogue of Paintings in the Folger Shakespeare Library: "As Imagination Bodies Forth."* New Haven: Yale University Press, 1993. A dense book intended for a scholarly audience, it nonetheless provides fascinating information on provenance and secrets revealed by restoration for a lay audience.

Schoenbaum, Samuel. *William Shakespeare: A Compact Documentary Life.* Oxford: Oxford University Press, 1987. The bible of modern biographies.

Spielmann, Marion Henry. Essay on portraiture for the "Shakespeare" entry. *Encyclopaedia Britannica,* 11th edition, vol. 24. London: Britannica Co., 1911.

Wilson, Ian. *Shakespeare: The Evidence.* New York: St. Martin's Griffin, 1993.

Wivell, Abraham. *An Inquiry into the Authenticity of the Shakespeare Portraits.* London: James S. Virtue Co., 1827.

Plate Credits

Every reasonable effort has been made to trace ownership of copyright materials. Information enabling the Publisher to rectify any reference or credit in future editions will be welcomed.

Book jacket front cover: The Sanders Portrait. Carlo Catenazzi, Art Gallery of Ontario.

Chapter opener illustrations: *Chirologia; or, The natural language of the hand, composed of the speaking motions and discoursing.* John Bulwer. London, 1648.

The Picture Gallery: p. *i*, X-ray photograph of the Sanders portrait. Photograph: Jeremy J. Powell, Senior Scientific Documentation Technologist, Analytical Research Laboratory, Canadian Conservation Institute, Department of Canadian Heritage. © All rights reserved. "Sanders portrait," Canadian Conservation Institute—Reproduced with the permission of the Minister of Public Works and Government Services, 2001; p. *ii*, *top* Droeshout engraving from the First Folio. By permission of the Folger Shakespeare Library; *bottom* The Flower portrait. Copyright RSC collection. From the RSC Collection with the permission of the Governors of the Royal Shakespeare Company; p. *iii*, *top* William Shakespeare attributed to John Taylor ("the Chandos portrait"). By courtesy of the National Portrait Gallery, London; *bottom* Monument/statue of William Shakespeare, in the church where his birth and death were registered, Holy Trinity Church © Dorling Kindersley, photograph Rob Reichenfeld; p. *iv*, *top left* The Felton Shakespeare portrait. By permission of the Folger Shakespeare Library; *top right* The Janssen Shakespeare portrait. By permission of the Folger Shakespeare Library; *bottom left* The Ashbourne portrait (Portrait of

Shakespeare/Sir Hugh Hammersley). By permission of the Folger Shakespeare Library; *bottom right* The Ashbourne portrait (photograph taken before restoration). By permission of the Folger Shakespeare Library; *centre right* The Zuccaro Shakespeare portrait. By permission of the Folger Shakespeare Library; p. *v*, The Grafton portrait of Shakespeare. Reproduced by courtesy of the Director and Librarian, the John Rylands University Library of Manchester; p. *vi, top left* The Burbage Shakespeare portrait. By permission of the Folger Shakespeare Library; *top right* The Lumley Shakespeare portrait. By permission of the Folger Shakespeare Library; *bottom left* The Gunther Shakespeare portrait. By permission of the Folger Shakespeare Library; *bottom right* The Shakespeare portrait. By permission of the Folger Shakespeare Library; p. *vii, top left* The Staunton Shakespeare portrait. By permission of the Folger Shakespeare Library; *top right* The Vroom Shakespeare portrait. By permission of the Folger Shakespeare Library; *bottom* The Chesterfield Portrait. By permission of the Shakespeare Birthplace Trust; p. *viii, top right* Detail of letter and number forms, Sanders portrait. Carlo Catenazzi, Art Gallery of Ontario; *bottom left* Detail of doublet. Carlo Catenazzi, Art Gallery of Ontario; *centre left* Photomicrograph of cross-section of paint from the collar under reflected light, Photomicrograph of cross-section of paint at collar under ultraviolet light; *top left* Photomicrograph of cross-section of paint at date of Sanders portrait. Photomicrographs: Dr. Marie-Claude Corbeil, Senior Conservation Scientist, Analytical Research Laboratory, Canadian Conservation Institute, Department of Canadian Heritage © All rights reserved. "Sanders Portrait," Canadian Conservation Institute—Reproduced with the permission of the Minister of Public Works and Government Services, 2001; p. *viii, centre right* The Sanders Portrait *and* p. *ix, top right* Ultraviolet induced colour fluorescence of label. Photographs: Jeremy J. Powell, Senior Scientific Documentation Technologist, Analytical Research Laboratory, Canadian Conservation Institute, Department of Canadian Heritage © All rights reserved. "Sanders Portrait," Canadian Conservation Institute—Reproduced with the permission of the Minister of Public Works and Government Services, 2001; p. *ix, centre left* Back of Sanders portrait by Patti Gower. Reprinted with permission from *The Globe and Mail*; *bottom right* Cross-section of wood panel from Sanders portrait. Carlo Catenazzi, Art Gallery of Ontario; p. *x*, John Fletcher, after unknown artist. By courtesy of the National Portrait Gallery, London; p. *xi, top* Ben Jonson, by Abraham van Blyenberch. By courtesy of the National Portrait Gallery, London; *bottom* Richard Burbage, British School. By permission of the Trustees of Dulwich Picture Gallery; p. *xii, top* Unknown man, Isaac Oliver. Private collection; *bottom* Elizabeth Harding, Mrs Oliver, painted 1610–15. Private collection; p. *xiii*, Henry Wriothesley, 3rd Earl of Southampton, by unknown artist.

PLATE CREDITS

By courtesy of the National Portrait Gallery, London; p. *xiv*, Portrait of unknown boy, 1605. Unknown artist. By courtesy of the National Portrait Gallery, London; p. *xv*, *top left* Portrait of William Burton, dated 1604. Ascribed to William Segar. Society of Antiquaries of London; *top right* Portrait of Lawrence Atwill, by unknown artist. Exeter City Museums & Art Gallery; *bottom* Portrait of a Gentleman of the Terrick Family. Private collection. Photograph: Photographic Survey, Courtauld Institute of Art; p. *xvi*, Ultraviolet fluorescence colour photograph of Sanders portrait *and* p. 276, Enhanced photograph of label. Photographs: Jeremy J. Powell, Senior Scientific Documentation Technologist, Analytical Research Laboratory, Canadian Conservation Institute, Department of Canadian Heritage © All rights reserved. "Sanders portrait," Canadian Conservation Institute—Reproduced with the permission of the Minister of Public Works and Government Services, 2001.

Acknowledgments

Many people helped to make *Shakespeare's Face* the book it is, and Alfred. A. Knopf Canada and I owe many debts of gratitude.

First, of course, to Lloyd Sullivan, who shared their portrait and their story. Lloyd was unfailingly generous with his time; he shared his research, provided me with access to the painting and took great care to relate its history.

At the Art Gallery of Ontario, Christina Corsiglia, Curator of European Art, provided unflagging support and encouragement, including allowing our contributors access to the Sanders portrait, putting us in touch with crucial sources of information and photographs and reading drafts of the manuscript. We also appreciate the support of Matthew Teitelbaum, Director and CEO of the AGO, and the help of Sandra Webster-Cook, Conservator of Paintings, and Akira Yoshikawa, Art Handler.

At the Canadian Conservation Institute, Marie-Claude Corbeil, Senior Conservation Scientist, was an invaluable source of information; she helped me to understand the institute's very complicated work and vetted the chapter on the scientific analysis of the painting. Ian Wainwright, Director of the Analytical Research Laboratory, was generous with his time and expertise.

At the Folger Shakespeare Library, Erin Blake, Curator of Art, was endlessly patient with my questions and provided many tips that helped unravel the mystery of the portrait. Heather Wolfe, Curator of Manuscripts, aided in the analysis of the label.

We benefited as well from the vast knowledge and enthusiasm of the team at the Records of Early Elizabethan Drama project at the University of Toronto: Alexandra F. Johnston, Director; Sally-Beth Maclean, Executive Editor; Arleane Ralph, Research Associate; and Abigail Anne Young, Research Associate.

Ian Lancashire, Professor of English Literature at the University of Toronto, graciously answered many Shakespeare questions and took a keen interest in the portrait. Roelf Beukens at the University of Toronto, Peter Klein at the University of Hamburg and Aileen Ribeiro at the Courtauld Institute were also patient with my questions.

At the National Portrait Gallery in London, Catharine MacLeod, Curator of Sixteenth- and Seventeenth-Century Paintings, provided assistance, as did Robin Francis, Archivist.

At the National Gallery of Canada, Chief Curator David Franklin, Curator of European and American Art Catherine Johnston, Associate Curator Michael Pantazzi and Archivist Cyndie Campbell all helped to bring clues about the painting to light.

Editor-in-chief Richard Addis and *The Globe and Mail* contributed the enthusiasm that first made the portrait famous, and then later information and images for this book, and graciously gave me the time to write it.

Within the publishing house of Alfred A. Knopf Canada, many people worked enthusiastically on the project, including Damián Tarnopolsky, Scott Richardson, Deirdre Molina, Astrid Otto, and Sharon Bailey.

And finally, I have a few personal thanks to add. To my parents, Jim and Barbara Nolen, who gave me, among many other things, the story of the portrait. To my marvellous fellow contributors, who provide a breadth of knowledge to this book, for which it and I are much the richer, and who were patient with my many, many questions; to Louise Dennys at Knopf Canada, who first envisioned *Shakespeare's Face*; to Rick Archbold, the Project Editor, who so capably filled the role of Master Tailor and stitched the book together. And to Marney McDiarmid, Andy Pedersen, Mona Thyagarajah, Ben Davies, Kathryn Morris, Jen McDonald, Stephanie Chambers, Monica Noy, and especially Andrea Clegg: "... you Mistake my fortunes; I am wealthy in my friends" (*Timon of Athens* 2.2).

Stephanie Nolen
Toronto, 2002

Index

Roman numeral page citations in **boldface** refer to the illustrations and text in the Picture Gallery, located between pages 206 and 207. Other roman numeral page citations refer to the preface and preliminary material.